GUILT
&
GRACE

GUILT

&

GRACE

A PSYCHOLOGICAL STUDY

by DR. PAUL TOURNIER

English Translation by Arthur W. Heathcote
assisted by J. J. Henry and P. J. Allcock

1817

HARPER & ROW, PUBLISHERS, San Francisco
Cambridge, Hagerstown, New York, Philadelphia
London, Mexico City, São Paulo, Sydney

FIRST U.S. PAPERBACK EDITION

The Scripture quotations and references in this publication are from *The Revised Standard Version of the Bible*, copyrighted 1946, 1952, © 1971, © 1973 by the Division of Christian Education of the National Council of the Churches of Christ in the U.Ş.A., and used by permission.

Library of Congress Cataloging in Publication Data

Tournier, Paul.
   Guilt and grace.

   1. Guilt—Psychological aspects.   2. Guilt—Religious aspects—Christianity.   3. Grace (Theology)
I. Title.   II. Title: Guilt and grace.
BF575.G8T6813   1983   233′.4   82-11882
ISBN 0-06-068331-7

85 86   10 9 8 7 6 5 4 3

CONTENTS

Part One

THE EXTENT OF GUILT

Chapter I

INFERIORITY AND GUILT

THIS book is a sequel to *Bible et Médecine* which I published in 1951. In fact, I drafted both of them following the studies which I presented at the 'Semaines médicales' at Bossey in 1957. The session was devoted to the problem of guilt and its place in medicine. It was my daily task to find in the Scriptures suitable material to guide our dèbates.

The reader will not find in this book an account of the meetings: the most important thing is lacking here, that is the clinical studies. What matters to doctors is the observation of patients. It was the observation of patients that set us all on that road of 'integrative medicine', that is to say a treatment which takes into account all the factors which play a part in illness and its cure.

Now the sense of guilt is one—and not the least—of those factors. It is enough for me to mention the simplest of cases, namely insomnia resulting from remorse. We can and should relieve such a patient by prescribing a soporific. But to stop at that would be very superficial medical practice. A conscientious doctor always seeks to attack the real cause of the illness and not merely the obvious symptoms.

But much more numerous and much more complex are cases in which guilt plays a pathogenic role and in which the resolution of the guilt helps in the cure. All the studies of recent years by the psychoanalysts or by the psychosomatic Schools have continually broadened our vision in this respect. This was shown by the speakers at Bossey. Dr. André Sarradon[36] of Marseilles dealt with the problem from the standpoint of general practice and gynaecology. Three psychiatrists presented it as it manifests itself in their special fields: Mme. Line Thévenin of Lyons, in child-psychiatry; Dr. Aloys d'Orelli of Zurich, in neuroses; and Dr. Paul Plattner of Berne, in psychoses. Finally, Dr. Théo Bovet of Bâle showed the broad, human aspect of guilt, which touches the doctor as well as his patients, personally in his own physical and moral health. I have in this book set aside the whole of the clinical aspect which is so important to the doctor. The talks for which I was responsible during that week, were only a complement to the medical studies, a juxtaposition of the problems under discussion with biblical revelation. Indeed, we cannot tackle the

problem of guilt without dealing with the religious questions
which it poses. Even doctors like Dr. Hesnard,[16] for example,
who strive to keep strictly to the psychological point of view,
are today prepared to discuss in medical circles the religious
doctrine of sin and the influence of the Churches.

Thus, under the pressure of medical progress, the rather artificial barriers raised between science and philosophy, medicine
and theology, are overturned. Is there really a conflict between
the facts of medical experience and the teaching of the Bible?
The question is so important and so topical that I have thought
fit to offer it to the public in a book. Any other information
about the meetings, or the reports of other lectures, must be
looked for elsewhere. What I am presenting here is only the
substance of my own lectures, developed after the event in the
light of our debates.

Although this is in no way a transcript, I have retained the style
of a friendly talk, as if I were still talking to the doctors gathered
at the Ecumenical Institute. I said 'You' to them, and 'you' is
now addressed to all of you who read this book, as if you too had
come to take your seats among our group.

This may be a fiction, but it is a fiction which expresses a deeply
felt reality. Even as I write I feel as though I were speaking, not
to an anonymous and impersonal public, but to each of you, my
readers; to be discussing with you questions which spring to
your minds as to mine, and which are, to neither of us, simple
debates of an academic or abstract type, but living, personal
preoccupations.

Now a guilty conscience is the seasoning of our daily life.

All upbringing is a cultivation of the sense of guilt on an
intensive scale. Especially the best education, that by parents
who are most anxious about the moral training of their children
and their success in life. It consists above all in scolding; and all
scolding, even if it is only discreet and silent reprobation, suggests
the feelings of guilt. 'Are you not ashamed to behave like that?'

At the beginning of this century, such an upbringing tended
to make children into showcase dolls, well-behaved, not heard,
well schooled in the social graces. 'I loathe Sundays,' was the
remark to me by a woman who was always kept from full
maturity by an inner check. 'When we were children, my sister
and I were made to wear our best clothes on Sundays; there were
flounces of starched lace and a ribbon for our hair with a very
complicated bow that was difficult to tie. And woe betide us if we
got dirty! And this always happened, although we were careful
not to play. The day ended with reprimand and punishment.'

At table, some time ago, I asked my wife why her face suddenly lit up with a strange smile. 'Look,' she said, 'I had cut into the butter at one end and you cut into it at the other end. I just thought of what would have been said if that had been done as a child: a well-brought-up child should continue to take the butter from the end already begun. Your action was like a blow for freedom!'

Today, upbringing is very different. The breath of liberty blows across the cradle itself. Under the influence of the psychologists, the meticulous upbringing of those days is frowned on. But the problem is very similar. Nowadays the parents are proud if the child is noisy, if he shows personality! But woe betide him if he does not show enough personality, if he does not do something, in some special field, of which his parents can be proud.

Their friends are very ready to adjudge the child as badly brought up, even though the pattern of the well-brought-up child has changed. The child senses in his parents the inevitable fear of 'what will people say?' Their social reputation is at stake in him and the responsibility weighs heavily upon him. He feels guilt if he brings shame upon them, or even if he has no exceptional gifts of which they can boast.

The school, with its bad marks and the sinister prospect of the moment when he must show his report to his parents, fills his childish mind with feelings of guilt. This can become such an obsession as to lure him into cheating, the source of a more genuine guilt. And often in drawing up the marks, the teacher takes more account of the pupil's faults than of his good qualities.

How many people whose spelling is bad have a lifelong aversion to writing letters. How many people always stand paralysed with confusion in the presence of any authority which reminds them of that of a father or of a stern schoolmaster! Even at the desk of some government office they tremble as they hand over to some lowly clerk the form which they have had to fill up. And at the first glance the clerk spots some heading which they have stupidly missed: 'Can't you read?'

The serious thing is that parents and teachers project their own prejudices, their own problems and their own guilts into education. For example, those who have most remorse over their sexual behaviour invest their warning counsel to their children with dramatic overtones which awaken in their hearts a veritable dread of sexuality.

Unhappy parents will find it difficult to tolerate their child and his exuberance. A hundred times a day, they will say, 'You silly boy! You are unbearable!' A father, burdened with professional care, will lose his temper with his daughter over nothing. A mother deceived by her husband, will, without realizing it, vent her spite on her son and will roundly scold him for some trivial misdeed. 'You're a liar like your father!' Intuitively the child will feel this unjust burden of reproach in the form of anxiety.

Saul reproaches Jonathan for his friendship with David: 'You son of a perverse, rebellious woman,' he says, 'do I not know that you have chosen the son of Jesse to your own shame, and to the shame of your mother?' (1 Sam. xx. 30). And notice the guile of 'shame of your mother', as if he himself had nothing to do with it.

Thus many parents, out of social prejudice when it is not through pure jealousy, make their children feel guilty in their friendships. The children are left with a choice between two guilts: towards their parents, if they are faithful to the friends: to their friends, if they submit to the parents—unless they resign themselves to keeping up the friendship secretly, with the burden of guilt which results from secrecy.

A courageous child will confess his fault immediately to his parents; he will accept a reprimand and all will be settled, whereas his brother, more sensitive and fearful will not dare to. He will carry a double burden of guilt: that of his fault and that of its concealment. He will withdraw into moral solitude and because of his shame will always be more fearful of being frank with his parents.

Sooner or later, the child must either run the risk of neurosis or free himself from his parents and follow his own devices, his own tastes, his own inclinations. Few parents welcome this awakening of individuality in their children. Almost all of them suggest to their children that it is wrong to like what their parents dislike, to desire what they disapprove of or to behave otherwise than they expect.

'Children, obey your parents,' writes St. Paul (Eph. vi. 1). Devout parents use this statement to demand servile submission from their children, even when they are no longer children. But these parents pay less attention to what the Apostle immediately adds: 'Fathers, do not provoke your children to anger' (Eph. vi. 4), or to what he adds elsewhere: 'lest they become discouraged' (Col. iii. 21).

By their behaviour as much as by their words, austere living parents suggest that anything that gives pleasure is sinful! Many people have told me how this idea from their upbringing has lingered on. It was inculcated like an inexorable adage: 'Enjoyment prohibited.' They can enjoy nothing without feeling conscience-stricken and this spoils their pleasure.

Alternatively, enjoyment is considered legitimate only if it is merited as a reward. Those who have received this idea through their upbringing burden themselves with tasks which are too heavy or with useless sacrifices, with the sole aim of enjoying a much desired pleasure without feeling conscience-stricken. Thus they keep a sort of complicated balance-sheet which is always more or less charged with anxiety; this anxiety is a check to their spontaneity, be it in an impulse to unselfish sacrifice or to the enjoyment of a pleasure they have not earned.

Yet unearned pleasures and unexpected gifts are the most appreciated. The Bible speaks not only of the fact that salvation is free. It speaks of all God's gifts, the small ones as well as the great. It reveals to us, contrary to the idea of those who have suffered from an over-severe upbringing, a heavenly Father who rejoices in His children's happiness and is pleased to give them pleasure.

But to return to the adolescent. Not a single one passes through this period of emancipation from parents without involving himself in a life of secrecy which is always guilt-ridden. He finds a book exciting and continues to read it far into the night, by the light of a candle, attentive for the sound of a creak on the stairs which will warn him that someone is coming whose approach he fears—rightly or wrongly. Or alternatively he will place the absorbing book over his open Latin grammar, ready to slip it quickly into the drawer if someone comes. Or again, as proof of his approaching manhood, he will go off to smoke his first cigarette secretly.

It is by having secrets that individuality is formed. So long as a child has no secrets from his parents, so long as he cannot tell a friend secrets which he withholds from his parents, he has no consciousness of being somebody distinct from them. Parents usually declare that a child should have no secrets from them; they consider it as wrong to have something hidden from them. They say bitterly, 'You have hurt us terribly'.

We are all constantly beset by criticism, sometimes keen and outspoken, sometimes silent, but not less painful for being so. We are all sensitive to it, even if we conceal the fact. Self-assured people are the best able to bear it. They defend themselves, they retort, they give criticism for criticism and then their critic is put in the wrong: 'My sister is so categorical in her opinions that one always feels rather guilty if one does not agree with her!' Or again: 'I find myself avoiding visiting my sister; for when I want to leave, she says, "What? Going already?" in such a reproachful tone that I feel quite guilty.'

Notice that those who are so absolute in their assertions and reproaches to others are seeking, without being fully aware of the fact, to reassure themselves. They rid themselves of their own doubts by awakening doubt in others. Thus the strong free themselves of their own guilt by rousing guilt in the weak, who are so ready to make comparisons to their own detriment.

Take the example of a very meticulous woman. She shows this quality of hers in doing very carefully all that she has to do. But she tells me that she always feels guilty for being so meticulous, for spending so much time on all that she does. She was brought up by a woman who was quite different, who did everything in a very hurried, rough and ready manner. The latter was certainly irritated by this girl who was so different from herself and made her feel guilty for being so meticulous, probably in an attempt to rid herself of the guilt she herself felt for not being sufficiently conscientious.

Everyone has his own rhythm, and people have different rhythms from one another. In an office, the great speed of one typist will constantly arouse in her slower fellow-workers a sense of guilt which will paralyse them still further in their work. Yet it is a simple fact of nature which should be seen objectively. There is no special merit in the speed of the rapid typist any more than there is culpability in the slowness of her colleagues. Moreover, if she is at all sensitive, the rapid typist will come to feel guilty for being the involuntary cause of umbrage among others and will do many little services for them to win their forgiveness.

Long-lasting feelings of guilt are thus continually put into the minds of the weak by the behaviour of others, by their assertions, their judgments, their contempt, even by their most unjust reproaches. For as retort follows retort, the criticism becomes harsher and more aggressive. Dr. Baruk[3] has shown that this law of defensive aggressiveness is universal: any repressed guilt evokes an aggressive response. Thus, when a husband feels aggressive towards his wife and annoyed with her, he can at once ask himself: 'What are my faults towards her?' With a little honesty, he will always find the answer. The same is also true of course, of a wife towards her husband, or of an employee towards his employer and vice-versa.

But it is just as possible to humble other people by advice as well as by reproach. Every piece of advice conceals a veiled criticism, unless it has been asked for. To tell someone, 'In your place, I should act in such and such a way', implies that his way of acting is not the right one. Thus many zealous parents paralyse their children with good advice. They give them to understand that they are incapable of finding the right way of behaving for themselves and sow seeds of inadequacy in their minds.

Martha and Mary, mentioned in the Gospel (Lk. x. 38–42), are

sisters of two well recognized types. The one is of a practical temperament who occupies herself about the house; the other has
more taste for things of the spirit and sits at the feet of Jesus to
listen to Him. I fancy, that for a few minutes, Martha has been
making a lot of noise with her dishes to let her sister know of her
bad temper. Suddenly she can bear it no longer and appeals to
Jesus Himself: 'Tell her to help me.'

Thus we find much criticism between members of a family,
between brothers and sisters, between husband and wife or between friends. We can easily see the part played by secret feelings
of inferiority and even of guilt. Martha feels less at ease than her
sister in spiritual discussions and takes refuge in her dishes. She is
probably not proud of it and consoles herself in showing off her
practical services and in criticizing her sister. The latter has perhaps sometimes flaunted her contempt for household duties in
order to relieve her bad conscience for having neither taste for
them nor skill in them.

Jesus lifts the discussion above these elementary psychological
mechanisms by raising the question of values: 'Mary has chosen
the good portion which shall not be taken away from her.' But
this does not imply any contempt on His part for housework,
since He did not think it beneath Him to cook for His friends
(Jn. xxi. 9).

There is not always as good a reason as Mary's for standing
aside from the kitchen. How many women are upset to be reading
a book or to be resting when someone else is making a stir with
furniture and a vacuum cleaner in the next room? Even if they
are inwardly convinced that it is right, even if they are acquiring
culture as they should, or are obeying the doctor's orders for rest,
they have a sense of guilt at leaving the responsibility of the household to someone else and at feeling or believing themselves
criticized.

Many women also deprive themselves and their husbands of
entertaining friends, even the friends of their children, for fear
of being criticized for the way their house is kept. They are often
the most conscientious housewives, so careful over the smallest
details of their tasks that they think that no shortcoming will
escape the notice of the visitors. While the latter will perhaps, on
the contrary, think that our housewife keeps her house so perfectly that it lacks life and charm.

Thus in everyday life we are continually soaked in this unhealthy atmosphere of mutual criticism, so much so that we are
not always aware of it and we find ourselves drawn unwittingly
into an implacable vicious circle: every reproach evokes a feeling
of guilt in the critic as much as in the one criticized, and each one

gains relief from his guilt in any way he can, by criticizing other people and in self-justification.

This daily guilt is of much interest to the doctor and the psychologist for it is linked with relationships with others, with criticism by others, with social scorn and with feelings of inferiority. Remorse, bad conscience, shame, embarrassment, uneasiness, confusion, shyness, even modesty: there is a link between all these terms which have no clear-cut frontier.

Chapter II

SOCIAL SUGGESTION

ALL men are continually making mutual accusations, because of the sole fact that they have life in common, in the family and in society, and that inevitably they make comparisons of one another and contrast their various temperaments, their conceptions of life and their convictions. Some time ago, my wife and I were lunching in France. On the menu was ox-tongue with Madeira sauce. My wife called the manageress: 'I do not like tongue; can you give me something else instead?'—'Certainly I have an excellent fillet of beef, if that is to your taste.'

During the meal, naturally, we spoke about guilt, my current subject of study. 'Do you know,' my wife said, 'it made me feel guilty when I asked for that change of menu in front of you. You always eat whatever is put before you and I have the impression that you think me capricious and difficult.'—'But I did not say a word!'—'No,' she answered, 'but your silence was most eloquent!'

My immediate reaction was to defend myself: 'What!' I said, 'I make myself the champion of everyone's right, even his duty, to be himself, unreservedly and without pretence, and you of all people do not dare to show your desires without being afraid of my criticism!' I thus threw back on her shoulders the responsibility for the sense of guilt which she had felt.

Yet she was right; in my troubled silence during her conversation with the manageress, that judgment was indeed present, hardly conscious it is true, but enough for her to be intuitively aware of it. I can make myself the zealous champion of every man's duty to be himself, and still be unaware of bringing silent criticism to bear on my wife when she behaves differently or shows herself different from me.

I am thus causing the growth in her of a false guilt. For true guilt is precisely the failure to dare to be oneself. It is the fear of other people's judgment that prevents us from being ourselves, from showing ourselves as we really are, from showing our tastes, our desires, our convictions, from developing ourselves and from expanding freely according to our own nature. It is the fear of other people's judgment that makes us sterile, and prevents our bearing all the fruits that we are called to bear. 'I was afraid', said the servant who hid his talent in the earth instead of putting it to use (Matt. xxv. 25).

Social suggestion is then the source of innumerable feelings of guilt. A disapproving silence, a scornful or mocking look, a remark, often thoughtlessly made, may well amount to a powerful suggestion. Thus, a girl is weeping on the day after her father's death. 'Don't cry for your father,' her mother flings at her; 'he died because you were not a good girl; now you will obey me!'

The last phrase provides a clue to the feelings that drive the mother, in her confusion, to say such things to her daughter: anguish at finding herself alone to bring up the child, and anxiety to make sure, from the start, that she will be obedient. But she does not calculate how ineradicable such a suggestion may be. Even without any such assertions by the parents, we often find that the idea grows in a child's mind that he is guilty of the death of a father, a brother or a sister, and that the death is a punishment for his own disobedience.

May some nerviness or severity of the parents in their grief have contributed to suggest this idea to him? Whatever the reason, once it has taken root in the mind, it remains there with incredible tenacity. More often than is believed parents or married people allow themselves to be drawn into a kind of blackmail: 'You will make me die of grief! And then when I'm dead you will be sorry; you'll see!' Words spoken in anger, and immediately forgotten by the speaker, but they leave a lasting scar on the one to whom they were said.

Illegitimate children also all feel more or less guilty for their position because of the scorn that comes their way. Terrible childhood memories! 'My friends left me one after the other,' a woman told me, 'telling me that their mothers had forbidden them to see me any more, because I had no father.'

But social suggestion of guilt does not operate merely in extreme cases. There are, for instance, few unmarried women who do not feel slightly guilty for not being married, as if it were their fault. Some defend themselves by taking the offensive, criticizing men as selfish and as very poor judges of a woman's qualities. Some need to make it quite clear that they have turned down several suitors. Others imagine that they have suitors, and believe it sincerely.

It must be recognized that some stupid and unfair discredit attaches to the unmarried woman. And if she is of a nervous type, she is the object of other very unpleasant innuendoes: 'We know what she wants!' Married women give them a further sense of guilt when they say: 'You are lucky to be free; no worries about a domineering husband or sick or noisy children; you can live a nice, quiet, pleasant life.'

Careful examination shows that a similar sense of guilt weighs on the sick, at any rate on many of them, especially on mental or nervous patients. Hence the uneasiness they so often experience about consulting a psychiatrist or psychologist and their care to keep it secret. It is also the reason why their families usually raise objections to their going away to a clinic or feel ashamed if a period in hospital becomes inevitable.

The world is generous in sympathy for the sick and the infirm, but this sympathy is far from being as altruistic as is thought. All kinds of contumely, repugnance and criticism are concealed behind this apparent charity and even sometimes in the conde-scension of the charity. I strive in vain to reassure a young woman who is obsessed by her short-sightedness and who is obliged to wear ugly glasses. I tell her that it is not important and that she ascribes to other people the feelings of contempt which she so fears because of her own obsession. At her very next visit she passes outside my door in front of some workmen busy in the street, who point her out to one another: 'Did you see those glasses?'

Indeed, the social unconscious has a certain defensive repugn-ance for sickness and infirmity, those reminders of human distress which we prefer to forget. Poverty, sickness and death present the human problem to our minds with a painful brutality that many, consciously or unconsciously, would like to ignore. Thus, when the youthful Buddha wished to leave his gilded palace and walk the streets of his capital, his father, the king, hurriedly tried to clear the streets of all the beggars, the sick and the dying. It was a vain attempt, however, and it was this experience which over-whelmed the Buddha and sent him on his grave, unremitting search for an answer to the problem of evil. But everyone does not have his moral stature. Illness sharpens the sensitivity of the sick who are intuitively aware, in many healthy people, of a secret restraint which they feel as contempt.

St. Paul who suffered from some unknown infirmity, thanks the Galatians for their welcome: 'Though my condition was a trial to you, you did not scorn or despise me, but received me as an angel of God, as Christ Jesus' (Gal. iv. 14).

With His usual realism, Jesus refers to this very human tendency to turn aside from suffering in the Parable of the Good Samaritan (Lk. x. 30), and in that of the Last Judgment (Matt. xxv. 43). In his devotion to his patients, the doctor is very ready to think himself exempt from such a complex. Yet he may find it reawakening when he is confronted with an incurable patient, for whom he can do nothing; suddenly he realizes that he is having to make an effort not to avoid him, or to bear his gaze; it is so painful to feel powerless before implacable suffering.

You may say that this unconscious contempt of illness has no connection with the sense of guilt. What an illusion! One always feels rather guilty at arousing revulsion in others, at causing, by illness, a disturbance in the family, an extra burden of work for one's colleagues at the office, extra work and worry for one's wife. Thus a majority of sick people at first refuse to admit that they are ill, they refuse to go to bed or to consult the doctor. All this false guilt about illness is a very common cause of culpable self-neglect.

Behind this false stoicism, there is nearly always the fear of being suspected of enjoying the illness, of coddling oneself. For there is some pleasure when life is hard in suddenly having the right, through illness, to step aside, to be looked after and cosseted. But even those who are conscious of enjoying it, also feel at the same time, a keen sense of guilt. The result is that those who are most ashamed of being ill take least care of themselves.

What is much more serious, however, is the judgment, sometimes expressed, sometimes veiled, which the sick sense in the healthy, even and especially in the best-intentioned of them, and in their words of comfort. Very often devout people are the ones who awaken baneful guilts. Re-read the book of Job and the fine speeches of his friends. At first they had the delicacy to remain silent for 'seven days and seven nights' (Job ii. 13) before his grief. They did not turn their backs on him; they came to 'condole with him and to comfort him'. But carried away by their very zeal, they begin to discourse, to philosophize and to exhort; they talk so much that they do more damage to Job with their fine words than all his misfortunes, so that he exclaims: 'Worthless physicians are you all' (xiii. 4).

Behind these noble sentiments of the healthy, the sick Job detects a terrible spirit of judgment, a continual insinuation that his misfortunes are a divine punishment. Even in their exhortations to faith Job feels an accusation. Thus Bildad says: 'If you will make supplication to the Almighty, if you are pure and upright, surely then he will rouse himself for you and reward you with a rightful habitation' (viii. 5–6). This obviously implies that if Job does not recover, it is because he does not make supplication to the Almighty or because he is not sufficiently zealous in his obedience. Job cries (xxi. 27):

> 'Behold, I know your thoughts,
> And your schemes to wrong me.'

In this way we see believers, theologians and laymen from all Churches and from all denominations, especially the most sincerely zealous in sick-visiting, crushing the sick with religious testimony. The forceful assertion of the power of God who cures those who put their trust in Him, conveys the idea that the sick person lacks faith. He was already feeling a false guilt for being ill; and now a much more serious one is added—a religious one this time: the idea that he is guilty of not recovering despite all the care and prayers lavished on him, the idea that if he does not recover it is because he is not worthy of God's grace or because some interdict, some mysterious unknown sin, stands in the way!

You can see how delicate the problem is. There are divine cures; there are miraculous cures; there are cures by prayer and by faith. Those who have experienced or witnessed such cures are right to speak of them to the glory of God and in order to sustain the hopes of the sick. But people all too quickly overstep the bounds of truth in such testimonies; they generalize as if God cures all those who call on Him, they suggest guiltiness in all those who have recourse to scientific medicine or to drugs, as if these were not also gifts from God.

Passions are quickly roused over questions in which the effective stakes are so high, as is shown by the controversy among Catholics about Lourdes or among Protestants about Pentecostalism. Everybody does not have the extreme discretion of the medical control commission at Lourdes or of a Protestant theologian such as Pastor Bernard Martin. [25] The motives which incite some believers to a kind of higher bid of testimony are so noble that they do not perceive the evil that they can do to their cause or to the sick.

Grave doubt exists in these medical minds of ours before some of the reports of miraculous cures. Sometimes it turns on a suspicion of wrong diagnosis; sometimes on a patient who proclaims himself cured, when it does not seem to us that he is really recovered; moreover he may have some doubts which he will not admit even to himself and he may need to proclaim his recovery all the more loudly in order to convince himself; sometimes it seems to us that there is more of the spirit of magic than of genuine faith in the cure.

Professor Jores of Hamburg[18] has forcefully shown the contrast between the spirit of magic and the spiritual maturity to which we are called by the Gospel and by psychotherapy. It is possible to recover from illness without recovering from the spirit of magic, which is also an illness; it is also possible to invest science and academic medicine with magical properties.

It is also very flattering to offer oneself as an example, to edify other people by one's example, to present oneself as the object of exceptional grace from God. A patient may gain from such things a very legitimate joy which may have real curative value. But then other patients, who have called on God in vain, may, as a result, experience increased sadness and even guilt. A doctor of materialistic outlook will perhaps be able to bring relief by declaring his scepticism of the genuineness of miraculous cures.

When the Gospel speaks of faith which heals, it sometimes refers to the faith of the sufferer: 'Do you believe that I am able to do this?', Jesus asks (Matt. ix. 28) when some blind men seek healing from Him. But more frequently it is a question of the faith of others, of parents or of those interceding for the sick person: the father of the epileptic (Mk. ix. 23–24), or the friends of the paralytic (Mk. ii. 5). When it speaks of prayer which heals, the Gospel sometimes refers to the prayer of the sufferer (Lk. xvii. 13), but more often to the prayers of others (Mk. ix. 29; vii. 26). And we see Jesus curing sick people who expected nothing from Him, the paralytic at Bethesda, for instance, who hoped only for a magical cure (Jn. v. 5–9).

I myself must confess that I feel a keen sense of guilt when we are discussing these problems of spiritual healing. I am fully aware that if I had more faith and were more faithful in prayer, I should more frequently be the instrument of direct divine healing. For we see clearly that without neglecting any technical or scientific help which we can bring to our patients, we should always add the benefits of our intercession.

The spiritual ministry to which we are all called, and which we cannot shirk without a bad conscience, is a highly dangerous one. Thus when we speak of the spiritual aspect of illness, as we do at gatherings of physicians concerned with integrative medicine, we run the risk of loading innocent patients with new and oppressive guilt. Some well-intentioned healthy people repeat our statements to them and recommend our books. Now if it is true that problems of living form a background to all sickness and that sickness may be the outward expression of a psychical or spiritual conflict, the patient feels weighed down with a crushing suspicion. It can never be said too often that there are as many problems of living presented by healthy people as by the sick.

Similarly, every fine exhortation arouses guilt. 'You must . . . you must . . . You must be patient; you must put up with it; you must accept it; you must hope; you must fight. . . .' And the sufferer feels guilty for not being patient, for not being able to hope, to react, to accept. Could the healthy visitor who speaks to him so finely do any better in his place? I speak of all this with deep emotion. For it is closely bound to the sufferings of innumerable lives which are unwittingly aggravated by the admonitions of the most kindly believers.

Take the case of a woman who was sent to me by her surgeon. He would probably have operated, had he not been enlightened on the part that the problems of life might play in her condition. Her confessor had, at an earlier date, sought to stop her marrying a divorced man. In his zeal, in his love for her, he had finished by saying: 'Do you not know that by marrying him you are bringing about his damnation and your own?' How heavily such a phrase can burden the whole life of a profoundly religious woman!

I hope that you will not misunderstand: I am not criticizing the confessor; I am not opening a debate on dogmatics which is not within my competence. I am speaking only as a psychologist and as a man. I cannot study this very serious problem of guilt with you without raising the very obvious and tragic fact that religion—my own as well as that of all believers—can crush instead of liberate. There is a kind of unavoidable reverse side to every declaration of faith, which follows it as faithfully as shadow follows sunshine. To say that one has found truth in Roman Catholic doctrine or in Reformed doctrine, in Pentecostalism or in Adventism, implies to those who do not share our faith that we consider them as lost in error. However little this may concern men tormented and in doubt, they nevertheless become a prey to contradictory guilts; in turn, they wonder if they are rejecting the call of God or if it would be more wrong to adhere to a doctrine which they cannot cordially accept. They reproach themselves still further for this honourable hesitation, thinking that it is guilty.

I recently met again a woman who had become burdened with feelings of inferiority and guilt by the stern upbringing of a domineering father, feelings from which I had tried to free her. While on holiday she had met a very dynamic minister and had told him about her difficulties. 'Have you been born again?' he asked her. She was again quite overcome with feelings of inferiority and guilt: 'It is true,' she mused, 'I have not been born again! But what must I do to achieve it? Others experience it and are freed, whereas it does not happen to me. My torment is proof of this.'

I am not contesting the Gospel message of rebirth, nor the experience of being born again which I have passed through myself, and which really this woman seemed to have done without realizing it as she gradually freed herself from the psychological mechanisms which had crushed her up till then, and as she achieved spiritual freedom. But it was to Nicodemus that Jesus spoke about rebirth (Jn. iii. 5), a scholar, a powerful man in the world, one of the 'strong', self-assured in the deference which surrounded him, just the very opposite of my patient.

This was the man to whom Jesus threw His challenge, a man well able to face up to Him, both in strength and in humility. Nicodemus was trying to achieve a skilful balance between his social character and his private character, his strength and his humility, and Jesus summoned him to choose; one cannot live two lives at once.

It seems important therefore, when we read the Gospel, to take notice not only of the words of Jesus, but also of the person to whom He is speaking. I believe that we doctors have a task, in this connection, in the Churches. For a doctor has the sense of individualization.

By their studies, by their very calling—the teaching of truth— theologians are orientated towards general ideas. They rightly insist on the universal value of the divine revelation. They preach 'broadcast'. I am alluding to a parable of Jesus Himself, the Parable of the Sower (Lk. viii. 5–8). The theologian makes it his business to sow the most excellent and purest possible seed.

We doctors, accustomed to thinking in 'cases', think of the ground on which the seed falls. The ground certainly contains thorns and stones, as Jesus said, the sins which can choke growth. But it also contains such varied qualities as the different temperaments of men, their physical and psychical make-up. A single biblical phrase can produce the most salutary shock in one soul and wound another.

This is what makes this problem of the connections between feelings of inferiority and guilt so complex and dramatic. I do not think that a clear line of demarcation can be drawn between them. All inferiority is experienced as guilt.

Chapter III

MATTERS OF TIME

IN the street I notice an old friend some distance away. For many years our work had brought us together very frequently, but this is no longer the case and I am afraid that he reproaches me for neglecting him. I may be wrong in ascribing this grievance to him, but I am none the less sensitive to it. I might be tempted to avoid him, yet this would put a more serious guilt upon me, that of disloyal action.

I greet him then with rather exaggerated eagerness, a lively joviality; I congratulate him on looking so well, and talk volubly in very friendly terms. I realize that it is to give him no chance of saying the dreaded words: 'It is a long time since you came to see me.' I feel guilty for my rather forced, superficial attitude, for I like to be honest with my friends. Moreover, I have a great genuine regard for the man and this is what makes my reactions look so bad. I should not like him to measure my friendship by the frequency of my visits. I shall never be able to say with complete sincerity, that I have no time to go and visit this friend. We can always find time to do what we really wish to do.

When I have a lecture to prepare, or a piece of work like this study, I always promise myself to take my time and do it carefully. Then I keep putting it off, I have difficulty in settling down to it, just because I am very keen on doing it well and am afraid of failing. I find all sorts of other things to do first.

The subtle thing about this is that by wasting time, I am building up a sense of guilt which I need to drive me to work. It is as though I were building up the power of an auxiliary motor which will get me moving. On the eve of the lecture a moment will come when I shall feel so conscience-stricken at having prepared it so badly that I shall rush to it, just as one must jump into the water from a burning ship. It will be a kind of excuse for the inadequacy of my work: it is a pity if it is less good than I would have wished, but I must be satisfied with what can be done in a hurry.

A friend of mine experiences the same sort of unease when he puts off an urgent and difficult task. What makes us different is that the unease stimulates me, and suddenly gives me wings when it reaches an intolerable level. In his case, however, a bad conscience paralyses him. All his work is hampered. He cannot settle to another task when the main one is incomplete, and the longer this is put off, the greater his paralysis becomes. It can be seen that the same feeling of guilt can be either a stimulant or a brake.

The stimulating role of guilt probably explains the pleasure that innumerable people feel and seek in the commission of mis-demeanours which they consider harmless, without being caught—customs frauds, for instance. This is why some people, without realizing it fully, will buy trifling articles abroad, merely for the pleasure of passing through the Customs without declaring them.

In such activity there is probably a need for revenge against the power of the State and Administration, an age-old Punch-com-plex which makes fun of the policeman. The proof of this often lies in the fact that duty would not have been levied by the Customs or would have been so trifling that it would not justify the delight which the offender feels in avoiding it. The same complex oper-ates in taxation fraud, which is so widespread in some countries that the legislators recognize it as normal and make provisions which would be absolutely unjust and insupportable if anyone were stupid enough to submit to them honestly.

In his turn, the taxpayer thinks that the State is robbing him enough to justify his robbing the State. Where is this delicate balance of reciprocal theft to end? Obviously it brings with it some demoralization in both State and people. For none of these rationalizations removes the sense of guilt.

Even in time of war, to deceive the invader appears as a great virtue, but is nevertheless accompanied by a sense of guilt. During and after the war I have seen many men who felt a need to confess such conduct, even while they were extremely proud of it and ready to do the same again, in similar circumstances.

If these so-called harmless frauds are so attractive to many people, it is because of the risk of prosecution. Hence comes what is popularly called enjoying the forbidden fruit: enjoying the risk and enjoying being free from it if one escaped the Customs' men.

But this game has another side to it—that of an antidote. It is an attempt to overcome guilt by familiarity. By resolutely multi-plying opportunities for minor guilt, we try to make ourselves sufficiently familiar with the emotion in order to be less subject to it in major cases, in which we are really ashamed because our true nature is then compromised. We confuse the issue so that the contrast between good and evil is weakened and the boundary between them blurred.

This brings me back to the guilt of wasted time. Just as I was writing these lines a former patient came and sat beside me. 'Am I disturbing you? Are you busy?'—'Oh no. What's been hap-pening to you?' I was really pleased to see him again, for he brought good news of the remaking of his own life, a process which had begun four or five years ago in my consulting room. And yet I could not give him my full attention for I was beset with mixed feelings of guilt.

During the whole conversation, I felt that I should have told him frankly: 'Please excuse me; I have urgent work to do. We shall be able to talk more easily another time.' I did not dare. I have always been rather ashamed of my timidity, because it limits my freedom. I felt guilty at putting down my pen at the moment when I should have been writing. But if I had not recently myself wasted much more time in my hesitations than this interview cost me, I would have been easier in my mind at parting from my visitor. Thus one first secret fault determines our behaviour and leads us into other faults which draw their venom and their power from the first unconfessed guilt.

The problem of organizing our time is rich in cross-currents of guilt. When I speak about it at a gathering of doctors, the whole audience laughs. This means that all of them feel remorse on this subject and relief at discovering that they are not alone. Yet we all feel its importance, that our real liberty is at stake and also the concrete sovereignty of God in our lives. Dr. Théo Bovet has dealt with it in a charming little book.[4]

Time belongs to God, and we are stewards of time, we are responsible to Him for every minute that He gives us. We all feel that if we listened to Him more carefully, our lives would be more harmonious.

We are all overworked and tired and the bad conscience over things that we cannot do wearies us as much as the things we can do. How many doctors' wives fret at seeing their husbands thus burdened? Long ago the wife of Moses was probably preoccupied with this matter (Ex. xviii. 13–24), but her husband paid no more attention to her than many present-day doctors pay to the good advice given by their wives. And so Moses' wife appealed to the authority of her father to warn him: 'You will wear yourself out!' he said to Moses. Fortunately Moses listened to him and wisely delegated to others the less important tasks which could be entrusted to them.

Friends are not the only ones to be neglected. Letters lie un-answered, professional journals and many other documents pile up on the desk, or in the cupboard if one cannot bear the sight of them any more. They should be scanned if we are to keep up to date. We try to persuade ourselves that we shall tackle it one day, but we are not deceived, for experience has taught us that it takes much more time than we think. The greater the pile, the fainter the hope.

One day in my life, I could bear it no longer. At a time of silent reflection it seemed to me that so much disorder and tardiness were a monumental denial of all that I ever said about a healthy, bright, free life, guided by God. For more than three months I did nothing outside my consultations except clear off the arrears to bring myself up to date. What a relief! But it is an ever-recurrent problem. I have become much more orderly, but for all that I am still not free from many guilty feelings.

I feel intolerable uneasiness when my mail piles up. To relieve my conscience, I have cancelled my subscription to many journals, but then I hardly dare admit that I no longer receive some particular great medical journal to which my serious-minded colleagues subscribe. Yes, a guilty conscience is indeed the inevitable seasoning of our daily life.

The whole problem of organization of our time becomes still more acute as our powers decrease with advancing years. It is one of the sufferings of old age and can become an obsession. Which activities should be given up? What should be continued in spite of fatigue? Are we betraying our task by giving up such and such an activity? Or do we show arrogance by carrying on with it, and a culpable contempt for our health?

This also applies to invalids. I have noticed something curious about them; very often they will ask, 'How far should I accept my infirmity, and how far should I fight, in an attempt to overcome it, to re-adapt myself?' As if accepting and reacting were mutually exclusive. In fact we see the opposite taking place—those who accept their infirmity also react best; whereas the rebellious ones make no effort at re-adaptation, just because of their rebelliousness.

Living means choosing. But do we always choose freely and consciously? Is our choice not frequently forced on us by circumstances, by our faint-heartedness, our habits or even our guilts? Thus if I have qualms of conscience towards a friend, I feel in his debt and shall not dare to refuse him a service which will occupy time that I ought to devote to other things. This will help to overburden me, to make me irritable, and to increase still further my sense of guilt.

Of course, I have had to learn to refuse my services, to turn down invitations to lecture for instance. But I always do it unwillingly. I am reluctant to disappoint other people, and feel remorseful when I do so. Could I not be rightly reproached for accepting, yesterday, another lecture which will take still more of my time? Thus if I refuse, I feel guilty towards those who were expecting something from me; but if I accept, I feel guilty towards myself for allowing myself to be swayed.

Do I not run the risk of giving in to the most importunate, to the detriment of the more reserved? Or—a more subtle risk—of giving in to the latter because I am touched by their reserve? I go abroad to medical congresses to which I am invited, and I almost never attend the Medical Society of Geneva; I have qualms of conscience about this, towards my colleagues, who are always so kind to me, and towards myself, for missing these opportunities of learning.

Then there are all the books which I should have read before venturing into writing myself, about subjects which other authors have studied carefully before me. I often make up my mind, not without embarrassment, to quote from them, on the strength of their reputation; but accuracy demands that I know them well before speaking about them. I am a slow reader and so read few books; each of these is sure to list the titles of a good dozen other books which I should read, and it makes me still more ashamed to confess that I have not read them.

On the other hand, others read a great deal; they devour book after book, not without a bad conscience about this insatiable appetite and the disproportion between what they receive and what they give out. If I gave up my writing, I too should feel guilty, for I should be spared criticism at the expense of a cowardly surrender, unfaithfulness to my vocation. The time that I give to writing cannot be given to patients whom I have to refuse, or to my wife who runs the risk of having only what is left over from my time.

These questions are a perpetual torment to many of my colleagues. When a doctor gives his wife a fine present, he may not admit that it is in order to win forgiveness for giving her so little of his time, because he is so absorbed by his profession. He is disappointed when she receives the gift with little show of enthusiasm. The reason is that she would infinitely prefer her husband to give her the time that a husband owes his wife.

Of course, gifts are not always a cloak for guilt; but probably more often than we think. Thus before Jacob goes to meet his brother whom he has treated so badly, we see him sending to Esau huge flocks, which he divides into successive batches in order to increase the effect! (Gen. xxxii. 13–32).

But Jacob is not thus freed from his bad conscience. It may even have been exacerbated by this crafty act. And while waiting to meet his brother, he spends a terrible night, a positive nightmare, a veritable battle! He wrestles with himself. More than that, he finds that he is wrestling with God. Then with the audacity that is so characteristic, he calls on God to bless him.

That is the great paradox which we find time after time in the Bible; the painful path of humiliation and guilt, with all the

heartache and rebellion against God which it brings, is the very
path which opens on to the royal road of grace. God loves those
who, instead of dodging the problem, face up to it, even to the
point of challenge and rebellion. 'I have seen God face to face,
and yet my life [*nephesh*, soul] is preserved,' cried Jacob.

Jacob has passed through the greatest experience possible: he
is a new man; that is why God gives him a new name—Israel.
From that moment, he is able to meet his brother with a security
that all his gifts could not assure—the blessing of God. 'Esau ran
to meet him, embraced him, and fell on his neck and kissed him,
and they wept' (Gen. xxxiii. 4).

From that moment also, Israel limps. It can so happen that an
illness may seem like a sequel to a spiritual combat.

But let us return to the doctor's family. Sometimes the children
too would rather have some really genuine contact with their
father than expensive gifts. The mother can vainly explain: 'Your
father is so dedicated, you understand; we must not bother him.'
The children come to the conclusion that the patients mean more
to their father than themselves. It is dangerous, moreover, to
have an absorbing vocation. It can often lead to self-deception and
to salving one's bad conscience towards one's family. It is sometimes many years, and in more or less tragic circumstances, that a
man realizes suddenly how far he has neglected his calling as a
father, and feels deeply remorseful as a result.

Is it not true, in a sense, that men seek refuge from a body of
diffused guilts in a frenzy of work, rather than face up to them?
Does not this overwork, this running about outside, provide a
fine alibi which we can invoke in self-exculpation? Or very often,
a kind of expiation by work? And when it is a seeking after gain
or social esteem or gratitude from those we serve that draws us
into this maelstrom, should we not see in this too, a cloak for
guilt? For this quest is the expression of a need to regain self-
esteem, as an antidote to the loss of it which guilt brings in its
train.

We see many people who are perpetually lamenting the lack of
time, without ever seriously considering what sacrifices they could
make to remedy the situation. They accuse civilization, modern
life, the motor car, machines, all the things which have been invented to save time, as if they were only the victims rather than
the culprits.

Deep down, we know that we all have our share of responsibility to this unhealthy climate of restlessness, that we allow
ourselves to be swept along by the current of life instead of
resisting it by the reform of our own lives, and that the problem
is a personal rather than a social one.

If we have qualms of conscience over wasting time, as we discussed a while ago, we also have them for not knowing how to waste time, not knowing how to take things easily, how to rest as God has ordered (Ex. xx. 10); or how to meditate, how to pray or spend time in quiet contemplation. It is at times of such contemplation that we rediscover the inward peace that the world of today so much needs. How can we give it to our patients if we do not have it ourselves? How can we teach them to organize their lives better if our own are so much of a bustle? In contemplation, we rediscover the correct order of values, a clear distinction between what is really important and what is secondary, or even dangerous.

When we open the Gospel, we see that Jesus Christ whose responsibilities were far greater than ours, seemed to be in much less of a hurry. He had plenty of time to speak to a foreign woman whom He met at a well (Jn. iv. 1–26). He had time to spend holidays with His disciples (Mk. viii. 27); time to admire the lilies of the field (Matt. vi. 28), or a sunset (Matt. xvi. 2); time to wash His disciples' feet (Jn. xiii. 5), and to answer their naïve questions without impatience (Jn. xiv. 5–10). Most important, He had time to go into the desert to pray (Lk. v. 16); or to spend a whole night in prayer before an important decision (Lk. vi. 12).

This time of silent meditation is always a good barometer of my own spiritual life. Periodically, I rediscover its decisive importance; periodically also, I weaken, not without a sterile sense of guilt. I am also struck to see how many people develop ingenious theories to clear their bad conscience in this connection; vainly, however, as is shown by the multiplicity of their arguments and their peremptory tone of voice. 'A guilty conscience needs no accuser,' says the proverb. One day, almost a year ago, I realized that I was doing myself harm because I had begun to read the newspaper before my morning meditation, the time when God was asking me to listen to Him before listening to the world. Rectifying this was simple, but it was enough to brighten again the climate of my life.

I have just read these last words to my wife. She immediately answered: 'It is just the opposite in my case; I listen first to the radio news and that thoroughly wakens me; after that I can meditate to some purpose.' So each one must sincerely seek his own way of making contact with God.

Jesus also knew how to slip away from the enthusiastic crowd which wanted to direct Him into a brilliant public career (Jn. vi. 15). He even knew how to refuse, with extraordinary calmness, a weeping mother, the Canaanite woman, and not to turn aside, on her account, from the path which God had set before Him (Matt.

xv. 22-28). Yet when He discovered her faith, He knew how to change His mind and thus show His true inner freedom.

It is this freedom that we yearn for: the freedom to act or not to act, to speak or to remain silent, to do one thing rather than another, to work or to rest, according to the way God moves us. Whether we are believers or not, we always feel guilty for letting ourselves be led by worldly considerations, however noble they may be, rather than by an inner, personal inspiration.

Chapter IV

MONEY MATTERS

I REMEMBER my first day at school. I was the only one wearing a wide-brimmed hat, and as a result, my new schoolfellows immediately nicknamed me 'devil-dodger'. This affected me deeply; I was an orphan and withdrawn and was here having my first experience of that pitiless society of a school class and of the need to make the difficult adaptation to its law. Its law is that of the herd, and any schoolboy who distinguishes himself from the herd by some eccentricity quickly becomes the object of attention. I felt ashamed and guilty at not being like the others.

At that age, a child is acutely sensitive to the shame of poverty when he compares himself with his better-dressed fellows who can buy sweets and fascinating toys for themselves. I have heard innumerable poignant accounts from those who suffered from misery in childhood and from all the outrages which childhood brings.

A mother, deserted by her husband, has run up such a debt at the grocer's that she dare not go to the shop herself. But the children must be fed, so she sends her little daughter. The child knows what to expect and at first refuses to go. But the mother scolds her! She feels guilty at disobeying and sets off.

'Have you any money?' asks the woman in the shop; 'Go home and bring some; I cannot let you have anything without money.' The child cannot make any answer; she goes away in tears. She feels guilty because she has no money like the other little girls who go to the grocer's; she feels guilty for being poor. She wanders about the streets, afraid of the terrible guilt which she will feel when she sees her mother weeping or scolding her for coming home empty-handed.

And if only the woman in the shop were the only one! Even the good ladies of the parish who bring parcels to help out unwittingly arouse, by their attitude, words and gestures, innumerable feelings of guilt in the little girl. They have a queer way of saying, 'You mustn't eat it all at once; your mother is very poor; you must make it last a long time,' Or they say to the mother: 'We thought it would be more useful to bring a few old clothes for the children rather than toys.'

And that goes on all through life. How many people dare not go to Church because they have only shabby clothes and cannot bear the scornful, condescending or pitiful look of the middle-class folks in their Sunday best! These latter are the guilty ones, of course, but the poor are the ones who look and feel guilty, whilst the others, imbued with the merit of their own piety, greet one another ceremoniously.

No one is immune to the judgment which lurks everywhere in society. If you are taciturn, you are called aloof; if you talk a lot, you are said to be ostentatious. A woman wearing severely cut clothes is scornfully considered as 'repressed'; if her dress is more daring, she is judged as an adventuress. All the guests are to be in evening dress and you knew nothing about it; you are the only one in a lounge suit. If you are wealthy, they will admire your simplicity and will think that you wanted to put them at their ease; but if you are poor, they will treat you as uncouth. If you make the contrary mistake and are the only one 'dressed', you will be just as upset. So the problem is not so much in poverty or wealth but in the inevitable comparisons mutually made between people.

Thus money is the source of innumerable feelings of guilt and of contradictory guilts at that. We feel shame because we lack money, we also feel shame at possessing it, at earning it. Many doctors have confessed to me that they cannot send off bills without a feeling of guilt. If the patient is not cured, it means being paid for services which have proved useless. If the patient is cured, it is almost worse: it is to exploit the service given and thereby destroy its value.

Many doctors hand over the task of dispatching bills to an accountant or to the secretary of their clinic; many have told me that they became missionary doctors or industrial doctors to be relieved of the problem of bills for fees, or that they opened clinics so that their fees could be concealed in the inclusive charge for treatment as an in-patient. Hence also the participation of doctors in the detailed and official price-fixing which has become general for all types of treatment. This relieves them of personal responsibility in fixing fees and in claiming payment from patients who are thus cut off by an impersonal ruling.

But it also removes from medicine the personal relationship; it turns patients into 'cases' and doctors into clerks. In Geneva, my colleagues found a way of preserving a relatively liberal system, but only at the cost of hard struggles and searching criticism. But then if the doctor has qualms about making the normal charge to people less rich than himself, and the patient is plunged into greater financial straits by the illness, the doctor feels guilty towards his own family if, as often happens, he gives the patient free treatment. This happens in all walks of life. A conscientious clerk has qualms about asking for an increase in salary which he is not sure is fully deserved by his work and qualms also because his wife must manage on an income which imposes restrictions and anxiety on her.

He walks round the town with her; she admires a pretty dress in a shop window and wants him to share her admiration: 'Look! It is beautiful!' He does not look. He takes the remark as a reproach. He tries to take her elsewhere, and buys her a little bunch of violets, as a kind of compensation for not buying her the dress.

Often the wife works and earns and buys pretty dresses with her own money. Then the children are left out in the street or are alone in the house when they return from school; they have to let themselves in with the key hung round their necks and there is no one to welcome them. Then again the husband has a feeling of guilt—so deeply ingrained in the human heart is the idea that a family-man should be the breadwinner, despite the evolution in customs.

All discussions of domestic finances are loaded with more, or less conscious guilts, from which such discussions draw their venom. When a woman speaks of the cost of living, her husband becomes nervous and abrupt, for he feels these complaints as rebukes. He shirks any serious discussion designed to help his wife in organizing her budget. He gives her a sum which he knows is insufficient and tells her to make do. He shuts his eyes to the problem and has a guilty conscience. Often, he does not even tell her how much he earns, for fear of provoking her to spend, whereas he squanders more money than he will admit on paltry pleasures. It is possible to complain loudly about being short of money and yet spend it foolishly.

Other husbands give it only grudgingly, bit by bit. Incessantly, their wives have to make unwelcome requests, until they feel really guilty for asking, as if it were their fault that children grow quickly and wear out their shoes. And many wives have no other resource than to falsify the household accounts in order to have enough for their personal needs. Complete financial truthfulness between husband and wife is very rare and their mutual concealments are always guilt-ridden. Each fears a critical judgment from the other partner about personal expenses.

By upbringing and complex, I am more given to spending than my wife. And so when she approves an expenditure, I am quick to consider it as legitimate. In this way I put responsibility on my wife which I wrongfully shed from my own shoulders. As in the organization of our time, we all feel that the genuineness of our submission to God operates daily and in concrete form in our decisions about money. Here too we are quick to say that what we possess is God's, and that we are not proprietors but stewards.

However true and sincere this thought may be, it can be for wealthy people a way of salving the bad conscience which they feel for being rich. It can be very convenient—or on the other hand, to a person of scruples, very disturbing—to consider oneself as a steward for the belongings of a far-off proprietor, whose instructions are only received in a confused kind of way. In all honesty, it must be confessed how hard it is in practice to judge God's will in the use of our money.

And so it is invaluable for married couples at least to seek divine inspiration together, by means of quiet communion. But those very psychological factors which I have mentioned deprive many couples of the calm necessary for that seeking of God's plan, when money is under discussion. A priest or a friend may be approached for advice. But J.-P. Sartre[37] does not seem mistaken when he says that we select our counsel by our choice of counsellor. We can almost always foresee who will approve our plans and who will advise against them.

I once had an interesting experience of this kind of thing. At the time, my wife and I were talking about taking the children for a cruise along the Dalmatian coast and on to Greece. Was such an expense legitimate, more particularly was it willed by God? Such a thing can be argued interminably in one's own mind, with a host of plausible arguments but without altogether silencing an inner doubt. It seemed to us also in our own meditations that if we submitted the question to a friend from the same social milieu as ourselves, this check would not be of much value.

At the time I had close links with a group of workers in a nearby factory. One evening I went to the home of one of them with all my household accounts; all my bank statements and my tax declarations. With his encouragement, we went for our cruise, but I shall never forget the wonderful evening I spent with that friend.

All of us in fact are usually so reserved, so rarely transparent, with so little inclination to talk freely about our financial problems, even to close friends, and especially to those who appear to be less privileged than ourselves. Important trade union officers will conceal from the workers the affluence they have achieved in serving the workers' cause. It is just this lack of frankness which is the source of a sense of guilt.

Then the whole of society becomes organized in an attempt to exorcise this guilt which is inexorably bound up with the privileges of freedom. Wages are fixed by collective agreements;

advancement becomes automatic with seniority. I am certainly not criticizing progress which reduces in any way the terrible guilt of social injustice.

For if there is a guilt of wretchedness, there is also a guilt of ownership which has fortunately developed as the cry of misery has become louder. But all the social legislation which the proletariat has forced out of the bourgeoisie, and which is still so cruelly insufficient, appears as an inadequate veil thrown over the guilty conscience of the privileged. The too noisy witnesses of social injustice are suppressed so that affluence can be enjoyed with less uneasiness.

A certain sense of guilt is a corollary of any privilege even when the privilege is deserved. An employee of quality feels it towards his fellows when an appreciative chief entrusts him with the highest responsibilities. A girl who is asked to sing in Church at Christmas has this feeling towards a friend who would have dearly liked to be invited instead. Any envy or jealousy of other people arouses some guilty conscience in us.

Similarly in the world of work, anyone who does not work feels a sense of guilt which he hides as best he can under ingratiating manners. So also do those who earn too much money, or who earn it too easily, and exculpate themselves by generous endowments to the Church, social works or by founding scholarships or prizes. We often find a sense of guilt also in a woman who has been too spoilt in life by her husband, and vice-versa.

So what separates people is not only the differences in their positions, nor merely the envy which the differences arouse in the less privileged, but also the fact that they awaken among those who are envied a guilty conscience which spoils their pleasure. By a curious paradox, the employee who fully deserves his advancement and who has not asked for it is more troubled before his fellows than another, without scruples, who has deliberately set out to achieve it, by more or less doubtful means.

You may think that I am contradicting myself, that I am openly admitting in this way that there are people without scruples and without guilt. I am using the expression in the popular way, but it is only a manner of speaking. Do not imagine that the careerist is really untouched by guilt. See how he needs to explain his conduct, to disparage others and to justify himself, to put forward to others as well as to himself a corrected account of events which exonerates him from all reproach. People who are apparently without scruples are people who have pushed their scruples out of clear consciousness.

I feel uneasy at being in good health when there are so many people sick; happy, when there are so many people unhappy;

at having money when so many are short of it. I feel a certain
discomfort too at having an interesting vocation when so many
people sigh beneath the burden of a job they hate; and even at
having been taken hold of by God and illuminated by faith, when
so many people suffer in anguish, isolation and obscurity.

I recently spoke of this to one of my colleagues, a psychiatrist.
With a knowing smile, full of kindness, he replied: 'I am your
friend, but I must also be your doctor to a certain extent.' He
said this to tell me kindly that he found my feelings of guilt really
morbid. I do not deny it. You have perhaps all thought the same
as you have followed my argument up to this point. He explained
to me what he meant. 'You are suffering,' he said, 'from a distorted
sense of responsibility. We are not responsible for the whole
world, but, more modestly, for a small immediate circle. If we are
faithful within these limits, we can have a clear conscience.'

At that, I was laden with fresh guilt. It is indeed true that we are
guilty of pride in feeling ourselves responsible in this way for the
whole world and all its injustices. Pharisaism also would ensnare
me: we can pity the Indians who are dying of hunger without
seeing the distresses close at hand which we ought to remedy.

But these reassuring considerations are not enough for me.
In the meantime, I received a letter from a foreign friend. He
wrote: 'I have just discovered that, according to statistics, a large
proportion of mankind is under-nourished; the good things of
the earth are badly distributed. As a consequence I am uneasy
when I eat and when I sleep in a bed; and I don't dare to seek
amusement on Sundays and holidays.'

Of course, my friend the psychiatrist will be able to say that
this man too, like me, is rather ill. But there is another illness as
well, a universal illness, a vast 'repression of conscience'. If there
is so much suffering in the world, is it not because so many good
people, who are very moral, even scrupulous in their immediate
responsibilities, reassure themselves too easily by telling themselves that those distant sufferings on such a grand scale are outside their radius of action? They persuade themselves that they
can do nothing about it. In this way flagrant injustices subsist
through a sort of universal complicity.

From time to time a prophet emerges, like the Abbé Pierre
recently in France, to stir people's consciences. He awakens a
sense of guilt which had been repressed in innumerable hearts, he
broadens once more the sense of responsibility and achieves
reforms believed to be impossible.

On hearing the voice of such a prophet many remember suddenly the story of Pilate who washed his hands in the presence of
the crowd to mark clearly the formal limits of his responsibilities.

'I am innocent of this righteous man's blood', he said (Matt. xxvii. 24). This dramatic ceremony did not relieve Pilate's bad conscience, however, and we see this afterwards by his having the inscription put on the Cross, 'Jesus of Nazareth, the King of the Jews' (Jn. xix. 19). It was a sort of atoning profession of faith. In this way many people who feel guilty at remaining cowardly inert in face of the evils of the world find relief in making empty verbal protests.

'There will always be somewhere a stray dog to prevent me from being happy,' cries the Sauvage in Anouilh's play.[42] And I admire Simone Weil's noble scruple about crossing the threshold of the Church 'like a sort of painful refusal to enter into the comfort of the elect when there exists the wretchedness of the outcasts'.

As long as there are injustices, crimes and sufferings in the world we all feel, consciously or not, that extensive sense of guilt which my friend called morbid, unless we assume another sense of guilt—that of dissociating ourselves from the responsibilities of others.

A theory of limited responsibility, the confession of our powerlessness in the face of so many evils, cannot really satisfy us. We need another answer to the problem. My friend felt this clearly himself and our conversation soon turned upon another topic: 'Where does the grace of God come in?' he asked me then. 'It is precisely because I am acutely aware of our guilt in all its extent,' I told him, 'that I am also acutely aware of grace, which is our sole help.'—'Well, that's all right,' he said.

But where is the limit to complicity? It is often a very delicate problem. Many employees, secretaries and salesmen, have confided in me about such heart-searchings. They know that their boss tricks customers or business partners. Must they carry out orders which they know are dishonest? Sometimes they go so far as to talk about it to their boss who usually takes great exception to a subordinate's interference in questions which do not concern him and about which he is not, in fact, always fully informed.

I always remember too a young woman pharmacist who suddenly realized that she was handing over an abortive product to a pregnant woman. In her consternation she confided in her boss about it. But very calmly he told her that she had only to make up doctors' prescriptions and not to discuss them. What they prescribed was their affair and not hers. She gave up her career as a pharmacist.

In reality, whatever the good reasons we may invoke to defend ourselves from other people's faults we always feel guilty of them. A sense of human solidarity is deeply infused in the soul of every man. He feels it more keenly when one of those near to him is involved. If his brother wins honour or glory through some striking act he is absolutely proud of him even if he has had nothing to do with it himself. On the contrary, if this brother commits a shameful crime he feels shame at it himself, even if he apparently has no hand in it.

Thus we see people who all their lives foster a social shame which they have contracted in their childhood because their father at that time went bankrupt, or because their parents were divorced. Their friends at school turned their backs on them, for if we ourselves can forget the solidarity uniting us to those near to us, the world can well remind us of it. And these children have felt the family dishonour like a guilt.

We feel this solidarity too on the national plane. If my federal government committed a grave error in its internal or international politics, I should disavow and criticize it in vain. Guilt would fall on me even if I were myself the first victim of this fault. And the zeal I can expend in criticizing the government if I am of the opposition has its origin precisely in the keen need I feel to push off on to it a guilt which affects me. Moreover, even if I read in the newspaper that a Swiss has committed a crime in Venezuela I feel a certain shame at it.

But must I not feel myself responsible also for other nations? In that respect I have a very vivid recollection. It was in Germany just after the war at a doctors' meeting. Transport was still disorganized and a speaker whose subject was to have been death had not been able to get there. A theologian, a German colleague and myself, combined to take his place. My colleague said, 'We must speak of the concentration camps and of the doctors who agreed to be the instruments of murder.' 'Well,' I replied' it is your job to deal with that subject; not mine as a Swiss. I'll talk on something else.' And that is what we decided to do.

But in the evening in my room I suddenly realized that that sentence which I had pronounced was tinged with Swiss Pharisaism. It was akin to the 'that is your affair' of Pontius Pilate. It let my colleague understand that because he was a German, and even though he had been persecuted and ruined himself by the Nazis, he was more allied than I was to the doctor-murderers. How upset I was! I got up, and went and woke him to ask him to forgive me.

The circle of these collective responsibilities grows wider and wider. Where is its limit? There is no limit. We have a guilty conscience in the eyes of our children and grandchildren in leaving them such a disturbing world to live in. And many physicists today in the face of threats of atomic weapons are rudely awakened to a general sense of the responsibilities of the scholar—an awareness which beautiful theories about the moral neutrality of science had hitherto stifled.

The more a stranger the guilty person is to me the more easily I can deceive myself and persuade myself that what concerns him is his affair alone. But this movement of dissociation appears to me, if I am honest, as a sort of guilty refusal of my human vocation, the dignity of which resides in the sense of responsibility.

This is the case in particular of a leader when he realizes the scope of his acts and that innocent people may pay for his mistakes. Thus David took a census of his people to pride himself on his power, which was displeasing to God. When the plague spread over the land, David cried: 'Lo, I have sinned, and I have done wickedly; but these sheep, what have they done?' (2 Sam. xxiv. 17).

The more acute this sense of responsibility becomes the keener too becomes the guilt we feel at all the evil in the world. 'Who is made to fall, and I am not indignant?' St. Paul exclaims (2 Cor. xi. 29). And St. Peter speaks of that righteous man Lot who 'was vexed in his righteous soul day after day' with the lawless deeds of his contemporaries (2 Pet. ii. 8). We ought to quote here the beautiful passages from the prophet Ezekiel who felt himself appointed as a watchman responsible for the sins of others (Ezek. iii. 16–21; xxxiii. 1–11); or again, Aaron who in his office of priest bore before God all the iniquities of his people. But it is in Jesus Christ that this sense of responsibility towards men reaches limitless extent. We feel this in His whole attitude—when He weeps over Jerusalem and her crimes (Matt. xxiii. 37); when He regards the crowd like sheep without a shepherd (Matt. ix. 36); when He refers to the shepherd's anguish for the least of his lost sheep until he finds it (Lk. xv. 4); when He adds mysteriously that He has yet other sheep which are not of this fold and that finally there will be but one flock and one shepherd (Jn. x. 16). We realize it above all when we see Him moving towards the Cross. He was innocent, burdened with the whole of human guilt, as Isaiah had prophesied: 'He was wounded for our transgressions, he was bruised for our iniquities; . . . he bore the sin of many' (Is. liii. 5, 12).

Thus the spiritual life and ministry, far from alleviating the burden of guilt, rather increase its weight. Moreover it is not a question, as with Jesus Christ, of the guilt of others only. The nearer we get to God the more we experience His grace, and the more we experience His grace, the more too we discover faults in ourselves which we did not discern before, and the more we suffer from them.

Chapter V

OUR INNER WORLD

WHILE I was preparing this study I suddenly received a telegram from America. I had promised to send an article for the month already passed, and there was the periodical in which it was to appear ready for printing! I had completely forgotten. I was full of embarrassment. The colleague who sent me the telegram will surely doubt my friendship, which is none the less real. But then, why did I not think of him? Thus, at any time, a telegram, a demand, can suddenly denounce an oversight, a piece of negligence, a mistake, of which we were already guilty without realizing it.

There is then a kind of latent, unconscious, yet fearful guilt. We live constantly under the threat of a revelation which is impossible to avert since we cannot think of everything. By delaying writing a letter we may have done someone an ill and we are suddenly aware of it when the damage can no longer be repaired. In the case of such and such a patient we did not think of making an additional examination which would have avoided a stupid error of diagnosis.

That is in fact the condition in which we live: the vague, anxious consciousness that to all the faults which we recognize we have there is certainly added a greater number still which some incident or other may suddenly bring to light. Thus St. Peter, when the cock crew, suddenly became fully aware of his denial when it was too late. 'And he went out and wept bitterly' (Matt. xxvi. 75).

We are continually beneath the threat of some cock-crow which will plunge us into embarrassment. This maintains within us a certain permanent anxiety. We feel ourselves in a state of presuming that we are continually in a condition of unforeseeable, transient guilt.

Moreover, into all anxiety there slips a little of that fear of being guilty without knowing it, which makes it all the more painful. A child is late returning home: I do hope nothing has happened to him! Perhaps I shouldn't have let him go so far? Perhaps I should have insisted more forcibly that he should repair his bicycle brakes? Perhaps I didn't give him all the necessary advice? Perhaps there is only a simple misunderstanding about the time of his return, but then, that means I didn't make myself clear enough; I am really still the same, as vague as ever! That will play me a bad trick some time! . . . What else? . . . I have perhaps other responsibilities of which I am not aware.

The child returns, full of smiles. He innocently dallied while talking to a friend. I am now quite confused, and my anxiety itself seems guilty to me. I risk standing in the light of the child's development if I am so lacking in confidence as that. My spate of questions disappears, but it will soon reappear on some other topic; it will turn about in my head in an intangible whirlwind of hypothetical guilts, which may even so be real.

What is annoying in forgetfulness is the feeling of powerlessness which it leaves. We cannot think of everything. We invoke forgetfulness as an excuse: 'I beg your pardon, dear Sir, I am sorry, I completely forgot.' But forgetfulness is also an accusation as much as an excuse. It is true that I ought not to have forgotten if I were conscientious, foreseeing, faithful, lucid, master of myself. Thus, for example, we are always confused when we do not succeed in remembering the name of one of our patients.

There is more to it than that. Freud has demonstrated to us that no omission, any more than a lapse, ever happens by chance. It betrays an unconscious impulse contrary to our conscious intentions. At bottom, well before psychoanalysis, men already had an inkling of it. Forgetfulness reveals a fault of agreement with oneself, the existence of an inner cunning and active force which bungles our conscious action; it is a force which escapes our will, which hides in the shadow and strikes us unexpectedly from behind.

And so we feel that we are, in a sense, not responsible for it, and yet at the same time guilty; it reveals to others, as to ourselves, the fact that we are not entirely such as we appear to be. We profess our friendship and suddenly our forgetfulness belies it and betrays a hostility which we should like to deny. Behind the virtues which we flaunt there are innumerable guilts which we should prefer to close our eyes to, and which we should not succeed in identifying exactly even if we wished.

The fear of forgetting something plunges certain people into real distress when they have to pack their bags before setting off on a journey. We also feel we are always guilty of our absent-mindedness. A friend told me he had met me yesterday in the street but I had not seen him. I am indeed not guilty, as I should have been if I had pretended not to see him in order to save myself, for example, the time spent in a little conversation. But I feel all the same that there is guilt in my absent-mindedness, namely a lack of availability to the outside world as I was too absorbed in my little inner world.

A man is driving a car. Suddenly the lorry in front of him brakes. Our driver realizes it just in time; another fraction of a second and there would have been an accident. It was because he was thinking of something else: his gaze was held by a woman, a foreign tourist in rather light attire, bending down to choose postcards on a stand. It was a very commonplace distraction! What normal man in similar circumstances does not at least glance?

But each one makes a secret of it. This is the conspiracy of silence which Bergson mentions somewhere. And so some readers will perhaps consider my mentioning it out of place. As Dr. Théo Bovet cunningly pointed out in a lecture, it is fitting to mention it only jokingly, in songs. He showed us that all men, in making it in this way a triviality, seek to avert the guilty conscience they have because of it. In a flash, our driver perceives the accident he narrowly missed, the investigation and enquiry as to the responsible party. Would he have had the courage to confess the cause of his absent-mindedness?

I do not forget the accurate distinction made by the theologians between temptation and sin. I am the first to expound it to an over-scrupulous patient. Temptation is not sin. The proof of this is that Christ Himself was tempted (Lk. iv. 1–13). Any idea, even the most impious and the most criminal, can surge up in our minds without our being able to do anything about it. The only fault lies in our accepting it, cultivating it and taking pleasure in it. I quote Luther's saying that we cannot prevent the birds from flying over our head, but we can prevent them from building their nests in our hair.

But where does the exact limit of complacency lie? In theory the distinction is very simple; in practice it is insidious and futile. The whole of the Sermon on the Mount (Matt. v–vii) overthrows the reassuring barriers which men hope to set up between the secret thought and the act, between the fault imagined and committed.

I do not know whether the theologians are more successful than I am; for my part I am struck by the ineffectualness of such explanations as theirs to reassure an over-scrupulous person. Of course, the spiritual authority of a priest over a penitent can be great enough to convince him that his guilty conscience is without foundation in such and such a case. But then the penitent will constantly have to return to his confessor to put before him his ever-recurring anxieties.

A man is much more soothed by an absolution pronounced

over his real faults than by all the explanations he may be given to exonerate him from his imaginary guilt. In vain you can tell an over-scrupulous man that his guilt is quite different and that it lies in his refusal to accept his human condition, and the weaknesses and temptations which that condition comprises. In his anxiety and in the very difficulty he experiences precisely in accepting himself as he is, he expresses an uneasiness from which no one is entirely exempt.

We thirst for a divine answer, not only to such and such a precise fault of which we recognize that we are guilty, but to our human condition itself. For it is clearly the inexorable drama of our existence which oppresses us, the fact that evil is inseparable from good. Faithfulness without temptation to infidelity is not true faithfulness. Faith without temptation of doubt is not true faith. Purity without temptation to impurity is not true purity.

But to appeal to our 'psychological complexes' never frees us from our guilty conscience. 'What can I do about it? I have a complex', seems to exonerate us. Yet we feel clearly that this secret mechanism which defies our mastery over ourselves contradicts our claim to liberty. It is like an inner enemy which humiliates us by the defeats it inflicts upon us. Dr. Sarano[35] has in fact stressed this 'guilt of non-liberty'.

The very notion of complex implies that behind these autonomatic repetitions of our conduct there are other deeper and more mysterious problems. It signifies that we do not know ourselves, that we have not had the courage to examine ourselves thoroughly, that we all have a certain fear in carrying out such an examination, of making unpleasant and unflattering discoveries about ourselves. And so, even though we know that everybody has complexes we are always a little ashamed of our own.

In inventing the word complex, Professor C. G. Jung has not exonerated man; he has simply displaced his guilt by revealing him to himself as being less free than he thought. It humiliates us to discover to what extent we remain prisoners of suggestions experienced in our childhood even though our conscious mind recognizes them now as erroneous. A man may understand perfectly that sexuality is divine and not diabolical, as it had been represented to him as being. He may adhere with all his soul and mind to a healthier vision of sexual love. He does not succeed all the same in giving himself up to it with the freedom and fullness to which he now aspires. He no longer believes himself guilty in having a sexual instinct, but a subtler guilt torments him; it is the guilt of being the plaything of his complexes, of inhibitions of which he disapproves, and of feeling himself so inwardly divided.

Think, for example, of the guilt of homosexuals. You tell them in vain that it is society which is guilty of making an undeserved scorn bear down upon them, that it is a matter of an accident which has occurred in their psychological development of which they are no more responsible than if they had broken their leg and a badly healed fracture had left a pseudo-arthritic condition; they maintain a tenacious feeling of guilt, even if they conceal it beneath beautiful Platonic theories; it is culpable to go against the order of nature.

We have seen this too in the problems of time and money, how much we are often in contradiction to ourselves, and how much this humiliates us. Such and such a man is extremely distressed about the future, anxious to economize. He will suddenly spend his money stupidly. He does not forgive himself, even if he realizes that an inferiority complex is the cause at one and the same time of his distress about the future and the expenditure he has made. To produce a large sum of money for a superfluous object is to give oneself the social importance which the appearance of wealth confers. It compensates for one's inferiority. Another man is a spendthrift, and he suddenly goes into a discussion about a minute sum of money with a meanness which surprises himself.

A man has been brought up with care for the strictest economy. His wife asks him for money to spend; he has a guilty conscience in refusing it to her because he considers it legitimate and is able to give it to her; but he also has a guilty conscience if he does so, because of the training he has received from his upbringing which leaves him with tenacious restraint. Another began when quite a child to buy himself sweets to console himself for not receiving from his parents the affection he needed. In spite of all the reprimands he may get now, and in spite of all the wise warnings from his wife, even in spite of all his resolutions or of the worst threats from his creditors, he continues to contract debts.

Our complexes influence us even in reading the Bible, when we seek in it inspiration for a line of conduct which is freer and more in conformity with the will of God. It is like what happens with the three-dimensional cinema where the spectator, in order to obtain a stereoscopic vision, wears glasses of two colours so that each eye sees only one part of the projected image. Thus, each one of us sees in the Bible what corresponds to his preconceived ideas and his complexes.

The prodigal will readily appeal to the words of Ecclesiastes: 'Cast your bread upon the waters, for you will find it after many days' (Eccl. xi. 1), or the story of the manna (Ex. xvi. 13-31) which indicates clearly that, if God gives his children each day what they need, He does not allow them to amass reserve supplies; or to Jesus' reply to His disciples in the house of Simon the leper when they were criticizing a poor woman who, in an outburst of generosity, had anointed Him with a perfume of great price. 'This ointment might have been sold for a large sum, and given to the poor.' Jesus rises up against this fine economists' reasoning and defends the woman they criticize so severely (Matt. xxvi. 6-13).

But reasonable people will be able to appeal to the Book of Proverbs: 'Go to the ant, O sluggard; consider her ways, and be wise . . . she prepares her food in summer, and gathers her sustenance in harvest' (Prov. vi. 6-8); or these words of Jesus: 'Which of you, desiring to build a tower, does not first sit down and count the cost, whether he has enough to complete it?' . . . (Lk. xiv. 28-30); or again, His strange parable of the Unjust Steward: 'The sons of this world are wiser in their own generation than the sons of light' (Lk. xvi. 1-13).

When He sends His disciples off on a mission, Jesus tells them: 'Be wise as serpents and innocent as doves' (Matt. x. 16). There are readers who retain only the first of these two recommendations, or the second, according to their temperament; whereas Jesus has purposely put them together. Thus we constantly risk being influenced by our psychological make-up in our interpretation of the Bible. Are we sincere in our desire to let ourselves be led by God if we claim to remain sole interpreters of His will?

We always risk seeking in the Bible passages which support our prejudices. And yet we all have the intuition that it must rather free us from our too narrow views or our psychic automatisms. The man who is more a serpent than a dove feels keenly at the bottom of his heart a certain guilt at not being a dove, at being too cunning, at having stifled his natural candour. But the man who is more of a dove than a serpent feels he is guilty too, even if he does not confess it, of not being sufficiently shrewd, of offering himself too naïvely to the wickedness of others.

Complexes, secret imaginations, temptations, vain and unconfessable dreams, a whole world of impulses more or less conscious, often of no clear form, develop within us. They defy the censorship of our will, as we realize with confusion. It is another self which lives in us, which we cannot stifle, and which we fear will be discovered. For we can even have such horrible thoughts that it seems we could not bear the shame should they be revealed.

Precisely because everyone keeps them secret, everyone believes also that he alone has them. He wonders with fright how it is possible that criminal desires, obscene images and shameful cowardice can arise in his mind. With the sick, this can become a veritable obsession; it seems to them that everyone can read their soul; they think they can discern frightful scorn in the look of some unknown person they meet in the street and are persuaded that he is an agent of the secret police.

But that is what often drives a normal man to the psychologist. He readily accepts that he experiences noble temptations like pride or jealousy, but not thoughts as revolting as these others. At bottom what he would like to be cured of is his human nature itself, for he cannot accept it just as it is.

He finds he is capable in the heat of a scene with his wife of speaking words of incredible wickedness, treachery and even coarseness. How is it possible? for he is always so refined, so distinguished, so master of himself! He would never behave in that way towards anybody else. And yet he loves his wife. It is precisely because he loves her that his frenzied passion can get the better of him to that extent. Strange reversal of love! He is upset not only at his behaviour but at disowning his better self too.

From this cause there springs too the painful emotion felt by everyone when telling his dreams, because he finds in them the thoughts which are disapproved of by his psychic censor, just as we find in a dustbin everything that a decent housewife has carefully swept out of her home. And when a neurotic dares to confide in us about the absurd thoughts which obsess him, we can recognize in them the most commonplace associations of ideas which develop in the mind of each one of us without our fortunately paying too much attention to them.

We have little fads and naïve dreams which are only just worthy of children; and little cowardlinesses which we conceal beneath jokes or evasive replies, for we do not dare show ourselves exactly as we are. As much as our dreams, we fear the Bible, even though we love it, because it delves into our secret being as X-rays into our body: 'For the word of God is living and active, sharper than any two-edged sword, piercing to the division of soul and spirit, of joints and marrow, and discerning the thoughts and intentions of the heart' (Heb. iv. 12).

What humiliates us is not only what we discover in ourselves, but still more our powerlessness to make a unity of ourselves, to efface the dualism of our hidden and our apparent being. This is no longer a case of guilt in the moral sense of the term but rather in an existentialist sense: guilt with regard to himself which every man vaguely feels because there are within him obscure forces, impulses and inhibitions which neither his will, nor his intelligence, nor his knowledge can master.

It is, moreover, striking to note when a man confesses with keen emotion his guilty behaviour, that he so often adds straightaway: 'I don't know how I could have done that.' He is nonplussed at his own behaviour, and this self-astonishment at the self reveals the disquieting dualism which exists even in people who are proud of their mastery over themselves. They feel with confusion that the judgment on their own actions which they clearly bring to bear after a lapse of time was totally suspended at the time they committed those actions; they underwent them blindly and too quickly for them to be considered actions.

A timid man is always ashamed of his timidity because it is stronger than he and falsifies his relations with other people exactly at the time when they depend on him most; and his shame aggravates his timidity. An emotional person is always ashamed of his emotion because it paralyses him just at the moment when he would like to be calm, and his shame aggravates his emotion. An impulsive person is always ashamed of his impulsiveness because it exposes him to unjust judgments, and his shame aggravates his impulsiveness.

A young woman comes and consults me about her shyness. She embarrasses me very much for she seems to expect me to free her from it magically in one session! I venture to inform her straightaway of my recent observations concerning this problem. It seems to me that in at least a large number of cases shyness is hereditary, inasmuch as when social shame weighs upon the parents a sensitive child may perceive it without knowing what it is, and it penetrates into him and makes him shy.

These few words immediately open the door to confidences: 'I know just what you mean,' the young woman says. 'My father was a workman. He was intelligent, hard-working and honourable, but he was a workman. My mother came from a middle-class family, full of prejudices. Her father, regarding her marriage as a bad match, shut his doors to her. And my mother never saw him again until he had breathed his last.' She adds: 'I myself only understood this tragedy later little by little when I was shown from a distance my grandfather who had gone into a side street in order not to meet us.'

So this banal problem of shyness illustrates well the inextricable mixture of true and false guilt, which, mutually interwined, are at play within us. Social scorn and the thousand and one suggestions we undergo determine it. But the shy person cannot take his stand against it, precisely because he feels that his real nature is not like that and that he feels guilty in showing himself to be other than he is.

We all experience this uneasiness. However spontaneous we may be, there always remains a certain divorce between our deep being and our apparent being. The more internal perspicacity we acquire and the more progress we make in the psychological analysis of ourselves, the more we are convinced of a lack of inner coherence, and the more we suffer because of it.

Chapter VI

OUR OUTWARD ACTIONS

I OUGHT to complete this survey of our daily guilt by including the blatant guilt everyone thinks of—violence and cruelty, hate and betrayal, deceit, injustice, adultery and all the other kinds. But that is without interest here. What is of more importance for us is the feeling of guilt which every man experiences not for the evil he has done but for the good he has not done. It is the theme of the Last Judgment as Christ has depicted it, in such a poetical passage that it seems like a parable (Matt. xxv. 31–46). Contrary to moralism which always imagines that we shall be reproached for the faults we have committed, Jesus Christ refers to the kind actions we shall have omitted to perform. Here is guilt which is singularly more extensive, even unlimited.

This account interests us doctors a great deal for it shows, together with other of His words, that Jesus Christ was acquainted with the unconscious mind well before modern psychology discovered it. Those he sets at His right hand and those He sets at His left both manifest the most lively astonishment: some have done good without knowing it; others have let slip the opportunities for doing good without knowing it either. In the presence of Jesus Christ there is a pang of conscience because of unconscious behaviour.

There is here too an opposition between 'duty' and life. Many people make a sort of religion of duty, that is to say of conventional conduct, conduct neither alive nor spontaneous. When you think of it, this morality of duty appears as a protection against guilt. It consists in fact of arbitrarily defining a certain number of tasks in order to have an easy conscience when they have been performed. These people say with a fine but naïve assurance: 'I have nothing to reproach myself with, I have done all I should have done.'

But the repression of guilt brings with it a hardening of the heart: we no longer see what God expects of us outside our conventional duty. It is precisely that which Jesus stresses in the Parable of the Last Judgment in order to sharpen in all its disquieting fullness the feeling of guilt in His legalistically minded hearers. We can compare with it the other saying of Jesus: 'When you have done all that is commanded you, say, "We are unworthy

servants; we have only done what was our duty"' (Lk.
xvii. 10).

What really affects our patients is what we do out of the
ordinary for them, what exceeds conventional duty in a spontaneous movement of the heart, even if it is only a personal word,
but a genuinely personal one. We constantly feel the danger of
routine, of charity which loses its savour in becoming a job.
Who amongst us has not felt some disquiet in the face of the
professionalization of devotion?

But the guilt of omission has a still more general effect. It comprises all that we had dreamed and have not attained, the poems
shoved into a secret drawer which still have a few lines missing
or a few corrections to be made; it comprises the promises made
in the mystical impetus of a short-lived moment; all that we have
attained only incompletely, begun and abandoned; all that is
unfinished, timid, unexpressed, shapeless.

As long as we are young we can still deceive ourselves; what
we do makes up for what we do not do; what we dream and hope,
for what is lacking in reality. We still discount from the future
a revenge on the past and the present. The more we advance in
years the more these mirages vanish. We have to confess to ourselves that we deceived ourselves by affecting to believe in realiza-
tions which will never come. On the threshold of maturity,
then of old age, terrible crises occur which are the sources of
illnesses as much psychological as physical.

And that is just when strength decreases, when the capacity for
work lessens, when social obligations increase leaving less room
for spontaneity. A man may feel that he has let himself be devoured by life, that a thousand and one secondary tasks have filled
his life more and more, and that from procrastination to procrastination what he wanted most to do in this world fades away
for ever. What remains of everything which absorbed him every
day? How many hours really count in a life-time and leave a
savour of fullness and development?

A friend comes to see me. He is a businessman of the same age
as myself. He has always had keen religious preoccupations.
Whereas so many Christian businessmen accommodate themselves strangely to an economic and social system which is so
deeply in contradiction with their faith, he has never ceased to be
tormented by it; tormented too because of the deficiency of the
Churches, their prudence and their timidity. For it is evident that
businessmen engaged in mundane affairs ought to collaborate
more actively and closely with the theologians to infuse fruitful
inspiration into our common life.

But his greatest distress is his own deficiency, because he has so often skimmed the surface of these problems secretly in his own mind, or occasionally in some interesting evening of discussion which had no practical consequences. Because he has never faced up to them with enough vigour to arrive at least at an outline of a solution, and because his aspirations have remained vague, ineffectual and academic.

Absorbed by a heavy professional task and by family worries, he has left lying fallow the thoughts he held most dear. He is very well looked after by an excellent doctor; and if the treatment is not more effective he wonders if it is not because of the vague guilt he feels over this balance-sheet of his life.

Jean-Paul Sartre[38] forcefully affirms that our life is nothing else than what we have made it. For my part, I believe on the contrary that all we should have liked to make of it and all the nebulous potentialities which we bear within us count. Even then, truly enough, the brutal contrast between the dream and what came out of it weighs upon us as a mass of guilt.

Who is not disappointed in himself? Who does not try to console himself by some cynical, disillusioned or bitter aphorism about life? I have just read in the newspaper a reply made by Simenon to an embittered writer. The latter had said to him: 'If you don't hope for anything from life you are never deceived!' 'How true that is,' Simenon smilingly agreed, 'and if you don't breathe you never swallow microbes!'

Other people try to reassure themselves by recalling at every turn, by allusions more or less discreet, what they have actually accomplished which is valid, courageous or original. Others again complain of their parents, their wife, their boss, or their friends, to blame them for the guilt of their failures and deficiencies. They affect to believe that external circumstances alone have prevented them from showing what they are capable of in life.

But at bottom all this bitterness expresses a dissatisfaction with oneself and with the limits of our human condition. I have just received a letter from a student: 'We can do absolutely nothing. Humility is resolved to recognize its pride, and sincerity to state its lie. Death alone will deliver us from the approximations which rend us. . . . Simplicity escapes us, and the pursuit of it complicates everything. . . . We soon succeed in realizing that we shall never know. . . . The expectation of grace can only be borne by grace. . . .' Who does not understand the gravity of this human drama?

'Vanity of vanities, saith the Preacher; vanity of vanities, all is vanity' (Eccl. i. 2). Who is not disappointed in himself? Who has not painfully felt the vanity of his efforts, even in the pursuit of the ideal which he held most dear? Even if we have succeeded in one respect, we perceive one day that the zeal we put into it was no more than a way of side-tracking many other failures. Our successes in one field do not make up for our disappointments in another. They rather sharpen them by contrast. I always remember a man who had achieved the greatest world celebrity and who lamentably repeated in my consulting room: 'I have wasted my life.'

Jean Guitton[13] speaks of Abbé Thellier de Poncheville as being 'innocence itself', yet he reveals himself in his Spiritual Journal as being 'weighed down by the thought of his mediocrity'. Guilt at the unfinished, the relative, the failure to develop, the talents left lying fallow; guilt at a certain betrayal of oneself, one's aspirations, convictions and human vocation. A husband says to his wife (or wife to her husband): 'I have only been a hindrance in your life instead of helping you to show what you are capable of. Why didn't you marry someone else!'

Open the Bible and you will see from beginning to end the men whom God's call has snatched from the banality of their lives, impelled into a great adventure and vested with a creative power which did not come from themselves. Then we feel clearly that our guilt at what is unfinished is a guilt of non-inspiration, of lack of contact with God, and of failure to respond to His call.

We meet again here a favourite theme in modern psychology; for modern psychology wanted to see man in the making, man's evolution and his dynamism. Freud reveals to us all that remains infantile and regressive in us, our fear of life and of responsibilities, our longing for a refuge in maternal consolation. We are all children, and we all feel guilty at being so lacking in courage, in virility, in adulthood. C. G. Jung widens these notions by talking of integration and by depicting man's destiny as the acceptance of all that is within him.

But the new birth of which Jesus Christ speaks, the transfiguration of man by the Holy Spirit which we see carried out in the primitive Church, contain and surpass the secular notions of Freud's 'becoming adult' and of Jung's 'integration'. Yet among the faithful of all Christian Churches there are so many immature, infantile, timid souls, and so few radiant, victorious, developed souls. By what deformation has Christianity succeeded in so often crushing men instead of freeing them?

We feel ourselves responsible for Christianity, guilty of the deformation we take part in, guilty of demonstrating so badly the power of Jesus Christ. We are weak, indeed, though perhaps not guilty of that weakness. But does not St. Paul say that it is precisely in our weakness that the power of God should break forth? (2 Cor. xii. 10).

It is in the face of God that we feel guilty at not having become what He expected of us; at letting ourselves be paralysed by fear, fashioned by our environment, petrified by routine, sterilized by conformity; at not having been ourselves, at having copied others instead of taking advantage of the particular gifts which God had entrusted to us. Here the opposition between false guilt suggested by society and the responsibility for oneself before God is made clear. A poet tells me that he does not begin writing his poems without a feeling of guilt—for he feels he is criticized for wasting his time scribbling on paper instead of earning his living, whereas he experiences a vaguer yet more authentic guilt in keeping secret the talent he has received (Matt. xxv. 18).

The drama may be still more disturbing, and I have seen examples of it which were resolved by illness. It is not only society and its prejudices which prevent us from being ourselves; it may sometimes be fellow believers, however good their intentions. There is, indeed, a virtue in humility and obedience; it would be false to act in our own way on pretext of being ourselves! But it can happen that a man afterwards discovers himself to be guilty of letting himself be stopped by his friends' advice or that of a too authoritarian confessor. Because of his inferiority complex he attributed more authority to the advice of others than to his own convictions.

I am not speaking now about monastic life in which obedience is chosen as a vow inspired by God, nor of the submission demanded of an ecclesiastic to his superiors. But when, as Christians who are equal before God, we seek together His proper inspiration, it happens that the man who is sure of himself paralyses the one he imposes upon. According to his own conceptions he may, with a word, deter his friend from the accomplishment of his own, without the latter even having dared to put them to him or to defend them. Then suddenly this friend will realize that his life, far from having become more fruitful, has been made sterile and that he has let himself be dominated, that he has obeyed men rather than God (Acts v. 29), and has not maintained his own opinions ardently enough but has betrayed himself.

This notion of faithfulness to oneself is deeply felt by every man whatever his beliefs or his unbelief, whether he is a Christian or an existentialist. And it is a universal source of guilt, for no one feels that he is always faithful to himself. It is a universal guilt, but hardly conscious; for it is indeed so painful to us that we have much difficulty in confessing it to ourselves. A thousand excuses come to mind to exonerate us from it.

I was talking about this recently to a French philosopher. I told him that cowardice seems to me to be one of the most common and the least conscious of sins. 'That is perhaps what explains the fact that courage was placed by the Ancients so high in the hierarchy of virtues,' he replied. But he also expressed his astonishment at my asking: 'Give me an example!'

I took the most banal example, that of a conflict between man and wife. At first you get lost in the analysis of numerous factors in the conflict—social, cultural, psychological, sexual—and their importance is real but not decisive. With a deeper pang of conscience the husband is reduced to seeing that at bottom he has capitulated in his vocation as a husband. In the face of these difficulties, and precisely instead of meeting them courageously, he eluded them. In order to restore peace and for fear of not being understood he broke off the mutual adjustment, shut himself up in secretiveness, and grew further and further away from his wife.

Well before being unfaithful to her in the banal sense of the term, he was unfaithful to the biblical command on which he had wanted to found his home: 'They shall become one flesh.' For this command specifies a single person, a total sharing by both parties. Whereas he shows himself to be so courageous in so many circumstances in his professional and social life, he realizes that he has been lacking in courage in the faithful construction of conjugal unity. He has been a coward. It is the same thing with the keen sense of guilt which an abortion always occasions either in the case of an unmarried woman or a married woman, or else in the case of the lover or the husband or even the parents-in-law who have often forced the woman to undergo abortion. There enters into it, certainly, the guilty conscience of an attempt against life, but the feeling of guilt is usually more keenly felt as the shame of having committed a cowardly act.

There is frequently a sense of guilt too in the case of a man in attaching himself to a woman, in making her his mistress, in dragging out their relationship without having the courage either to break it off or to marry her. He clearly feels that he is the really guilty one, whereas it is she who lives in an atmosphere of guiltiness the life she has sacrificed to him, because he has condemned her to secretiveness. There is no lack of innumerable excuses. Péguy wrote: 'A capitulation is essentially an operation by means of which we begin to explain instead of acting. And cowards are people who are overflowing with explanations.'

Guiltiness at all our capitulations. From the moment a man recognizes values he necessarily finds himself guilty of betraying them on a thousand occasions. And man cannot fail to recognize values.

Much courage is necessary to maintain to the end a genuine relationship with one's wife or with one's best friends. Much courage is necessary in order to be true, to recognize one's own faults, to assume all one's responsibilities, to forgive, or to maintain the solidarity uniting us to our friends even when they deceive us. I am always struck by the unfailing faithfulness of Jesus to His disciples. He chose them at the inspiration of God (Jn. xv. 15–16). In vain do they fail to understand much of what He tells them, ask Him stupid questions, show themselves to be ambitious or cowardly. He continues to trust them, to count on them alone, and to entrust them with the whole accomplishment of His ministry on earth (Matt. xxviii. 19–20).

Men are in flight all the day long. All of us flee continually: in silence or in gossip; in inertia or in boredom; in the pleasures of the table or those of the library; in the reading of a newspaper or in a piece of knitting; in sports or by the fireside; in witty sayings or idle discussions (2 Tim. ii. 23). We hide behind an official regulation to 'cover our responsibility', that is, to protect ourselves against guilt, and this very flight of ours is guiltier still; we hide now in anger, now in kindness; in self-sufficiency or in modesty; in sentimentality or in aggressiveness; in conformism or in bohemianism; in an attack of nerves or in mastery of the self; in sickness or in stoicism.

To be faithful to oneself would mean to be always like oneself in all circumstances, in the presence of any interlocutor. We remain silent in turn about either our deepest convictions or the doubts which inevitably arise concerning them. We hide our feelings, or else we show them to be more ardent than they really are. To be faithful to oneself would mean to be natural, spontaneous, fearless of the opinion of others.

We envy King David who dared in his joy to leap and dance in the open street behind the Ark of the Lord which he was bringing to Jerusalem. He was not afraid of his wife Michal who scornfully watched him from her window (2 Sam. vi. 16). But spontaneity also has its inconveniences and it is perhaps because he felt thus scorned by her that David deceived her later with the wife of Uriah, after he had treacherously exposed Uriah to death (2 Sam. xi. 14–27).

The manifestation of feelings gives rise in turn to contradictory guilts. There are many people who are ashamed of crying. There are families in which crying is considered blameworthy, as is also any outburst of joy. Some patients have confessed that they hesitated a long time before coming to see me for fear of crying in my consulting room. Jesus wept quite simply as He drew near the tomb of his friend Lazarus (Jn. xi. 35), although He had said

equally simply on hearing of his death that He rejoiced at not
having been there (Jn. xi. 15).

Many husbands, once the honeymoon is over, take care not to
tell their wives they love them, as if it were a guilty weakness on
their part, and unworthy of a man. And at the same time, they
feel vaguely guilty for the nerviness of their wives which betrays
their need of affection. And the wives are ashamed too to bother
their husbands or their friends with the effusiveness of their
feelings.

We flee also from God. Often we catch ourselves bargaining
with Him or cheating Him. 'Cursed be the cheat who sacrifices
to the Lord what is blemished,' says the prophet Malachi (Mal.
i. 14). There are moments when the piety we flaunt appears to us
as the worst of lies. We fail to keep time for recollection in order
not to hear what He has to say to us. Or else we claim that He
does not speak when what He tells us is displeasing to us.

Thus King Ahab had the prophet Micaiah thrown into prison.
It was through him that God foretold his death in the battle he
wanted to undertake. But the King was uneasy all the same. He
wanted to be cunning with God; so he disguised himself and
exchanged his royal robes for those of Jehoshaphat. But in the
confusion of the battle, Jehoshaphat was not killed, whereas an
arrow shot at random killed the King who thought he was too
cunning (1 Kgs. xxii. 15–38).

But it is not enough to listen to God. We must obey Him. The
guilt of omission constantly harasses us in our professional
activity. Do we give our patients all that God wills us to give
them? Are we not contented too often with superficial treatment?
Do we not feel sometimes that the medicine we prescribe is no
more than a very insufficient palliative? Should we not delve
more deeply and tackle the problems in our patient's life which we
suspect are at the back of his distress?

But there we are—it will perhaps be long and difficult, and we
shall not perhaps know what to say in delicate problems. It might
lead us on to unfamiliar territory, even to moral and religious
questions on which we do not feel ourselves to be very clear.
A prescription for the chemist's shop, a piece of advice about
hygiene, a good word of sprightly encouragement or of keen
sympathy is itself at least a beginning. We try to reassure ourselves
by telling ourselves that we have done our duty as doctors. A
priest, a pastor or a friend will be able to do the rest better than
we can. But did the patient not expect it from us?

A Dutch colleague was talking recently to a gynaecologist about
integrative medicine. The latter objected sincerely: 'For my part,
I am more modest,' he said, 'I am only a technician, and in order

to do my work well I have to deal exclusively with what relates to my speciality. There are colleagues and clergy who can deal with the individual, the whole organism, psychology and the spiritual life. Each man to his trade.'

At that moment the gynaecologist was called to the telephone. He was dumbfounded on putting down the receiver. 'There,' he told my friend, 'the other day I examined a woman sent to me by her doctor to establish whether she was pregnant. She was not. I told her so. She left. Now her doctor rings me up to tell me that she committed suicide on returning home.'

Pregnant or not? The question seemed purely technical. But a human question is never purely technical. For that woman it doubtless had immense repercussions. It brought into play all her conceptions of life, values and happiness. I ask all my colleagues, and the theologians who reproach me for encouraging doctors to go beyond the limits of their job, where they set these limits and in the name of what criterion.

But I who make myself a champion of integrative medicine, even I catch myself doing guilty, cowardly deeds. The other day a woman patient whom I have been tending for years and with whom I have the most intimate conversations was summoned after a haemorrhage to see the surgeon for a rectum examination. I easily realized what she was thinking of, what she feared, and what was causing the emotion she showed. I thought of it too. She knew I was thinking of it. I knew that she knew. However, out of a certain mutual complicity we let our conversation turn upon other subjects less laden with distress and uncertainty. Seized with remorse I timidly said to her on the doorstep as she departed: 'I'll think of you at the surgeon's examination.' It was afterwards when she brought me the reassuring result of the examination that I asked her forgiveness for not having been a doctor to the whole personality.

Suffering knows no frontier, that is living suffering, the suffering of man, of the whole personality of man. Our vocation is to reply to human suffering. We have a technical task and we could not neglect it without a keen feeling of guilt. But we all feel that our task is broader, less narrowly defined, and we also feel guilty in evading it. We are often perfectly conscious, when we write out a prescription, that the medicine prescribed, however appropriate it may be, serves to elude a problem which ought to be solved. We feel how insufficient such purely technical medical treatment is.

We readily appeal to a religious shame which may be no more than a covering reaction to exonerate ourselves. It is not a question of taking the clergyman's place, of teaching, preaching, indoctrinating, admonishing or proselytizing. Neither is it enough in many cases to entrust a patient to a psychiatrist or a priest. 'You give them something to eat,' Jesus said to his disciples (Matt. xiv. 16).

Look at the review *Présences*. Number LIX[31] takes account of the extensive enquiry sponsored by it into the personal contact between patient and doctor and into what the sick expect from the doctors in that respect. It is a question of perceiving the whole of our patients' suffering and of facing up to it without cowardice, without subterfuge. And if that suffering is a feeling of guilt, it is not enough to say that it is no longer in the doctor's sphere.

The clinical experiences of which we have heard in our Conference show the enormous part played by the feelings of guilt in the destiny of our patients, in the emergence of many illnesses and in the failure of much treatment.

Open your eyes! and you will see among your patients that huge crowd of wounded, distressed, crushed men and women, laden with secret guilts, real or false, definite or vague; even a sort of guilt at being alive, which is more common than we think.

Part Two

THE SPIRIT OF JUDGMENT

Chapter VII

TRUE OR FALSE GUILT

WE must now make the attempt to see things more clearly. The terms 'true guilt' and 'false guilt' have come easily to our lips from the beginning of our study. What do they mean exactly? That it is possible to feel guilty without being so? Or to be guilty without feeling it, without even knowing it? Then what relationship is there between the reality of the fault and the feeling of guilt? How are we to define the reality of the fault? What criterion are we to adopt in order to say whether the person who adjudges himself guilty really is guilty or not?

Think, for instance, of the case of a manic-depressive, who alternates between phases of exaltation and depression. In an exalted period he commits, without the slightest remorse, all sorts of moral faults for which he will evince the most terrible regrets during the period of depression. Yet you cannot deny the genuineness of his remorse in his depression. In any event, to tell him that it is morbid 'false guilt' will be of no comfort whatsoever.

Conversely, if he passes suddenly from depression to a fresh period of exaltation, he evinces such wonderful relief that he may describe it as a real spiritual experience. With an impressive ring of sincerity, he may say that he has at last understood divine grace and will never doubt it again. Yet here again, one cannot claim that every experience of God's forgiveness is pathological! Medical practice makes us very reserved before this great mystery of the sense of guilt.

We must, however, try to understand whence these feelings of guilt spring. You are acquainted with Freud's explanation: according to him, feelings of guilt are the result of social constraint. The feelings are born in the mind of the child when his parents scold him, and are nothing other than the fear of losing the love of parents who have become suddenly hostile. No one to-day contests the reality of this mechanism, nor the importance of Freud's discovery, which only confirms what the Bible had already told us—how much the human being needs to feel loved. This explanation remains valid in our view so far as the guilt of a child is concerned, at least of the little child, or of those who remain infantile all their lives. It is the guilt produced by upbringing, which we can also find among animals. Our colleague Robert Giscard has told us, in this connection, about his dogs and their obvious signs of guilt when disobedient, even before being scolded.

We have just seen too many examples of guilt-feelings aroused by the suggestion of educators and society to deny the mechanism described by Freud and his school. It is the guilt produced by fear of taboos. The question then arises: does this mechanism of social constraint which is opposed to the instinctive drives of the individual explain all cases of guilt-feelings or merely some of them? Many Freudians now accept, contrary to their master's theories, the distinction proposed by Odier [29] between 'functions' and 'values'.

A feeling of 'functional guilt' is one which results from social suggestion, fear of taboos or of losing the love of others. A feeling of 'value guilt' is the genuine consciousness of having betrayed an authentic standard; it is a free judgment of the self by the self. On this assumption, there is a complete opposition between these two guilt-producing mechanisms, the one acting by social suggestion, the other by moral conviction. Odier went out of his way to draw up tables as a guide to the clear diagnosis of these two orders of phenomena.

Functional guilt, normal in children, continues, at an intense level in all neurotics, and at a lower level in all normal adults. So it appears in Freudian doctrine as the sign of infantile fixation or regression, of childish dependence on parents, or other human authorities, which is abnormal in the adult. It seems then, that it may well be labelled 'false guilt'. And yet, it is frequently through training that we recognize ourselves as guilty of real faults, a judgment suggested certainly by other people, but authenticated by our own inner conviction, with the result that the term 'false guilt' is no longer adequate. You see how delicate the problem is!

I have a high regard for this work by Odier. None the less, the question seems to me even more complex. Indeed, all human conduct, however genuine it may be from a moral point of view, can be considered as 'functional', that is, it may be studied objectively with a concern for the mechanism of its origin. Conversely, even a neurotic syndrome which is functional in Odier's sense, may be, for the subject, the occasion for a genuine religious experience of divine grace. There are many instances in the lives of the saints.

In Odier's view, functional guilt becomes synonymous with neurotic guilt and 'false guilt'; value-guilt, synonymous with 'true guilt'. There is some truth in this view, of course, but the problem is less clear-cut. It becomes even more complicated if we take into account theories from other schools of psychoanalysis on the genesis of guilt feelings. For Adler, the sense of guilt stems from a refusal to accept one's inferiority. For Jung, from a refusal to accept oneself wholly, to integrate into consciousness that unpleasing part of ourselves which Jung calls the 'shadow'. We are still in the realm of 'function', in the realm of a purely psychological description which refers to the reality of phenomena but not to values.

And yet, even in Jung's view, there appears the idea of a 'true' guilt, a guilt in no way suggested by society, namely of a fault with regard to oneself, a violation of the normal relationship of the self to the self. What Dr. Paul Plattner of Berne has told us about guilt feelings in the psychoses should be recalled in this connection. He has reported a series of impressive case-histories of mental patients who suffer martyrdom with terrible self-accusations—accusations which appear to us to have no foundation in fact and to be absurd. These patients declare themselves to be damned, and are completely untouched by any word of comfort or any assurance of grace. The priest himself, armed with all the authority of the Church, does not succeed in bringing relief.

With extreme caution, keeping strictly to observation of the facts, and shunning any bold generalization, Dr. Plattner has shown us that such patients can be cured when they become aware of a guilt very different from the one obsessing them, which was secretly poisoning their being. Thus a 'false guilt' seems likely to blanket a 'true guilt' and to draw its implacable venom therefrom. In all these cases, this true guilt consisted in a certain refusal to develop, to assume full selfhood or total responsibility in a given situation. So it is a guilt of self towards self, which is to be found in the purview of C. G. Jung's psychology. This Jungian notion of guilt towards oneself is already to be found in the Bible. Thus the prophet Habakkuk cries: 'Thou hast . . . sinned against thy soul' (Hab. ii. 10).

Martin Buber goes further than Jung. In Scharfenberg's[40] words, Buber asks that psychotherapy should recognize the existence of 'genuine guilt' alongside 'neurotic' or 'unreal' (*grundlos*) guilt. What characterizes genuine guilt in Buber's eyes is that it always turns on some violation of human relationships, it constitutes a breakdown of the I-Thou relationship. It is thus a guilt towards others.

Hence, the frequency of the occurrence of taboo-guilt and especially of Oedipus guilt is shown to us by the Freudians; that of inferiority-guilt by the Adler School; that of the refusal to give

full acceptance to the self by the Jung School; and that of refusal
to accept others by Martin Buber. In the majority of cases, it
seems to me that in reality all these elements mingle and over-
lap; that, in a word, distinct phenomena are less in question than
different aspects of one complex mechanism in which each viewer
sees what supports his own psychological theory, his own conception of mankind.

Thus in the movement of the same cloud, or in the same
Rorschach blot, several observers will say they see, according to
their own different complexes, the representation of different
things. Or again, if you place a triangle between three observers,
each one will name as its base a different side, and as its apex a
different angle. I believe that it is possible to speak of a Freudian,
an Adlerian or a Jungian complex, which will lead a psychologist,
according to his affiliation, to view all men from one or other
particular angle.

But the Maeder School, and the Rank School, and some psychotherapists with an outlook akin to Jung's such as Aloys d'Orelli
or Plattner, whom I quoted above, have added a new depth to
this vision—that of guilt towards God. Whether it be conscious
or not, they recognize it as a truly genuine guilt; it falls within
the jurisdiction of the 'cure of souls', but it can be tracked down
by psychological techniques.

It can be seen that what differs from one school to another is
the interpretation and definition of guilt; but all admit its psychological reality. This is precisely the way by which the word guilt
came into the medical vocabulary, when psychoanalysts, even the
unbelievers, began to speak, like Allendy,[1] of an 'inner tribunal'
(*justice intérieure*). It has been made abundantly clear by the clinical
work which has been reported at the Bossey Conference, for
which the material of this book was prepared, and by the
associated discussions.

A century ago, at the time of the triumph of Positivism in its
earliest form, doctors discussing as we did the role of guilt in
medicine would have been regarded as old fogeys. Medicine was
striving to eliminate all moral expressions from its vocabulary.
Today we are at the cross-roads of medical progress, for medicine is thirsting for a still more positive positivism—to rediscover
the whole man and not merely an arbitrarily circumscribed part of
man.

Medical outlook must therefore incorporate the religious outline of the specific character of man. In the light of the Bible,
'true' guilt appears as guilt towards God, a breakdown in the
order of man's dependency towards God. For my part, I do not
think we should set these three definitions of genuine guilt

against one another. We are dealing, it seems to me, with one and the same assertion expressed in three different linguistic forms: guilt towards oneself is the psychological language of C. G. Jung; guilt towards others is the existentialist language of Martin Buber; guilt towards God is the religious language of the Bible.

Thus the true guilt of men comes from the things with which they are reproached by God in their innermost hearts. Only they can discover what these things are. And they are usually very different from the things with which they are reproached by men. The reference to God brought to us by the Bible illuminates our problem in a remarkable way: from now on, 'false guilt' is that which comes as a result of the judgments and suggestions of men. 'True guilt' is that which results from divine judgment. In fact, the guilt towards oneself of the Jung School is indeed at the same time a guilt towards God, since it is a refusal to accept oneself as God wishes us to be; and the guilt towards others of Martin Buber is also a guilt towards God since it is a refusal of the divine order of human relationships.

A true, genuine guilt can even be observed in the child, along with the infantile 'functional' guilts described by Freud, and quite distinct from them. In this connection, you will remember the many cases reported by Mme Line Thévenin, the child-psychiatrist from Lyons. You will also recall those of Mlle Madeleine Rambert, the psychoanalyst of Lausanne, and in particular the case of Zizi, the six-year-old girl who could not work at school or learn to read, who was difficult, unco-operative and sullen.

Miss Rambert uses a technique with marionettes, which represent the various characters in the child's environment. While playing with the puppets, the child can externalize his feelings towards these characters. Zizi threw the puppets across the room crying, 'Naughty mummy, naughty daddy, naughty Peter'. She beat them, trampled and stamped on them. The same game went on for several weeks.

Suddenly one day Zizi scrambled into the analyst's arms and began sucking a button on her blouse: a symbolic action of returning to the mother's breast, to the time of security prior to the birth of her brother. But she quickly regained control of herself and said: 'No, no, Zizi is naughty; no one can love her; she killed mummy, daddy and Peter.'

The child showed obvious violent guilt and asked to be punished: 'Smack Zizi; whip her!' No explanation could quieten her until the analyst had made the symbolic gesture of smacking her lightly on the hand. From that moment Zizi made rapid progress. She returned to her mother, she was relaxed and amenable at home, she worked at school, and expressed the wish to become a big girl!

The older a child grows, the more fully should this autonomous sense of true guilt develop, and in so far as he governs his life and conduct according to that sense he will free himself from false guilts suggested by society or parental reproof. A story from the Bible will illustrate this in a striking way. It concerns Jesus Himself, at the age of twelve, which marks exactly the transition between childish dependence and adult autonomy.

What I have said will remind you of the parents who blamed their child saying, 'You have made us very anxious'. Now Jesus made his mother anxious, very anxious, when He began to be less preoccupied with her than with His own vocation. When His parents were leaving Jerusalem where they had gone for the feast, He remained behind, in order to learn from the doctors of the Law. Think of the mother's worry when she noticed that He was not with the party! But to her reproaches, Jesus replied with unexpected firmness: '. . . I must be about my Father's business' (Lk. ii. 42–51).

Not to cause His mother any worry—that was the law of the little child, and He must now free Himself from it in order to assume shortly the law of the adult: to accomplish the mission to which God called Him, and to begin preparing Himself for it now. From that moment, true guilt would have been to neglect that inner call, to remain dependent on His parents, bound by all their demands.

You will notice that Jesus really did throw His mother into the most acute uneasiness. She might well have considered Him as guilty towards her for the worry He had caused her. And this is no imaginary guilt, but very real. The term 'unreal guilt' suggested by Paul Ricoeur seems to me therefore, at least in this connection, to be less adequate than 'infantile guilt'. Now Jesus rejects this infantile guilt; He does not admit Himself as guilty. He justifies Himself with terse assurance. And here we can grasp a truth of great importance: the objective reality of the wrong done to others cannot make the guilt genuine. The distinction between 'false' and 'true' guilt is in no way the distinction between an imaginary and a real wrong done to others. The criterion is quite different. It must be known whether the conduct was contrary to, or in accordance with, the will of God.

St. Luke, the doctor Evangelist, adds a little later, however, that Jesus was 'subject' to His parents. Is there a contradiction? I think not; just the opposite. No other child passes through that necessary period of emancipation without disharmony. He must throw off the false guilts with which his parents burden him. But in his attempts he loses his sense of proportion, he pours scorn on his parents, he rebels. It is this which gives to adolescence its stormy and contradictory character. It is the critical period of conflict between the law of the child and the law of the adult.

On the other hand, as Jesus Himself says, it is clear that His perfect psychological health derives from the fact of His true and total dependence on God. This dependence is what frees Him from excessive parental demands, but it also saves Him from rebellion. The result is that even the conflict with His mother in no way embitters her: 'His mother kept all these things in her heart', the Gospel writer adds, on a quieter note.

Thus the crisis of adolescence can end either in a neurosis of opposition, when the adolescent becomes his own god, or in a neurosis of submission, when like a child, he continues to look on his father and mother as gods. We find here the whole biblical point of view and the light which it throws on this very complex problem of guilt: the only true guilt is not to depend on God, and on God alone—'You shall have no other gods before me' (Ex. xx. 3).

Certainly the Bible brings us laws from God, but they are never unrelated to the person of God Himself, incarnate in Jesus Christ. Its standpoint is that of a perpetual reference to a person, to a living God, and not to a mere thing like a law. And it is the personal dependence on God which frees us from the weight of laws, judgments and social constraints.

In the Bible we find many stories which scandalize the moralists, examples of conduct condemned by society, by the law, even by the law of God, which are presented as not culpable, but as just the opposite—as heroic obedience to a personal order from God. Thus the divine law proclaims 'Thou shalt not kill' (Ex. xx. 13). And we see in the Bible many men who did kill at God's command.

A theologian like Karl Barth,[46] who points out this fact, suggests that there is no question of murder in such cases. Yet a murder is a murder. May we not rather say, quite frankly, that in view of the Bible it is, in such a case, a non-culpable murder because it is ordered by God. It can be seen then how categorically the Bible affirms that the only true guilt is disobedience to God or any dependence other than on God alone.

With murder I have taken an extreme case. But innumerable other examples can be found of conduct universally considered as culpable, which are presented in the Bible as so many cases of faithful obedience to divine inspiration: lies, stratagems, violence, revenge. What matters is not the knowledge of whether a particular line of conduct is judged as blameworthy or not by society, but whether it is ordered or not by God!

It can be understood that there is here the real principle of emancipation sought by the psychoanalysts from the false guilt generated by social sanctions. How are we to separate what is relative and often falsified in human conduct from what is true, absolute and inevitable? What is relative is the law or social judgment—things which change with the times, with custom and fashion, even when the moral law is more or less inspired by divine revelation. It is this legalistic guilt which is pathogenic.

What is considered as culpable in one society, is not in another. What is considered as culpable at one period is not at another. You cannot, for instance, separate what is a genuine feeling of modesty from what is social suggestion. A style of dress which is judged and felt as immodest in one country is readily accepted in another. Indeed, any guilt suggested by the judgment of men is a false guilt if it does not receive inner support by a judgment of God.

Therefore, real guilt is often something quite different from that which constantly weighs us down, because of our fear of social judgment and the disapproval of men. We become independent of them in proportion as we depend on God. You are aware, from all the work of psychotherapists, how vitally important is this emancipation from society and its constraints. Thus, for instance, everyone feels a special pleasure in using a well-placed slang or swearword. It is defiance hurled at the over-rigorous, crushing tutelage of good form, a healthy affirmation of independence in the face of social pressure.

I remember a lecture by Dr. A. Stocker to the Philosophical Society of Geneva. In the discussion, one of the philosophers asked my colleague for a short simple definition of neurosis. 'Neurotics,' he said with epigrammatic terseness, 'are people who cannot say d——' This very unacademic word sounded well in that scholarly assembly, and in its terseness expressed a penetrating truth, namely that, sooner or later, in order to fulfil his destiny in the way God has planned, every man must brave the judgment of others, even that of his parents, his masters, and perhaps of the religious authorities.

For instance, we shall see Jesus Himself show that same unbending firmness towards His mother when she was driven by the need which every mother has, of keeping her child from suffering, and sought to keep Him from His dangerous career. At that very moment He speaks of His utter dependence on His 'Father in heaven' (Matt. xii. 46–50). And yet, He is full of infinite tenderness for that mother who suffers because of His obedience, as His word from the Cross shows (Jn. xix. 26–27).

His reply to Peter is even more vigorous when the apostle reproaches Him for becoming involved in a conflict with the religious authorities which will lead to death on the Cross: 'Get thee behind me, Satan! You are a hindrance to me; for you are not on the side of God, but of men' (Matt. xvi. 22–23). God's thoughts and men's thoughts; judgments of God and judgments of men; that is a clear formulation of the opposition between true guilt and false guilt.

Chapter VIII

EVERYONE MAKES ACCUSATIONS

THE misfortune is that all men claim to express, through their own judgments, the judgment of God Himself. It is an absolutely universal phenomenon. Men make a monopoly of God, even those who do not believe in Him, but especially those who wish to serve Him and lead men to Him. When they judge the conduct of others, they all do it in a peremptory manner, implying that God Himself could not judge them otherwise. They are so strongly convinced in their opinion of what is good or evil that it seems to them that God would betray Himself if He did not share their opinion. For this reason false guilts arising from human judgments, and true guilt which depends on the divine judgment, become constantly and dangerously entangled and confused.

A child cannot receive his first lessons in morality directly from God; he receives them from his parents to whom he then ascribes a divine authority. There are indeed genuine divine truths which parents thus hand on to their children, for instance that in general lying is culpable. But parents and educators thus inevitably assume the flattering role of infallible mouthpieces of God. When the child later begins to express other tastes, other opinions, other moral judgments, they will be opposed with the same energy as if by opposing the parental judgments, the child were opposing God Himself.

They condemn with zeal, sincerity and in all good faith; and they seek to convince others that their condemnation is in line with that of God, that what they judge as wrong is evil in the sight of God. They are equally condemnatory of their neighbours, their friends, their enemies—of everyone. They are absolutely sure that what they denounce as evil is undoubtably evil in God's eyes.

They will probably approve of the definition just given of 'true' guilt: that it is not guilt suggested by human judgment, but is indeed guilt before God. But they will claim to be the interpreters of God's thought. If true guilt is our sense of God's reproach, they will make it their business to tell us what is the reason for God's reproach, to set themselves up as adjudicators of good and evil.

They will be all the more zealous in this because they have a deep sense of their didactic responsibility, that of guiding their children in the right way, to rectify the conduct of their friends and to denounce the faults of their enemies. And thus, throughout the world, accusations are flung about from all sides and become hopelessly entangled, all pronounced with conviction and all from the best of motives, for the triumph of good over evil, of truth over error. And all men hold one another as guilty.

If true guilt is God's reproach, what I can do for a patient is to help him to approach God, to listen to Him himself, and not to expect divine judgment from my lips. To make any claim of exercising moral arbitrament, to tell him whether he should feel guilty or not, whether he is guilty or not, is to step outside my role of doctor and even to close the door on all effective help. Was this not the ambition which a certain serpent awoke in our distant ancestors, by encouraging them to eat of the fruit of the tree of knowledge of good and evil? 'You will be like God,' he said, 'knowing good and evil' (Gen. iii. 5).

This is more than an epigram. We are touching on a fundamental point of the biblical message and one which is very illuminating for our subject of guilt. You remember that Dr. Bovet told us in this conference that 'the Fall was the invention of morality'. We have here a mysterious paradox which is very difficult to explain. I am afraid that I shall shock many people, the best people, believers for whom the moral and spiritual life of obedience to God is the most vital matter.

The more highly we value the cause of God and right, of helping people to serve Him and be subject to Him, the more we are driven to denounce evil and praise good, to expose the wicked and do homage to the righteous; in a word, to set ourselves up as arbiters of good and evil. And that is just what the Bible forbids us to do, by a strange inversion of perspective.

Read the newspapers and listen to conversation, and everywhere you hear the denunciation of injustice, abuses, vice, lying and selfishness. Indignation is spontaneous, quivering with sincerity and usually well-founded. Appeals are made to the conscience of mankind, it is impossible to be silent before such iniquity or to abandon the victims; would not silence condone the evil?

All the folk around us call on us to play the part of lovers of justice, and to bear our witness. See a married couple in conflict, and inevitably they appeal to us as to an arbitrator. See a brother who complains of his brother, or a son of his father, or a workman of his foreman or employer, or an employer of his competitor, and we have excited, indignant indictments, with detailed, blunt-spoken stories piling up; if we refuse to sit in judgment we are considered as cowardly, as condoning evil and quietly ignoring the promptings of conscience.

In all these innumerable conflicts, and amid all these reproaches and accusations which men hurl at one another, there is a real intention of holding other people culpable, of convicting the one under criticism as guilty and of making him recognize his short-comings. If we refuse to take part in this blackballing, we are accused, in turn, of being guilty, of betraying justice, morals and truth by remaining silent when they are reprehensibly violated.

On the other hand, see others who spring to the defence of an innocent victim, who desire to exonerate a man from the unjust accusations heaped upon him, to rehabilitate him, to explain his conduct and to show that he is not guilty. The same fervour is apparent, the same appeal to our conscience, the same indignation if we refuse to sit in judgment. Such reluctance appears to be really unethical, unworthy of a Christian or even of a gentleman.

The conscience of these people, a conscience which is so readily taken as the voice of God, is revolted before the reserve we show and cannot remain silent. There is no neutral position between good and evil; we must pass judgment, pronounce a verdict, say who is guilty and who is not, under pain of denying our faith, our morality and our humanity. Evil must be denounced in the very interests of the one who commits it, so that he may be freed from it: 'Let me take the speck out of your eye' (Matt. vii. 4).

You will understand that I do not deny this; I do not contest the existence of righteous anger, nor that God sometimes calls a man to take an inflexible stand against evil. Think only of *Uncle Tom's Cabin* and the suppression of slavery. I do not deny that God may put a whip in our hands; Jesus Himself took one once (Jn. ii. 15). But remember, we feel that Jesus could wield it with a clear conscience, whereas we cannot ever be quite free of doubt, if not about the justice of our cause, then at least about all the means which we use perchance to defend it, and especially about our right to place ourselves, as we do, in the position of accusers while others might advance reproaches against us.

The opponent replies with equal conviction and equal warmth. Certainly, we can brave it out; we can try to persuade ourselves that we are indifferent to his attacks, and say that they are utter calumny. That is part of the struggle. But there is no one who does not suffer, more or less secretly, from being in conflict with others and from being an agent of division rather than of harmony among men, even though he is quite certain of being in the right.

And conflicts do exist, not only between interest-groups or opposing ideologies, between the right and the left; they exist in the most homogeneous societies, in committees for social, humanitarian, idealist or pacifist objects, and in Church councils. These are often the most distressing, the most exhausting and the most charged with guilt. In order to show charity to an opponent, a man swallows his anger and aggressiveness; it turns to gall, and his charity to hypocrisy.

To be spared all conflict, a man would have to withdraw from life altogether—the supreme guilt of backing-out or surrendering. All life brings conflict, indeed it is based on conflict, even for the humblest cell which can only subsist by defending itself constantly against its environment. What does not eat others is itself devoured. And yet we cannot defend ourselves from a sense of guilt for having to hit out so frequently. Even a Gandhi with the rare courage to refuse the whip of physical force, had to use the whip of the spirit, and this does not always hurt less.

When passions have cooled, reconciliation may be attempted. But it is not always possible. We always think that the responsibility for this lies in our opponent. It is his intransigence which makes reconciliation impossible. But am I not just as uncompromising? If I yield for the sake of peace, I betray myself, and burden myself with fresh guilt. False forgiveness weighs more heavily than conflicts which at best have the merit of frankness.

There are people too with whom one has relations of a superficial kind only; one speaks of the weather, of the price of carrots or the children's schooling. One carefully avoids any expression of deeper feelings in order to spare oneself as well as the other any discussion which might prove painful. Thus some married couples can gradually become strangers to one another. They seek reassurance by flattering themselves about the apparent harmony which they thus safeguard. But we always have qualms of conscience about playing hide-and-seek with others.

Thus we have only the choice between several guilts: guilt from asserting ourselves or guilt from being silent. So it can be understood that the aim of this study cannot be to bring forward a recipe of which we are always secretly dreaming, a recipe for living without guilt! It will be more of a brave appraisal of our human condition, laden as it inexorably is with guilt.

There is no life without conflict; no conflict without guilt. We constantly try to reassure ourselves. We fall back on popular wisdom: 'You cannot make an omelet without breaking eggs.'

We fall back on psychology which strives to consider aggressiveness coldly as a simple force of nature, exempt from any moral standard, which causes still more harm by being repressed than by being expressed. We fall back on cynical or existentialist philosophical doctrines.

All these prevarications appear as proof of the secret guilt suffered by everyone by reason of the conflicts which are for ever setting one person against another, a guilt against which all seek to defend themselves. But from the mouth of Jesus Christ Himself come these words: 'Judge not . . .' (Matt. vii. 1). Without being fully aware of it we mentally twist this commandment, as if Jesus had said: 'Judge not unjustly.' He said: 'Judge not.' He did not deny that there is a mote in my neighbour's eye, but he asks that I should first concern myself only with the beam in my own. This abdication of all spirit of judgment is extremely difficult for us, and seems like surrendering before evil.

It appears almost impossible for us not to express our opinion on the guiltiness of men. All the more impossible as we believe ourselves enlightened by biblical revelation and our own psychological knowledge. Do we not, as psychologists, have close to our hearts the desire to free men from their false guilts? But, notice, to tell them in what they are guiltless, implies telling them inevitably in what they are guilty! To mark out the frontiers of Switzerland is to mark out also the frontiers of contiguous countries. To trace the boundaries of false guilt implies the tracing of the boundaries of true guilt.

Thus our very zeal to help enlighten and free others can lead us to play the part of guide and judge which involves the sin of judgment. It is our Swiss national failing, this need to speak bluntly to everyone, under the pretext of frankness, and of teaching everybody. Call it the Pestalozzi complex, if you wish, for in every Swiss there is a schoolmaster, even though Pestalozzi himself was less given to the spirit of judgment than the majority of his confederates!

In a lecture entitled 'The Marignan Complex' I ventured an even deeper explanation. Switzerland was a redoubtable military power until it was heavily defeated by Francis I at Marignan. By a psychological mechanism of concealment, Marignan is presented to our schoolchildren almost as a victory, because of the tribute paid by the victorious king to the courage of the Swiss, and the order and dignity with which the remains of the Swiss armies withdrew from Italy. But, from that day, Switzerland finally withdrew also from the main political scene of Europe.

Now, we always see that those who take no active part in affairs begin to criticize those who do. In this there is a certain need to offset the qualms of conscience which such folk feel when they avoid responsibility, by judging those who accept it and claiming that in their place, they would do better. Some of these passive people give the impression that they alone always know how a thing should be done for it to be done well, but they teach it, rather than do it.

This is perhaps one of the reasons why there are more neurotics in Switzerland than in other countries where there is more respect for the freedom of each man to behave in his own way without being showered with criticism and advice. This note of superiority always irritates foreign visitors; and it is probably a compensation for the rather insignificant part to which our weakness restricts us among the nations. By writing such a book as this, do I not give way to such presumptuousness?

Does not the Bible bring us the law of God? Does not conscience, enlightened by revelation, cry out in us? Then I would be sorely tempted, in my consulting-room, under the pretext of helping my patient, to tell him in what he is guilty and in what he is not, and whether his guilt is true or false.

Now, when a man appeals to our judgment he is at the same time afraid of it. When a man feels that he is misunderstood, as he puts it, it means that he feels that he is being judged, that we do not see things as he does, that we judge him guilty when he feels innocent. Because recriminations and reproach fill the world, everyone feels under constant criticism, or at any rate threatened with judgment, and he fears its repercussions. No one is indifferent to it; all are hurt by some word, by some look or some opinion contrary to their own.

Yes, this fear of being judged is intense and universal. Its importance became more and more striking to me, even overwhelming, while I was preparing this study. If all men are afraid of each other, pupils of teachers, teachers of pupils, husbands of wives, wives of husbands, ministers or priests of their parishioners, and parishioners of their spiritual leaders, it is because all are afraid of being judged.

And this fear plays a decisive part in all the conflicts, public or private, which divide mankind; for all men defend themselves and do it by attacking. The fearful do not attack openly, but brood over their indignation until the day when it breaks out in a still more violent way. And everywhere in the world we can see 'this aggressive behaviour which is the despair of families and peoples alike', as Dr. Nodet writes. [27] Even the Churches fear one another, because they are afraid of being convicted of unfaithfulness.

When a diplomatic incident occurs between two nations, each

country denounces the other's faults with prodigious energy. The proof is logical, ruthless, irrefutable, the unanimity of public opinion and the Press is most impressive, the wealth and ingenuity of argument is boundless.

The one which has formal right on its side, which is the victim of a violation of a treaty, flourishes that right with a legal vigour which seems unanswerable. But the other appeals, beyond the law, to equity, beyond the immediate and formal causation to a deeper more distant one. Recriminations become entangled and tension mounts. If war breaks out, each country will wage it in the name of justice. Beyond a certain threshold of passion, 'the guns go off on their own' as the saying has it.

This terrifying intensity of indignation and mutual recrimination is a fair measure of the intolerable anguish felt by everyone at the idea of being judged guilty. The classical formula of the social and political struggle can be translated into terms of guilt: men are reduced to pillory others in order to exculpate themselves. Everyone is smirched and none is cleansed.

Do not get the idea that those who assume a look of indifference or defiance are free from this fear of being judged. Rather their behaviour betrays the fear. They practise a strategy of diversion. By their eccentricities they attract criticism which does not touch them, since it is deliberately encouraged in order to divert criticism which they fear from other and more vulnerable and sensitive spots of the battle front which they defend against social judgment.

Human guilt is not produced, as is claimed, by science, positivism, an objective vision of things and their universal causality, historical determinism or psychological determinism. It 'fills our life', as Dr. Sarano says; 'for is not the best of our time spent in rationalizing and accusing?' Quite rightly, he labels our age as the 'century of the bad conscience', which makes a striking contrast with the nineteenth century, 'whose good conscience we find shocking'.

'About 1880', writes Jean Guitton,[12] 'the results of moral analysis could have been summed up in the following aphorism: even the guilty are innocent. In 1945, it would be necessary to reverse the terms; even the innocent are guilty. . . . We are in the age of the judges.'

See how the philosophy and literature of our day are burdened with bad conscience. Novels, essays, plays, films all deal with the problem of guilt—formal guilt and the impossibility of determining who is really guilty, and the deep-seated guilt, diffused and poignant, the guilt of being alive and the revolt which it induces. Simon[42] evokes the despair and cynicism of present-day writers. 'It is perhaps better,' he suggests, 'not to have a sense of sin when one does not have a sense of grace to balance it out.' The 'free-thinkers' of the beginning of the century were optimists. They could reject God with a smile because they had confidence in man and little consciousness of his guilt. Today, the atheists have an acute sense of guilt, and they are more pessimistic about man than the Calvinists.

Chapter IX

EVERYONE DEFENDS HIMSELF

EVERY judgment that I make of a man, even if I am careful to say nothing to him, even if I hide it deep in my heart, and even if I am almost or entirely unaware of it myself, makes between him and me an unbridgeable gulf and hopelessly prevents my giving him any effective assistance. By my judgment, I drive him more deeply into his faults rather than free him from them.

I am not thinking here of those frank explanations during which two opponents, a married couple or two friends for example, air their grievances. However stormy and painful such exchanges of accumulated reproach may be, they are necessary and salutary. It is an act of honesty. It is the price of real peace, the condition of true mutual forgiveness, of a rebirth of reciprocal confidence. No conflict is more unhealthy than those which breed in secret, products of mental brooding, under cover of a superficial courtesy or friendship. Observe the vigour with which Jesus Christ addresses the Pharisees! (Matt. xxiii. 13–36).

What I am contesting here is a very widespread illusion. The illusion that it is possible to help people by denouncing their faults, without even being asked to do so. We all fall into this error, at any time and in all good faith, and the more so when we have a higher moral ideal or more zeal in helping others. We are convinced that we act only for their good and for love of them. Because we love them, we wish to see them perfect, we suffer through their imperfections and exhort them to correct them.

In reality we always have the confused intuition of being on the wrong track. We need to reassure ourselves. This criticism of others is qualified, to our advantage, as 'constructive', in order to justify it. We say: 'I don't want to criticize, but——' And all that follows the 'but' well and truly gives the lie to this benevolent introduction. We seek to persuade ourselves that by denouncing a man's faults we are going to bring him to his senses, to make him recognize his guilt and to reform his conduct.

What a hope! Just the opposite effect is induced! Any man under the rebuff of accusation, has a defensive reflex of self-justification. A reply to the accusation immediately springs to mind. Arguments come flooding up, fill his thoughts and leave no room for humiliation or a confession of his faults. He can offer a thousand good reasons to exculpate himself. He is accused of cowardice: every occasion on which he has shown courage crowds into his memory. He is accused of lying: the recollection of other people's lies is what is present in his mind, and he judges himself, on the contrary as being too frank; it is those who, by their unjust conduct towards him have caused him to lie who are really responsible.

Such, at least, is the reaction of the normal man. One who, under reproof, immediately hauls down his flag and accepts the verdict without discussion appears as sick. He is a prey to an inhibition of his instinct of self-defence. His behaviour augurs badly for the future. A too-ready repentance is not repentance, but surrender. His perpetual *mea culpa* will bear no living fruit, for it is the product of a neurotic mechanism, not of an authentic movement of the spirit. It is a sign of defeat, and not a victory.

Admittedly, good people may be deceived and will praise his humility. If these be his parents, they will congratulate themselves on having such an amenable child and will set him up as an example to his rebellious brothers and sisters. He may possibly deceive himself and take as a high virtue what is really paralysis of his psychical energies. Real repentance does not grow so quickly. It does not have the automatic character of something psychologically determined. It is only reached after a long struggle, after a stormy defence. It is reached, above all, only when conviction of sin grows from within and not from without, when it rises from the depths of our own being, from intimate communion with God, from the prompting of the Holy Spirit, and not from the judgment of men.

In a healthy person, such judgments have just the opposite effect; they release an inexorable mechanism of self-justification whatever the benevolence of the critic and the purity of his intentions. This defence mechanism has the precision and universality of a law of nature. It is manifested as surely as a dog bares his teeth when threatened or a hare runs when the gun is aimed. Aggressiveness or flight are the immediate and ineluctable responses to criticism.

All criticism is destructive. This is probably why we all have such fear of the judgment of men. As with every fear, we are dealing with a manifestation of the instinct of self-preservation. We defend ourselves against criticism with the same energy as we employ in defending ourselves against hunger, cold or wild beasts, for it is a mortal threat.

Dr. Andreas of Hanover, the forensic expert, was telling us in Geneva, in connection with the delinquents sent to him by the courts, that in no case did he find any expression of the least sense of guilt. All of them showed but one concern—that of exculpating themselves, to bring forward extenuating circumstances, and to order their behaviour, words and silences with a view to obtaining, if possible, some lightening of the sentence which threatened them. It could be said, then, in analogy with the physiology of the heart, that there is in a man under accusation a phase of in-excitability of conscience.

This is not surprising. After the verdict, when the man is working out his sentence, he may experience a real heart-searching. But it is rare beforehand, when he is like a quarry sought by the claws of justice. At that moment, a movement of repentance is always a little suspect; it might be looked on as a mere manœuvre, conscious or otherwise, to obtain the indulgence of the court. Those who can bring him to this state are his chaplain or his counsel, those who seek to understand him and to defend him, not those who accuse him.

This address of Dr. Andreas in Geneva reminded me of an incident from my military service. It was during the war. One day my commanding officer said to me: 'There is a man whom I have to punish. I do not like it but I cannot evade it. He will spend twenty-four hours in the village cell. But that is not enough. What he needs is an opportunity to examine himself and to discover why he behaved in this way, instead of brooding over his insubordination. Will you go with him and help him to do it?' So I spent some hours which I shall never forget. We had plenty of time—a thing which is so often lacking outside; time to try and understand. But above all, we found in that confined place a certain fellowship, a real contact between man and man which is so rare outside.

I was therefore much struck by the conclusions of Dr. Andreas. He can glimpse, he told us, how far the personal relationship in medicine, which animated all of us at that Conference, can transfigure his relationships with the delinquents sent to him. They must feel welcomed with no sign of criticism, as people rather than delinquents, so that a salutary sense of guilt may be generated in their hearts.

Thus the most tragic consequence of our criticism of a man is to block his way to humiliation and grace, precisely to drive him into the mechanisms of self-justification and into his faults instead of freeing him from them. For him, our voice drowns the voice of God. We put him beyond the reach of the divine voice which can only be heard in the silence. The impassioned response which our criticism triggers off in his soul makes too much noise.

In fact, very paradoxically, by our very ardour to show him his fault, and by the justification-reflex which we thus set in motion within him, we provoke a veritable eclipse of the moral sense. As a result he comes to believe sincerely that his conduct, far from being guilty, is rather virtuous and excellent, and that he would have been guilty to behave otherwise. In the dialogue, he no longer listens to our voice, but to his own which refutes us.

You may think that I am exaggerating. But I would ask you to open your ears and eyes to see and hear the world as it is. If it occurs that a man recognizes his wrongdoings, he does it in the quiet of recollection, or the benevolent atmosphere of a *tête-à-tête* with someone who will not criticize. But in the heat of the debates which fill the world, each one proclaims his own rectitude and the wrongs of others, the excellence of his own cause, the purity of his motives and the moral concern which inspires him.

Dr. Hesnard[16] has an eloquent description of this universal phenomenon of self-justification—a phenomenon which is such that men lose the most elementary awareness of the moral faults which they commit. They may make a display of a scruple concerning 'inward sin', which this analyst denounces, namely a false or imaginary guilt unrelated to their real conduct. And in their real conduct they remain blind to their most obvious faults, and they outspokenly justify their actions in the presence of their accusers.

Like Dr. Andreas, Dr. Hesnard observes the frequency of this mechanism in delinquents and criminals and the amazing absence of remorse which they show. He speaks of that long drawn-out labour of self-justification which has developed in their hearts even before the crime, and which has finished by presenting it as permissible and even virtuous to their own conscience, so that after perpetrating the deed, the culprit experiences a kind of relief and no regret at all.

Dr. Hesnard describes this phenomenon of the 'justificatory conscience' not only on the individual plane but also on the collective social and international plane. He shows us that it is the only possible explanation of a universal fact which otherwise seems inexplicable: that men can commit the greatest crime of all, war, in which they massacre innocent women and children in great numbers, without feeling the slightest remorse. In fact, they are proud of having heroically served the highest values, the highest virtues, and of satisfying morality; they are absolutely convinced that they have served humanity.

Such then is the universal process, individual and collective, which can be constantly observed, implacably unfolding itself. Everyone censures his fellow, and each at the same time, defends himself and fears the other's criticism which he feels to be unjust.

At the same time, each exercises upon himself quite a different judgment of guilt, which turns on faults quite different from those which his critic set out to denounce. And the energy with which each man defends himself against other people's criticism which he finds unjust, and the atmosphere of conflict and threat which thus develops, prevent him from confessing the faults of which he accuses himself, just when that very confession would bring about the collapse of his critic's censure and his own aggressive reaction.

Study, for example, that frank explanation between two friends to which I referred a while ago. When it ends in reconciliation, it is by a very different route from any which either could have anticipated. After the event they are both at a loss to explain exactly what happened, even to make a clear summary of the grievances which, shortly before, they were reeling off with such apparent objectivity and logic.

Take a simple concrete example. Suppose the first accused the second of cowardice. It was an obvious fact. With relentless logic, rehearsing point after point like some theorem or other, he reached the inevitable conclusion—you are a coward. Any reconciliation appeared impossible and immoral until after some admission of cowardice by the other. But notice that such an admission is not enough for reconciliation. Thus, faced with the evidence, his defendant may say, 'Well, yes, I have been a coward, but . . .' And with that 'but' he immediately replies with his 'theorem', which has a no less rigorous or logical exposition of his grievances, and by which he hopes to drag another admission from his accuser.

Thus the 'theorems' cross without meeting. And so such discussions always appear more or less like dialogues between deaf people. Then, suddenly, miraculously, the atmosphere may be eased. What has happened? The 'defendant' having unburdened himself of all his grievances and mental reservations, has begun to talk of something completely different—of his real difficulties, his own failings, of what really weighs him down, of what he is not at all proud. In tones of sincerity he admits faults, not those which others wished to make him recognize at any cost, but other faults, much more secret and much more of a burden. And the tone of this admission is very different from that of the admission of cowardice such a short time ago.

Notice that neither contests the cowardice, neither the one who was guilty of it nor the one who voiced the reproach. But the emotive accent has shifted to other problems, much less formal, much deeper, much more complex. Here we touch on a very important question about which I am often asked: How are we to free ourselves of this spirit of judgment?—'I understand quite clearly,' says a woman to me, for example, 'that you are calling on us to give up our spirit of judgment. But my husband is an inveterate liar. I should have to be blindfolded not to see it. And I cannot consider my husband as truthful when he lies so openly.' Who cannot see that that woman's severity drives her husband to tell lies? It is almost always through fear of being criticized that people tell lies.

You understand now by the story of our two friends that to shed the spirit of judgment is not to close our eyes altogether to the faults which men commit, nor to deny them, nor to call good what is evil.

Further, no one can get rid of the spirit of judgment by an effort of will. As long as I am obsessed by a friend's fault which has shocked me and made me reproach him, no matter how much I say to myself: 'I do not wish to judge him,' I judge him none the less. But the spirit of judgment evaporates as soon as I become conscious of my own faults and speak freely of them to my friend, as he speaks to me of those which make him reproach himself.

That is what happened to our two speakers. The problem of cowardice which seemed so decisive, becomes strangely blurred. It appears, thenceforward, no longer as the root of the conflict, but the fruit of a whole chain of sufferings which arouse the sympathy of the one who a while ago was accusing him so harshly. From censor, the latter is suddenly transmuted into helpful friend, full of understanding, solicitude and zeal. Confidence for confidence, he begins in his turn to open up about his own difficulties and his own secret guilts.

For nothing is more contagious than confession. It is such that anyone who aspires to the role of confessor should himself confess with great care. Otherwise he will experience the most lively uneasiness at each confession made to him for it will awaken within him the painful memory of personal faults, and he would feel dishonest to keep silent about them before a penitent who is so frank in confessing his own.

The spirit of judgment can thus suddenly collapse and give way to a spirit of charity, and that not by the admission which the whole logical theorem of the accusation sought to extract, but by a very different way. Precisely, by abandoning the field of logic in which accusations crossed without meeting and by the genuine meeting of people, by a sincere revelation by each one of his real problems.

The one who, a while ago, was accusing the other now sees his friend in a very different light. He seems to have changed in appearance and in character. But in fact it is the accuser who has changed. This confirms the truth that a man's judgment of another depends more on the one judging and on his passions than on the one being judged and his conduct.

This often spectacular change is called 'metanoia' in the Bible. The word is usually translated by 'repentance'. Literally it means 'change of mind'. The logical attitude of accusation by others and of self-defence has changed into an attitude of mind in which each one talks freely about his own difficulties and seeks to understand those of the other. And the two friends will now ask one another's forgiveness for showing that spirit of judgment which neither wished to give up a while ago.

For the cutting arrogant attitude of the accuser, an attitude of humility is suddenly substituted, in which he recognizes his own faults. This is the 'metanoeite' of the Gospel (Matt. iii. 2), 'change your mind' or 'repent'. It is a reversal, a turning-in upon the self, and it is also a transcendence of the self, as the metaphysical transcends the physical and introduces points of view unknown to it.

Religious conversion itself often seems like a similar unravelling of a 'frank explanation' with God. The course of events is very similar to the one just outlined. We all have grievances against God, whether we are believers or not. Believers are often more reluctant to formulate them, and yet they are the ones who feel them very keenly, just because they have put their trust in God and believe in His power. But if we have enough honesty and courage not to inhibit them, we wield them with the same logical rigour as our two erstwhile opponents. And it also seems to us that no reconciliation with God is possible so long as He does not reply to the defiance we hurl at Him.

Think of the story of Job. His pleadings are also like a theorem: he is innocent and struck down by misfortune and illness; God is almighty and yet does not answer his prayer; he who could help the innocent sufferer and does not do so, is unjust; therefore God is unjust. Now, what do we see at the end of the book? God speaks to Job of something quite different: 'Where were you when I laid the foundation of the earth?' He evokes the grandeur and mystery of His creative work (Job xxxviii–xli). And suddenly Job's accusations collapse (Job xlii. 3).

In fact Job has not received any logical answer to the precise questions which he asked. This is what gives to so many rational minds the impression that faith is inadmissible sharp practice. They do not realize that they have themselves experienced such trickery a hundred times in the course of reconciliation with a friend. For God's answer is not an idea, a proposition, like the conclusion of a theorem; it is Himself. He revealed Himself to Job; Job found personal contact with Him (Job xlii. 5).

You can see that there is the same shift from the plane of rational discussion to the plane of reciprocal confiding. Job, who a while ago, was fiercely defending himself against the accusations of his friends, now accuses himself, but of something quite different. His friends claimed to be God's mouthpieces and wished at any price to drive Job to the confession of some sin by which he might have drawn upon himself the unjust misfortunes he is suffering. Against such a suggestion Job was revolted, for he felt himself innocent of what his friends accused him.

But the very fervour with which he defended himself against unjust accusations, hardened him in an attitude of recrimination against God and prevented him from hearing God's real reproach which turned on something quite different—his pretension to contend with God. It was necessary for Job's friends to be silent so that Job could hear God's voice and be reconciled with Him. Similarly our voice must be silenced, our judgment of a man must be broken off, so that he may hear the voice of God, whose judgment is quite different from our own.

Chapter X

THE UNITY OF GUILT

YES, the things for which God reproaches us in our secret heart are usually very different from those which men condemn! The ministry of confession which I have practised for so many years has abundantly convinced me of that. Men judge one another in an amazingly superficial and unjust way.

One man, for instance, is held to be proud by all his acquaintances, because of his constant and naïve display of vanity. In reality he reproaches himself for something very different: one day, many years ago, he was guilty of the cowardly betrayal of a friend who trusted him. Even today he has not understood his own conduct nor been able to forgive himself. He is a prey to the remorse which he has never dared confess. The arrogant behaviour which annoys those around him is, in his case, only a façade behind which he hides his real inner drama.

In fact, he looks on himself with contempt. He is much less arrogant than I am. The flattering poses which he strikes, and which everyone holds against him are only perpetual yet vain attempts to regain his own self-esteem. The contempt which he affects for other people masks a need to make them feel small in compensation for his inability to feel big himself. He will only become conscious of his own real value as a man through the experience of God's pardon. But that forgiveness will turn on the secret fault of which he was so ashamed and not on the so-called pride with which men reproached him. Against this reproach he always defended himself stubbornly for he felt it to be unjust, and the defence reflex prevented him from confessing his real fault.

A woman is judged as flighty, frivolous and sensual because she flirts with all the men she meets and embarks incessantly on fresh affairs of the heart. Yet, paradoxically enough, the reproach which she holds against herself is a strange timidity. When quite young, she passed through a period of intense religious fervour and felt herself called to adopt the religious life. But she never dared to speak of it to anyone. She has a sense of having denied her vocation and she is pursued by remorse. The worldly turmoil into which she plunged is only a perpetual diversion. In order to gain reassurance, she needs the attentions of men whom she cannot really love and who take advantage of her.

Let us take another look in the light of these observations at the type-situation of the parent-child relationship in education. Parents judge the children's conduct from their adult standpoint, with all the experience of life which they have and which their children have not. As a result they accuse one of lying because he tells as true stories which he has made up. They insist, so that he shall recognize his guilt. Now the child has no sense of guilt about it, for to him the world of make-believe is as real as that of reality. Suspicion creates what it imputes. That child may well become a confirmed liar through having been wrongly suspected of lying.

But perhaps that child already bears within himself other much more genuine guilts which pass unnoticed by the parents. He may discover them by listening to the voice of God already speaking in his heart. Will not the important thing for his future moral life be the fact that he has learned to listen thus to God, to depend on Him and not on the judgment of men? And that is just where the voice of his parents, anxious as they are about his moral education, muffles the voice of God, and their judgments prevent his becoming aware of that of God.

So for each of us there are, on the one hand, the reproaches held against us by men, and on the other, our own very different convictions of sin. But there becomes established a mysterious relationship between the two, a kind of emotional fusion. If we are so afraid of the criticism of men, it is because we have a chronically bad conscience. We may have a good conscience on the specific point on which we are judged, and have good reasons to justify ourselves and assert as unjust the reproaches levelled at us. But we have a bad conscience *elsewhere*, on other points; to be precise, those on which God, not men, speaks to us. That bad conscience may be obscure, veiled behind our protestations, or even completely unconscious. But it is that which envenoms our protestations of innocency with aggressiveness.

You can see how inextricably entangled are the links between false guilt and true guilt. Certainly, in the dread of true guilt, there is always a certain reference back to the dread of infantile guilt, a fear of losing the esteem and love of other people. Psychologists have amply proved it. But inversely, in the most truly neurotic guilt, there is also a reference back to the most genuinely human guilt and anguish against which we always defend ourselves and which give the intensity to our fear of criticism.

So guilt seems to be completely subjective. None of us can say with certainty to a friend: 'You are guilty on such and such counts.' Such a pretension to give objective foundations to guilt, constitutes, in a word, an attack on the person, on the person's autonomy, on each one's personal responsibility, a negation of the psychological truth that only the subject himself can recognize himself as guilty or not, and on what count.

In our Geneva Conference Professor Pierre-L. Mounier-Kuhn of Lyons related a moving episode. A patient of his was to go abroad and had asked him whether she might go by plane. He had examined her and felt compelled to advise her to go by sea. That is what she did. The boat was wrecked. 'I assure you,' added our friend, 'that I spent some dreadful days until I learned that my patient was among the survivors.'

I can read your thoughts! 'But that is not guilt! There is no guilt, since there was no professional fault. There would have been if the doctor had not given the wisest advice following his scientific examination of the patient. He gave the best advice; the boat may sink, but it does not change that fact.'

Obviously, I understand these objections raised by rational minds. But I also understand perfectly Dr. Mounier-Kuhn's deep emotion, and I think that it was indeed a sense of guilt that he felt so intensely. Logic has nothing to do with it. He was already imagining the death of his patient and could not help thinking: 'This misfortune has overtaken her because of the advice I gave her.'

The sense of guilt is linked to this feeling of causality, of responsibility, to the consciousness of unavoidable consequences. 'I did that.' A host of explanations of the objective causation of things may be reviewed without eradicating that sense of guilt. Neither excuses, proofs nor hypotheses can change anything. 'I did that, and now I cannot act as though it did not happen.'

We must therefore take this subject of guilt in its full breadth, in all its ambiguity and in its full unity. To tell someone who is a prey to guilt: 'It is not guilt', is like saying to a sick person: 'You have no temperature,' instead of taking a thermometer to see if he has.

Yes, it is right and expedient to distinguish, as we did in Chapter 7, and even to contrast false and true guilt, infantile and adult or moral guilt. All present-day psychologists arrive at this distinction and at this contrast. To elucidate it, they make a point of using different terms. Thus what I have called false guilt is, by Dr. Sarano,[35] called 'sense of guilt' or 'sickness-guilt' in opposition to what he calls 'consciousness of guilt' or 'value-guilt', corresponding to our true guilt. In certain respects, it may be said that what Dr. Hesnard[16] calls 'sin' answers to our false guilt, whereas he calls the true guilt 'morality without sin' or 'concrete morality'. Paul Ricoeur[33] answers him by proposing to call the first 'unreal guilt' and the second 'real guilt'.

But I think you will agree with me that this opposition of

words always has something artificial and intellectual about it. I do not, for example, reject Dr. Sarano's suggestions for he gives a good explanation of what he means by 'consciousness' of guilt on the one hand and 'sense' of guilt on the other. But when we have a 'consciousness' of guilt, we also, of necessity, experience a 'sense' of guilt. The distinction which we have ourselves made, so useful for clarity of understanding, is not so easy to make in practice. False and true guilts meet and become confused, in the patient, into one single emotion.

So Dr. Sarano[35] rightly speaks of a 'continuity' between the two guilts. Although suggested by education, our child-guilts have awakened us to a world of morality, trained us to a sensitiveness of conscience which comes into play now in our most genuine guilts. We have unwittingly passed from the one set to the other, without ever clearly determining their respective frontiers. And Dr. Hesnard[17] also writes: 'There is every intermediate stage between the endogenous guilt of the normal individual and the totally unreal guilt of the mentally sick.'

But Dr. Nodet[27] makes an even more penetrating observation on the connection between infantile and adult guilt: 'It is probably', he writes, 'by the fact that there is in the child the potentiality of becoming an adult capable of moral guilt that the child shows guilt reactions before anything which reminds him of his dread of his inferiority and weakness.'

You see how far we are from Freud, with this psychoanalyst who calls himself a Freudian! While Freud was reducing all genuine guilt to infantile guilt, Dr. Nodet is already catching a shadowy glimpse, in infantile guilt, of genuine guilt. Thus, inferiority-guilt, false in itself, is the embryo of true guilt. It does not mean that Freud's inverse views are thereby unfounded.

Indeed in true guilt, there is always a residuum of its infantile origins. What adult, even one who has been analysed, even a psychoanalyst, could boast that the guilt feelings which he experiences have no admixture of infantile guilt whatever? In the most genuine, the most moral and adult guilt, when we are ashamed of our very real and concrete behaviour, there always comes into that shame a little of the fear of losing the love and esteem of others, which constituted infantile guilt. In this connection the works of Zulliger[47] and Häfner[15] may be particularly recommended.

There is, then, practical continuity between the guilt feelings which we separate in theoretical analysis. This is an uncomfortable situation. 'Religious and Christian experience of sin', writes Father Daniélou,[8] 'and morbid phenomena, offer formal analogies, but are of absolutely different orders.' Alas, no! We quite understand that the theologian would like it so, but it does not correspond to reality as we observe it.

Though it is possible to make, to some extent, a diagnosis that differentiates true from false guilt, this cannot be done, as in all medical diagnosis, on one particular decisive criterion, but rather by considering the case in its entirety, by an all-embracing reference to the personality and to all that we know and observe in it. I must stress here that to believe oneself guilty has exactly the same effect as being guilty, just as believing oneself to be less loved has exactly the same effect as being less loved.

Beyond all our theories, we must get back our clinical attitude and talk to the patient. To exercise our calling as doctors we must observe without prejudice what happens and try to understand. Now, in this matter, only the patient can tell us what goes on, and he needs to be believed and understood, not contradicted.

Of course, I can help him by bringing an objective view which he lacks, on psychological mechanisms for example which may be active within him, just as I am doing in these pages. But he alone can say what he feels. If he experiences a sense of guilt, to tell him that the feeling is false only gives him the troublesome impression of not being understood.

To assert, as I heard some do in our Conference in connection with some of the cases brought to our notice: 'That is not guilt, but shame', brings a man no relief. You do not relieve minds with dictionaries. We are dealing with life; and life is something which is borne and felt rather than thought.

In the Conference Dr. Tina Rabaglia of Parma showed us, for instance, that in the poor class districts which she has studied, a prostitute experiences no sense of guilt and is the object of no contempt. Life is hard for people in Italy. There is respect for anyone who assumes responsibility for his life and family. On the other hand, if that prostitute is unemployed, if she finds no clients and becomes a burden upon somebody else, she feels very guilty. And from an example like this and many others, our colleague concluded with the assertion which I believe to be true, namely that a man feels a sense of guilt every time he fails in a cause with which he has identified himself.

On hearing these words, I at once understood why I had made a note, while preparing this study, that I feel a sense of guilt whenever my wife is ill or upset by some annoyance, even though I am in no way responsible. To make her happy, to shelter her from pain and sickness, is a cause with which I identify myself. It is legitimate for a husband! At such times I feel guilty of not having carried out my intentions, even though I am objectively guilty of no fault or negligence.

Dr. Rabaglia's arguments make us understand the terrible sense of guilt felt by children whose parents are in conflict. I have had innumerable such cases. However absurd it may appear, a child whose parents quarrel feels guilty. He sobs secretly under the bedclothes and it is not just from grief. The noise of the scenes, the outbursts and the tears strike him like an accusation.

It is because harmony and peace between his parents is a cause with which he identifies himself, so vital to him is the need for harmony between his parents. And he feels, as a fault, his own powerlessness to reconcile them. Even if he risks a word to his father in defence of his mother, when he is treating her too unjustly, he only succeeds in aggravating the conflict. He increases his father's anger tenfold and holds himself responsible. And he gets himself scolded: 'You mind your own business,' exclaims his father, 'and first of all, mind your manners. What impertinence! I won't have you speak to me in that tone. Show some respect to your father. You ought to be ashamed of yourself.'

And we doctors lead a long hard struggle to save a life. That is indeed a cause with which we identify ourselves. And when death comes along and clinches our defeat, even before the death occurs, when we find ourselves powerless before its inexorable approach, we feel a strong sense of guilt. We turn the case over and over in our minds. Would it have been better not to operate? —But then, we should have taken away, through cowardice, the patient's only chance of recovery.

The public generally does not realize how much torment the majority of doctors suffer, nor how much worry they may have over a case; they are in a perpetual state of alertness: Did I overlook some useful point in my examination? Did I make a mistake in diagnosis? Is there some effective method of treatment unknown to me or that I have not thought of? They mull it over in their minds to the point of obsession.

Similarly with the parents of a child who is the victim of an accident. Questions crowd into their minds. They weigh the circumstances of the drama, which such a little thing might have obviated. They remember some little fact that they might have taken as a presentiment, but which they did not bother about.

It may seem brutal to say so, but there is no grave beside which a flood of guilt feelings does not assail the mind. All that one reproaches oneself for having done and all that one reproaches oneself for having failed to do on behalf of the departed. One gets over these things as best one can, either by repressing them, or by admitting them under cover of some convenient philosophy. It is clear that there is no true and complete answer but the forgiveness of God.

It also happens that a doctor undertakes with fine zeal the treatment of a difficult case. He extends his researches, examines the literature, has discussions with colleagues and tries new drugs. The case interests him enormously and he evinces the most lively solicitude for his patient. But when the patient returns, despite all, with the same symptoms and the same complaints, the reactions of the doctor undergo a sudden change.

He shows bad temper which upsets the patient. The latter was expecting a still more kindly sympathy, and he is spoken to quite roughly; the doctor even comes to a point of scolding him, of suspecting him of exaggerating his sufferings or of inducing them by disobedience to his instructions. This very often happens with nervous or allergic cases, whose sufferings are difficult to define and even more difficult to overcome, and who react in unexpected ways to drugs.

Neither the doctor nor the patient quite realizes that the storm, so regrettable for the treatment, is due to an unconscious sense of guilt weighing on the doctor's mind. The patient believes himself unjustly scolded and suspected and experiences a mixture of revolt and guilt. Indeed, it needs a good deal of courage to bear the setback. Could it not be said that a man's moral stature is shown by the way in which he accepts his faults and setbacks?

Who will ever know whether another doctor would have succeeded where I failed? Should I have sent the patient to him instead of proudly taking on the case myself? And I too have made mistakes, clear-cut faults; I should have to be very dishonest not to recognize that. If I do not see them, the patient will be able to point them out; no one sees other people's faults more clearly than a neurotic. It is too late to put them right.

And then, there are all my unconscious faults, the tricks played on me by my own complexes which blind me. The most highly experienced psychoanalysts are no more exempt than I am from such things. Am I not myself a victim of 'conduct-failure', and my patient with me?

It can be seen that all these debates are vain. They take place on the rational plane and guilt gnaws at us on the affective plane. The two planes do not intersect. Indeed if every failure arouses, as Dr. Rabaglia says, a sense of guilt, it means that we become brutally aware of our weakness and powerlessness, the limitations of our human condition. Is not this guilt the unavoidable reverse of the joy we feel in the event of success?

Chapter XI

JUDGMENT IS DESTRUCTIVE

WE cannot escape judgment of ourselves which is forced upon us all the time by the judgment of others. The Bible is a school of courage: courage to recognize our wrong-doings; courage also, at times, to stand by our convictions unflinchingly, despite the inevitable sense of guilt which any conflict arouses. 'Even if I made you sorry with my letter, I do not regret it,' writes the Apostle Paul to the Corinthians (2 Cor. vii. 8). And we see him uncompromisingly resisting the demands of the Jerusalem Christians, even Peter himself, when the 'truth of the Gospel' is at stake (Gal. ii. 5, 11).

For the Bible also lays upon us the duty of defending ourselves, of not allowing ourselves to be crushed by the judgment of others, by the constant pretension of others to take our place as judges of our conduct and to exercise a moral oversight of our life. In our turn we are called to observe the same reserve towards other people, to resist setting ourselves up as judges of other people's conduct.

Jesus Christ Himself refused this role of judge when he was asked to act as such—even He, who will return to judge the quick and the dead. 'One of the multitude said to him, "Teacher, bid my brother divide the inheritance with me". But he said to him, "Man, who made me a judge or divider over you?" And he said to them, "Take heed, and beware of all covetousness" ' (Lk. xii. 13–15). This man was denouncing his brother's avarice. Jesus refuses to pronounce any judgment. But He at once awakens in His audience the awareness of their own avarice.

We find, in many other places, this same reversal, a turning from the objective to the subjective, from other people's sin to our own, in the mouth of Christ. 'Rabbi, who sinned, this man or his parents?' the disciples ask when confronted with the man blind from birth. 'It was not that this man sinned, or his parents', He replies categorically (Jn. ix. 2–3). There was the same question concerning eighteen people killed when a tower fell—and the same answer: 'Do you think that these were worse offenders than all the others who dwelt in Jerusalem? I tell you, No' (Lk. xiii. 4–5). But Jesus also adds: 'Unless you repent you will all likewise perish.' He brings back to a consideration of their own sin, those who were discussing the presumed sin of others.

We always go outside the biblical terms of reference and obedience to Christ, when we claim to discuss sin and guilt objectively. We become enmeshed in problems which cannot be disentangled and ourselves fall into the sin of judgment. Guilt is quite subjective. Our sin is in question, not the sin of others. We are not judges.

A man tells me openly and simply of an adulterous liaison which he has carried on for several years. He adds with obvious sincerity that he feels no remorse about it. Am I to consider him as an unscrupulous man? Not at all! A moment later, a prey to the keenest emotion, he goes on to confess that the other day he was guilty of coveting a woman with whom he had merely exchanged a glance.

We can understand now how naïve and vain was that urgent desire we felt to separate objectively true from false guilt, to formulate a criterion, even by propping it up with revelation or psychology. Law, morals, social constraint can vary with time and with people. They may be more or less in harmony with the voice of conscience or the word of God. They may depend on prejudices which seem absurd to us. But a perfectly sure sorting can be done only by God.

Try and do that sorting with an over-scrupulous man, or with a melancholic! He comes and asks you to do so. He accuses himself of things which seem quite without foundation. But you will merely exhaust yourself in vain if you seek to reassure him by logical objective proof. And what do you know about it? You are not inside his skin or his soul. Perhaps this fruitless debate in which you spend yourself in an effort to free him from false guilt is merely creating between you and him a gulf which will prevent you from curing him.

Moreover, the patient often has a lively awareness of the illogical character of his sense of guilt. And it is that which may hold him back from unbosoming himself either to the doctor or in confession. He foresees that his hearer will make light of his admission and discuss it rationally, as he has done a thousand times within himself. He feels that such a discussion would be utterly inadequate and would bring, not relief, but further suffering. When he has confidence of being listened to, understood and believed without discussion, then he dares to confess what weighs him down and to unburden himself.

It is especially in the sexual sphere that our contemporaries most fear social judgment, because it is particularly crushing, unjust and productive of mental anguish. All psychotherapists, analysts or not, and to whatever school they belong, are agreed on this point. They all denounce the false shame, still so widespread today, which presents sexuality in its entirety as culpable, a false shame which so many people believe to be biblical in origin, whereas the Bible speaks of sexuality with such simplicity and realism as to scandalize these same good people.

Yet, however false this social suggestion may be, it generates real guilt. A woman has been struggling secretly since childhood with onanism. Finally, in desperation, she undertakes a long journey to come and speak to me about it. True enough, there is more of false shame in her than of true guilt. There is also the pharisaism of society which overlays all sexuality with shame in order to hide a bad conscience. Further, there is, as Dr. Bovet has shown us, a false interpretation of the biblical narrative of Onan, whose fault was not sexual but simply greed: he did not wish to reduce the inheritance of his own children by giving children to his brother's widow! (Gen. xxxviii. 9).

Yet even so it was a real sense of guilt which had poisoned that woman's life for so many years and against which she still had a long and dramatic struggle in my consulting-room before she managed to unbosom herself to me. And in all the sexual shocks of childhood, in all the innocent victims of some sadist, exhibitionist or homosexual, in a girl seduced and basely abandoned by a man who has made her a mother, or obliged her to commit abortion, a sense of guilt remains, ineradicable and crushing.

The story of Onan has a sequel (Gen. xxxviii. 2–26) which is also of great interest to us doctors, for it clarifies the role of social pharisaism in the inception of guilt: the contempt poured on the prostitute actually strikes the victim and not the real culprit. Onan was Judah's second son, and should, by the law of the time, have raised up a posterity for Tamar, widow of his elder brother Er. After Onan's death, Judah himself violates the law in his turn: for fear of seeing his third son Shelah die also, he sends Tamar, his daughter-in-law, back to her parents, instead of giving her to Shelah.

Then Tamar disguises herself as a prostitute and places herself in her father-in-law's way. Three months later, Judah is told: 'Tamar your daughter-in-law has played the harlot; and moreover she is with child by harlotry.' 'Bring her out, and let her be burned,' exclaims Judah. But Tamar has kept a token: the signet, cord and staff of Judah. She shows them to him. 'By the man to whom these belong, I am with child,' she says to him. 'She is more righteous than I,' Judah then exclaims, 'inasmuch as I did not give her to my son Shelah.'

The reversal and quite subjective nature of guilt can be seen: in face of the evidence, Judah recognizes himself as the real culprit, whereas previously he was going to burn his daughter-in-law, who was pregnant by him.

Later there was another Tamar, a daughter of King David, whose story (2 Sam. xiii. 1–20) also illustrates the links between social contempt and false guilt. Tamar has been violated by her brother Amnon. This affair is also of interest to doctors. For to achieve his purpose, Amnon pretended to be ill, so that his sister had to bring a meal to his bedside. In spite of her resistance, 'he forced her, and lay with her'. Then he drove her out. 'No, my brother; for this wrong in sending me away is greater than the other which you did me,' exclaims Tamar. Fortunately she had another brother Absalom, a clever psychologist, who guessed what had happened; 'Now hold your peace, my sister; he is your brother,' he says to her. And he adds the touching phrase: 'Do not take this to heart.'

Absalom is the one who has taken it to heart. He is going to kill Amnon, the real culprit, to avenge Tamar, his sister, and that at the price of a mortal quarrel with King David his father and even at the price of his throne. I do not know whether Absalom succeeded, by exhortation, and then by revenge in bringing peace to Tamar's heart. What I do know is the incredible tenacity of feelings of guilt and shame, even when they seem unfounded. Perhaps Tamar, as often happens, takes the fault upon herself, reproving herself for being caught in Amnon's trap. Perhaps she does not forgive herself, although it was King David himself who instructed her to take the meal to the man who feigned sickness.

I have taken these examples from the sexual field because it is here that social suggestion causes the greatest ravages, awakening the most distressing and tenacious false guilts, all that 'inward sin', unconnected with real behaviour which Dr. Hesnard denounces. It is here that other people's judgment shows at its most destructive.

But in all fields, even those of culture and art, other people's judgment exercises a paralysing effect. Fear of criticism kills spontaneity; it prevents men from showing themselves and expressing themselves freely, as they are. Much courage is needed to paint a picture, to write a book, to erect a building designed along new architectural lines, or to formulate an independent opinion or an original idea.

Any new concept, any creation falls foul of a host of critics. Those who criticize the most are the ones who create nothing. But they form a powerful wall which we all fear to run into more than we admit and against which we can hurt ourselves badly. Again, we are less afraid of open contradiction which can stimulate us, than of mockery or contempt or of people who judge us as stupid or arrogant, neurotic or dangerous.

Judgment is always destructive. My wife said recently, 'At bottom, we must always ask ourselves, not whether what we say to someone is well-founded or not, but whether it is constructive or destructive for him.' I am very pleased that my wife has a constructive attitude towards me. How many married couples destroy one another by saying hard truths or by subtle mockery!

On reflection, we can realize how this fear of being criticized impoverishes mankind. It is the source of all the conformism which levels men and locks them away in impersonal modes of behaviour. How many very sensitive authors have never dared to face public criticism and have locked their masterpieces away? How many employees have a fair idea of what could be done to improve the atmosphere of their office or workshop, but will not express it for fear of being laughed at by the management and treated as intriguers by their fellows?

Take a look at that girl now engaged and blossoming out. What is happening? Certainly, the miracle of love and happiness. But something else is happening too. She has found a man who does not criticize her. Until that occurred, she was as silent as her sister was talkative. The latter was the pride of her parents because of her scholastic success and her display of learning. She herself was treated as stupid, because she hated school and had been unable to develop her studies as far as Advanced Level. And so she was always afraid that if she opened her mouth she would betray her lack of culture by some foolish remark.

And now, suddenly, to her fiancé she dares to say all that goes through her mind, and he exclaims, 'You know, you are very intelligent!' Even if she says something foolish, he finds it charming, original, ingenuous. It is extraordinary—and such a cultivated man too! She tells him all sorts of childhood memories which she has never dared to mention, for fear of being made fun of. And he finds it all so interesting. He understands her so well!

She can even tell him unpleasant things which she is not at all proud to remember, and he finds that they are not so serious after all. He at once tells her that he has done much worse things himself. He is extraordinarily humble and puts her quite at ease. Through knowing him, she feels herself a better woman. She could embrace the whole world, and begins to pray again, a thing she has not done for a long time.

There are things too of which she is proud; she would not speak of them to her parents because they would have said, 'You are proud; you should be ashamed.' And here is her fiancé exclaiming, 'That's marvellous! You are a wonderful woman!'

By seeing the tremendous blossoming which a being can experience when surrounded by love and confidence, when it does not feel judged, we can measure the stifling power of other people's criticism. And also realize that in turn, each judges others and stifles them because he is himself stifled. Nor does our girl criticize her fiancé; she admires him. She admires him so much that her parents are quite irritated by it and say spitefully: 'You are not so generous with us, you criticize us pretty severely! It almost looks as though your fiancé has every good quality and no faults. We'll see what you say after ten years of marriage.'

Indeed, the honeymoon does not go on for ever. It begins to change on the day a wife notices that her husband is selfish, or that a husband notices that his wife talks too much. Neither of them can say anything in order not to disturb the harmony which still reigns between them. But their eyes are opened and they make a mental note daily of other little things which confirm their judgment.

Yes one day, they will need, as did those friends of whom we were speaking a while ago, a frank discussion and that 'metanoia', that miraculous change of heart, in order that their unity may revive. Then they admit that they were afraid of each other. Fear was born of judgment, and judgment of fear. Even love could not resist it. If their sexual life had remained intact, it seemed to be more and more of a comedy which each played for the other's benefit. And by making a display of more love than one really has, one soon begins to doubt the love which the other still gives.

You see the destructive power of judgment. It insinuates itself surreptitiously, unnoticed, and secretly eats away at the structure of an apparently happy marriage, long before any conflict breaks out between the two partners. They can flush out this sly enemy and destroy it if they act together. In the light of God, in an atmosphere of prayer and spiritual communion, in prolonged silence, they may pass from the humdrum round of their everyday thoughts to deeper and less flattering reflections.

The voice of God is heard. Each partner becomes aware of personal faults which can then be unburdened to the other. It is very unpleasant. But there is nothing like it for bringing down the spirit of judgment. It is just at the moment of its fall that it is identified as judgment, and it is perceived how much the other partner was being judged, without its being realized. This is 'metanoia', the change of heart, the passing from the kingdom of this world into the Kingdom of God. A new, overwhelming love bursts out between the partners.

We find the same implacable phenomenon of judgment in a religious community. In the first flush of conversion, a man feels himself unreservedly welcomed into it. He has a boundless admiration for the spiritual leader who has opened such wide horizons to him, and revealed the truth to him. And in the joy which that man brings him, by his conversion, the leader gives him his unreserved confidence.

Our convert deserves it; indeed, he is transformed. He blossoms out; he wins over himself victories that he would never have thought possible. He understands that grace is more effective than all the efforts which he had so far made. And he experiences brotherly communion. In the religious community which he is entering, he finds men who speak with open hearts, even about their own difficulties and their own faults. By hearing these, he also discovers his own, which for so long he had hidden from himself, and he realizes how superficial and even mendacious were the social contacts which had satisfied him previously.

But little by little, disillusionment creeps in. He notices that his spiritual leader is not faultless, that he shows pettiness and moods which are really surprising in such a religious man. And then, in the community, there are some rather unpleasant people, who make pretty speeches and a display of virtue, but who lack charity. The thought comes into his mind that they are Pharisees. There are cliques, opposing theological tendencies, intrigues. Backbiting flourishes more than anywhere else. Our convert feels judged because he has taken the part of one against another. And soon he notices that there is in the Church, more than in the world outside, mutual criticism which charges the atmosphere and which none dare bring into the open for fear of being accused in turn of a lack of charity.

And then, he begins to doubt the efficacy of grace. The brilliant experience which made a better man of him loses lustre. He relapses into his old faults. Judgment has done its destructive work. In his Church, they still play the fraternal community game, they still proclaim loudly the mutual charity to which they are still seeking to conform; but it is only a façade which hides innumerable repressed judgments. All the members hold one another as guilty, all are crushed.

Chapter XII

THE DOCTOR DOES NOT JUDGE

IT is through fear of being judged that so many people today go to the doctor or the psychotherapist rather than to the clergyman. Rightly or wrongly, they invest the parson with a spirit of judgment which they fear. Is he not the guardian of morality, the one who must denounce evil in order to root it out, the one who should exhort to good? The doctor seems more neutral, just because he does not meddle with morality. He tries to understand a man's behaviour as an astronomer strives to understand that of the stars or why an eclipse takes place.

With our scientific and objective spirit, we flatter ourselves as beings stripped of all judgment. To whichever psychotherapeutic school we may give our allegiance, we know quite well that the essential condition for recovery is, on the doctor's side, a widely receptive attitude, free from all judgment. This is what allows our visitor, whether he be sick or not, to unbosom himself unreservedly in a way that he has never done before, not even (if he is a Catholic) to his confessor.

First he has spoken at length of all the injustice which has been heaped upon him. Then the morbid guilt feelings have come crowding in: all those mysterious brakes which check his spontaneity, the deep distress aroused in him by the taboos which education has created within him. Then sooner or later he comes to speak about what really makes him feel guilty, and he does so just because he feels that he is not being judged. He is reborn to life, and he blossoms out just like our fiancée a while ago.

The virtue of psychotherapy is the virtue of non-judgment. We are overwhelmed by it and overjoyed, every time that we experience it afresh. We see in it a sign of God's grace. We can be proud of it. But is it not just at the moment when we are flattering ourselves about some virtue that we most run the risk of blinding ourselves to the times when we are unfaithful to that very virtue? No one, I think, is more subtly exposed than we psychotherapists to the repression of judgment into the unconscious, and just because we attach so much importance to showing ourselves as uncritical of our patients.

This assertion may surprise you. You may think that this does not happen to you, that you are safe from any temptation to judge your patients. I think for my own part that I fall into it more often than I care to admit, more often than I am aware of. It is easy, at first, to listen without prejudice. It is even easier because the patient gives us his confidence; it is all the easier because we still know nothing about him; but it is more difficult if we are dealing with an old acquaintance whose family and environment, with their problems, are known to us. Patients are well aware of this, and are more ready to consult a psychotherapist elsewhere than in their own town.

But gradually, inevitably, we form an opinion about the patient. Some of his reactions disappoint us. Then, and notice this carefully, it is just because we know what a disaster it would be for him to know himself judged that we avoid telling him so. Moreover, in all good faith, we may repress this incipient judgment from our consciousness and not realize fully that the spirit of judgment has crept into our heart.

The other day, a patient of mine told me a remark of a doctor who had attended her with incomparable devotion for ten years and to whom she was deeply grateful. Following some incident or other, she had reproached him with being less patient with her than hitherto. 'What can you expect,' he said, 'in the long run it wears out.' What wears out a psychotherapeutic treatment, or a marriage, or life in a religious community? Is it not the spirit of judgment which creeps in, insidiously, unconsciously, unnoticed?

This is, I believe, the source of all our failures. It is then that progress in treatment flags. With the best will in the world we try to understand, to forgive, to regain mutual confidence. But the decisive effect, the miraculous impulse are gone; both doctor and patient are disappointed, and the disappointment weighs heavily. We steer a middle course, as in the humdrum relationships of everyday life, between the better and the worse—probably a little nearer the better; but that cannot count as enough.

I had this experience quite recently with a former patient whom I have continued to see for many years, because I am interested not only in her illness but also in the person herself and in the spiritual adventure of her life. For a long time the atmosphere of our meetings had lost its lustre. The glow of the earlier times had faded. There was still light, but there were shadows as well, small difficulties and discussions. Very honestly, we both tried to discover in what way we were responsible. But these explanations did not bear the expected fruit.

I had brought her to self-realization, to adulthood, and the success of her life was the fruit of this. But, inevitably, she came to assert herself against me and to hurt me, and I myself came to be less careful with her than when she seemed like a child to me. Then suddenly, she suggested that we should make a retreat together. It was many years since we had done such a thing. We did read the Bible together and pray together. But to go into retreat was something altogether different. We had given it up because, at the time, she still had too strong a sense of inferiority towards me to feel on an equal footing before God and to feel at ease in retreat.

In this retreat, God showed me that I was judging her and had been doing so for a long time. I was quite dumbfounded, for I flattered myself on having done just the opposite. The list of my criticisms grew longer under my pen. It was terrible. But when God has us in His grasp, He does not let us escape. And afterwards, I had to read the whole list to my companion. But she had written one just as lengthy. She too had perceived, in the course of the retreat, that she had begun to judge me.

It was 'metanoia'. In both of us there was a change of heart. In a flash all judgment fell away, spiritual communion was re-established, spiritual adventure sprang up afresh, sweeping away all that for so long we had tried to catalogue, analyse, explain and resolve. I am not belittling the value of sincerely meant analysis and discussion, but it is possible to get lost in it, if the breath of the Spirit is absent. For the intellectual plane of science and psychology, even of morals or of religion, is different from the spiritual plane. It may lead to the spiritual plane, and that is its chief virtue. But intellectual objectivity, of itself, always has a certain content of judgment.

Two months ago, I discussed this with a group of friends. They were all colleagues who place great trust and affection in me. They are interested in all that touches me closely; for instance, in the book that I am now writing. I had just arrived at the point where I was agog with the discovery of the universal importance of the spirit of judgment under which all men are crushed, and I spoke about this. We spent the whole evening discussing it, very seriously, very pleasantly. Our discussion was in the best possible spirit, but it was *discussion*.

What was for me personally a disturbing awareness or feeling, a confused intuition, was becoming a collection of ideas and propositions to be debated. When one discovers a living truth, one has great difficulty in putting it into words. Every artist suffers from the contrast between his finished work and the infinitely more complex reality which he first experienced in his inner being. An intellectual exposition is far more abstract and impersonal. In a work of art, what is put out for other people's judgment is much more rooted in the person of its creator and leaves a very sensitive raw place.

I have seen many artists stop short in their creation for having prematurely displayed their work—even before it had taken definite shape. It loses its lustre in their eyes, as a photograph fades when taken from the darkroom before being made insensitive to light by the fixing bath. Even praise can sterilize the creative impulse as much as blame. This proves that the stoppage stems from the fact that the work is taken as an object, as a thing which can be discussed, filed, pigeon-holed and judged.

This happened to me at the time of the discussion with my friends. Very judiciously they raised some objections. They told me that I generalize too much, that people can often be helped if their faults and mistakes are pointed out and if a judgment of them is formulated, provided that it is done with a helpful, non-critical approach. The more love one has for somebody, the more one can and should, in many instances, be severe, so that this severity appears as the measure of the love.

I was in full agreement. This was not the sort of thing I had in mind when I denounced the crushing effect of judgment. But then, we were in the abstract world of dialectic, of thesis and antithesis, not of life which communicates itself. My creative emotion wilted. It was two months before I could take up my pen again. Of course, I had other obstacles, but I should have overcome them if my flame had remained bright enough.

My friends may also think that I am too sensitive, and that in trying to point out the gaps in what I wanted to put forward they were only trying to help. But could I have my present position if I were not sensitive? Would I understand my patients if I were less vulnerable, less liable to the paralysis which bound me for two months, just because an objective scholarly discussion shifted the accent from the realm of the heart into that of ideas?

One of my friends said very gently: 'If you feel the destructive element of judgment so keenly, it is because you have within a pitiless judge, an overpowerful super-ego.' That is true, of course. I prefer to have a too-severe super-ego than one which is inadequate. But then, I put myself in the place of my patients. To hear it said that everything stems from a too-powerful super-ego, is to feel oneself pigeon-holed. A psychological diagnosis, in so far as it is of necessity something neat and rather trenchant, can also be felt as a kind of judgment.

This friend, who is also very sensitive, though perhaps he shows it less than I do, must have realized this. For he quickly went on to tell me a story to prove that on the contrary a diagnosis brings freedom from judgment. He said that he had a servant-girl to whom his wife could only be agreeable with difficulty. 'That girl must have suffered some mental disturbance in childhood, which must explain her behaviour,' he said to his wife recently. 'If only you had told me that earlier,' she exclaimed; 'I can put up with her much more easily now that I can blame on to illness what I took for a fault of character.'

It is true that the medical or psychological approach can override the moral judgment, and the servant in question must now feel much more at ease with her employers. 'But don't you think,' I asked my friend, 'that a day may come when that servant will be as unpleasantly sensitive of the fact that she is looked upon as a sick woman, and that she wears, as it were, a label of her former mental disturbance?' Certainly it is easier to bear than moral judgment; but it also can be very paralysing.

We all thirst for life and lively easy relationships with others; let them regard us without any preconceived ideas, directly and not blinkered by any moral doctrine, scientific theory or medical diagnosis. Does not God look at us in this way?

Thus any objective opinion, be it moral or psychological, always has in some degree the nature and weight of judgment. It is a man's opinion of a man, a claim of arbitrament, a claim of superiority by the giver of the opinion over the other. It calls necessarily for a rejoinder. Any intellectual discussion, even conducted in the best spirit of a common search for truth, has also in a greater or lesser degree, the sense of a struggle for domination, a fight for power. Each feels bigger by proving that he is right, and that the other party is consequently wrong and is guilty for being wrong.

Strictly speaking it is impossible not to judge. It is as impossible to live without judging as to live without breathing. 'I think, therefore I am.' Now, 'I think' necessarily means 'I judge'. I have just read these last pages to my wife. She remarked: 'To me, this problem of judgment is insoluble. How can we rid ourselves of all spirit of judgment? I really have tried, and it was quite in vain.' Certainly, it is insoluble! I too have had no more success in ridding myself of it. You thought so, no doubt, a while ago when you noticed the severity of my strictures against the spirit of judgment which is prevalent everywhere: I was judging those who judge. At the very moment when I was pleading against the spirit of judgment, I was thoroughly soaked in it myself, since I was pleading a case. Thus we see pacifists who became so inflamed for the cause of pacifism that they are very aggressive to those who, in their eyes, commit some crime against peace; or apostles of tolerance whose ardour makes them very intolerant of those who do not share their idea of tolerance.

It was my polemical attitude which provoked the retort from my friends. Yes, they were right, I was generalizing too much, I was not admitting the true worth of a severe, but thoughtful and kindly judgment. And my two months' halt stemmed from the fact that I felt they were right, with the result that after their warning, I could no longer be sufficiently partisan to plead my cause with the necessary liveliness. Nothing would ever be written if we were all the time conscious of every aspect of everything! But I only needed to pick up my pen again to find my aggressive verve, so clearly did I see political and social misfortunes striking humanity and men stifled by the judgment of others!

We must therefore be resolved to be guilty of partisanship, of passions and of judgment, under penalty of betraying our vocation as human beings. If my friends had remained silent in order to humour my sensitiveness they would not have been true friends. If I, in trying not to expose myself to the reproach of partisanship, had talked to them only of innocuous and impersonal topics, prudently avoiding those things which most closely touched and moved me, I too would have been lacking in friendship.

Artists who show their work to nobody, through fear of criticism, see their talents atrophy. For life is a matter of give-and-take, struggle and involvement. It is through intercourse that the character is formed, as I showed in my book *Le personnage et la personne*. And that intercourse is not an innocuous or sentimental conversation, but a costly engagement. It means standing up to others and their judgments. Living means choosing, and choosing means running the risk of making mistakes, and accepting the risk of being guilty of making mistakes. Fear of responsibility is fear of the eventual guilt arising from any involvement. So in wishing to spare oneself the destructive effect of judgment one takes the path of a greater and more certain destruction— that of flight and cowardice.

Judgment can vanish, as we have seen after a frank explanation, in retreat or in an outburst of love; but it reappears immediately. Such moments are fleeting and seem like signs of grace. But states of grace never last. Grace cannot be hoarded; we have only some preliminary instalments, as St. Paul says in a passage in which he evokes that strange mingling of super-abundance and poverty, of life and death, of the eternal and the fleeting which characterizes our human condition (2 Cor. iv. 7–v. 5). Yet these samples have sufficient savour to let us grasp what true human relationship is and to give us the yearning for it.

Part Three

THE REVERSAL

Chapter XIII

THE DEFENCE OF THE DESPISED

IN the biblical message, taken as a whole, there is a kind of extraordinary paradoxical inversion of things which I am very keen to bring to your notice, so convinced am I that it sheds light on our subject and brings the answer to this problem of inferiority-guilt which we have been studying.

A story from St. John is a particular illustration of this—the narrative of the woman taken in adultery who was dragged before Jesus (Jn. viii. 3–11). We have on the one side the woman, taken in the very act, accused and convicted of adultery, and on the other side the Scribes and Pharisees, who were scholars and theologians, moral, austere and sincere bourgeois. They accuse the woman, but they also want to drive Jesus into condemning her, or to be able to accuse Him if He evades this role of judge.

Notice that the accusation by these men does not rest on social or moralistic prejudice, but well and truly on the divine revelation: 'Moses', they said, 'commanded us to stone such. What do you say about her?' The challenge is terrible. Jesus took time to collect Himself; a moment of silence in which He wrote on the ground—'Jesus bent down and wrote with his finger on the ground'.

Thus this woman symbolizes all the despised people of the world, all those whom we see daily, crushed by judgments which weigh heavily upon them, by a thousand and one arbitrary or unjust prejudices, but also by fair judgments, based on the healthiest morality and the most authentic divine law. She symbolizes all psychological, social and spiritual inferiority. And her accusers symbolize the whole of judging, condemnatory contemptuous humanity.

It is as if the presence of Christ brought about the strangest of inversions: He wipes out the guilt in the woman who was crushed by it, and arouses guilt in those who felt none.

To the woman, taken in the act, convicted of sin, dumb with shame under accusations she cannot refute, Christ pronounces with divine authority, the word of absolution. He does not deny her guilt, He blots it out. He delivers her from her position of inferiority and of culprit before those who denounced her: 'Has no one condemned you? Neither do I condemn you; go, and do not sin again.' He does not suggest that she has not sinned, but he refuses to pronounce any condemnation.

But earlier, to the woman's accusers, He had spoken another word, calculated to awaken their own repressed sense of guilt: 'Let him who is without sin among you be the first to throw a stone at her.' And one after another, they slunk away. Before Jesus there are not two opposed human categories, the guilty and the righteous; there are only the guilty—the woman to whom Jesus speaks God's pardon, and the men who will receive it in their turn, since by their silent withdrawal they admit their own guilt. Such is the great reversal which is so strikingly presented by the story of the woman taken in adultery, yet which is also found throughout the Bible. In psychological terms, we could formulate it thus: God blots out conscious guilt, but He brings to consciousness repressed guilt. From a philosophical and clinical starting-point, Dr. Sarano[35] reaches exactly the same conclusion. He writes: 'There will be one guilt to be alleviated, but another to be awakened and recovered.'

Yet I am over-simplifying things by presenting, through the picture of this story, such a striking contrast between the accused and her accusers. In actual fact, we are all, not by turns, but at the same time, accused and accusers, condemners and condemned. Long before the discoveries of depth psychology, psychiatrists had observed that the persecuted became persecutors. We are accusers because we are accused, and accused because we are accusers.

To offer grace only is to cut off half the Gospel. Grace is for the woman trembling at her guilt. But her accusers will be able to find grace only by rediscovering for themselves the shudder of guilt. On the other hand, to present only the sternness of God also cuts off half the Gospel. Jesus does not awaken guilt in order to condemn, but to save, for grace is given to him who humbles himself, and becomes aware of his guilt.

Jesus Himself formulates this paradoxical inversion of things in these words: 'So the last will be first, and the first last' (Matt. xx. 16). How many times I have thought about it when a man has been sobbing in my consulting-room as he has given expression to his disappointment with himself, his faults and failures, his despair and his feelings of inferiority! He is nearer to the Kingdom of God than I who listen to him; and I come nearer—to the Kingdom, as well as to the man—only in so far as I recognize that I am as guilty, as powerless, as inferior and as desperate as he is. Only then also can I help him, for I am delivered from all spirit of judgment, I am his companion in repentance and in waiting for grace.

We see this inversion throughout the Bible. It was a murderer whom God chose to lead His people and successfully outface the Pharaoh of Egypt (Ex. iii. 10); Moses, a murderer, who had to flee into exile to escape social reprobation and the Pharaoh's justice (Ex. ii. 13–15); he was also a shy man, not a ready speaker but lacking in confidence (Ex. iv. 10).

It was a man held in contempt, Gideon, whom God chose as Judge and military leader; a humble man who exclaimed, 'My clan is the weakest in Manasseh, and I am the least in my family' (Jg. vi. 15). What an answer to those who are borne down by feelings of inferiority! It was a child, Samuel, whom God chose to reprove the priest Eli, and to become the prophet and leader of His people (1 Sam. iii).

It was a shepherd lad, David, scorned and persecuted by King Saul, whom God chose to be king in Saul's place (1 Sam. xvi. 6–13). He was the humblest among his brothers, the one whom his father, Jesse, had even forgotten to present to the prophet, for he was in the fields pasturing the sheep. It seemed incredible to the prophet also that God should prefer this stripling to the majestic giant King Saul; to convince him God had to say to him, 'Do not look on his appearance or on the height of his stature, because I have rejected him; for the Lord sees not as man sees; man looks on the outward appearance, but the Lord looks on the heart' (1 Sam. xvi. 7).

Another timid man, Jeremiah, was called by God to the dangerous mission of prophet in time of war, to a degenerate people who closed their eyes to threatening catastrophe. He was an emotional man too: 'My heart is beating wildly,' he says (Jer. iv. 19); he is lacking in confidence, he would like to hide and to remain silent (Jer. xx. 9), yet he is the one chosen by God and obliged to speak, to announce 'disaster upon disaster' (Jer. iv. 20), to denounce the false security with an answering boldness which is to lead him to prison: 'They have healed the wound of my people lightly, saying, "Peace, peace", when there is no peace' (Jer. vi. 14).

Another unimportant shepherd, Amos, is touched by God as he follows his sheep, and is sent to prophesy at Bethel, the holy place of King Jeroboam, before the priest Amaziah. Amaziah scorns and persecutes him and seeks to drive him out of the 'king's sanctuary' (Amos vii. 10–17). Time after time we find God choosing the weak, the timid, the ignorant and the despised to confound the great and wise and powerful of this world (1 Cor. i. 27–29). 'Hear, O our God, for we are despised,' cries Nehemiah (Neh. iv. 4). And God protects him and protects His people in their trial. 'In the thought of one who is at ease there is contempt for misfortune,' exclaims Job (xii. 5). In the teeth of all these social prejudices, God comes to the scorned and entrusts His Kingdom to them. As early as the Mosaic legislation, the heart of the law was the protection of the weak (Lev. xxv. 35–37).

But it is in the person of Jesus Christ that the inversion of values bursts upon us. He who was equal with God humbles Himself 'in the likeness of men' (Phil. ii. 6–8); like the most wretched of men, born in a stable, dying on a Cross, 'despised and rejected' (Is. liii. 3). For disciples, He chooses humble fishermen like St. Peter (Matt. iv. 18), or a tax-collector like St. Matthew (Matt. ix. 9), in the service of the Roman overlords. He is at home in the company of prostitutes and sinners to the scandal of virtuous people (Matt. ix. 10–13). 'I thank thee, Father, Lord of heaven and earth, that thou hast hidden these things from the wise and understanding and revealed them to babes' (Matt. xi. 25).

There indeed is a reversal—God prefers the poor, the weak, the despised. What religious people have much more difficulty in admitting, is that He prefers sinners to the righteous. This is explained precisely by the biblical viewpoint and is confirmed by modern psychology; namely, that all men are equally burdened with guilt. Those called righteous are not free from it but have repressed it; those called sinners are aware of it and are, for that reason, ready to receive pardon and grace.

Everywhere, Jesus defends despised people, the adulteress of whom we spoke, Mary the prostitute in the house of Simon the Pharisee whom she shocks not only by her past conduct, but by her lack of restraint in showing her feelings (Lk. vii. 36–50). To Simon, He speaks with severity; and to the woman He says: 'Your sins are forgiven.' He defends children, saying, 'See that you do not despise one of these little ones' (Matt. xviii. 10).

In the Church of Corinth, St. Paul finds that there are 'not many wise, not many powerful, not many of noble birth' (1 Cor. i. 26). And so, following His Master's example, he makes himself weak that he might 'win the weak' (1 Cor. ix. 22), he knows 'how to be abased' (Phil. iv. 12), he emancipates himself from the judgment of men (1 Cor. iv. 3). He frees his disciple Timothy from his sense of inferiority: 'Let no one despise your youth,' he writes to him (1 Tim. iv. 12); and elsewhere, 'God did not give us a spirit of timidity' (2 Tim. i. 7). And St. James in his turn stigmatizes those who honour the rich and vilify the poor (Jas. ii. 1–7).

I could multiply examples. It is Joseph, the eleventh son of Jacob, hated by his brothers for the provoking pride he flaunted before them, who becomes God's chosen one, and the Pharaoh's powerful minister (Gen. xxxvii); a prostitute, Rahab, is the instrument of God's plan (Jos. ii. 1–14); a humble widow of Zarephath has divine grace showered upon her (1 Kgs. xvii. 8–24); it is to a foreigner of easy virtue, the Samaritan woman, to whom Jesus reveals that He is the Messiah (Jn. iv. 1–26); the Prodigal Son in the parable is the one for whom the father's arms are opened wide, to the great scandal of his virtuous brother (Lk. xv. 11–32); Lydia, the first European to receive Christian baptism is an inconspicuous street-hawker (Acts xvi. 11–15); it is a refugee, Aquila, who first welcomes St. Paul to Corinth (Acts xviii. 2).

From one end of the Bible to the other, the answer is similar, a clear unambiguous answer, unconditional and without restriction, to those feelings of inferiority and guilt which we have been studying. We have seen how closely linked they are to each other. The answer also covers all of them. There is no learned discussion about false or true guilt, but in His grace God receives all those who are ashamed. Social rehabilitation and absolution are all one. At one and the same time, grace frees us from social contempt which burdens us from without, and from remorse which gnaws at us from within.

God is with the weak, the poor, the humble, the sinners who recognize themselves as such, and this adoption by God delivers them both from self-contempt and the contempt of others: 'If God is for us, who is against us?' (Rom. viii. 31). He is the unbreakable rock (Ps. lxii. 2)—the word recurs more than thirty times in the Bible—against which all self-judgments and all judgments of men are broken.

When a doctor bends sympathetically over a lonely downcast patient, a victim of the cruelty of men and circumstances, he is the instrument of the restorative power of God. Whether he is a believer or not does not alter the position, for Jesus Christ said: 'Whoever does the will of my Father in heaven is my brother, and sister, and mother' (Matt. xii. 50). Never has the patient met anyone who is so keenly interested in him, who listens with so much attention, who seeks to understand instead of judging him, who, far from showing contempt, displays real respect for him as a person. In the doctor's presence, he finds security and the consciousness of his value as a man—a true reflection of the esteem of God.

But this restoration to the outcast of their human dignity has more than personal repercussions. Consider that all the social and political upheavals which are disturbing the world today are in a sense a revolt and revenge of the outcast. The proletariat, coloured peoples, former colonies rise up against their masters from the Western world, who looked down on them even while

giving them benefits. Consider how keenly these racial prejudices
are still felt, even in Christian missions in distant lands.

But the West itself, at the height of its power at the beginning
of this century, the proud West, may perhaps discover a healthy
renewal in this cruel setback to its conquering enterprise; the
West—so proud of its technical, rational, cultural, military and
economic achievement that it thought it had no further need of
God and which developed that good middle-class conscience
which characterized the period of our childhood.

You see, we again meet the failure-guilt of Dr. Rabaglia, but now
we find a purpose in it. Grace is for the humble, not for the self-
satisfied. So a setback, a serious check, the crumbling of a whole
majestic world, may be the necessary road to a renaissance. For
each of us, a setback can become the opportunity of a return to
oneself and a personal meeting with God.

Now we have a much deeper understanding of the reason for
the existence of those close links which we have already discovered between inferiority feelings and guilt feelings. It seems
absurd and beyond reason that we should feel ourselves guilty of
a weakness inherent in our human nature which is suddenly
revealed to us by some failure. But that is how things are. A Bible
story will make the point clearer.

It is the incident of the miraculous draught of fishes (Lk.
v. 4–11). Catching fish is a cause with which the fisherman identifies himself. Now, Simon Peter and his friends have 'toiled all
night and taken nothing'. Yet Simon trusts Jesus who tells him
to sail into deep water and cast the nets there. Then our fishermen
take so many fish that the nets are breaking and they fill two boats.
'But when Simon Peter saw it, he fell down at Jesus' knees, saying,
"Depart from me, for I am a sinful man, O Lord".'

Simon Peter's reaction is immediate, spontaneous, almost
instinctive. He does not stop to study the reasons for his failure,
or for Jesus' success, he does not accuse himself of a professional
fault, for not casting the net in the right place. He does not say,
'I have made' a mistake, but 'I am' a sinful man. We have moved
from a guilt of 'doing' with its casuistry and endless rationaliza-
tion which I mentioned earlier, to quite another plane, a quite
different conviction of guilt, the guilt of 'being'.

There is a personal meeting of two beings—Simon Peter in all
his human wretchedness, and Jesus, God incarnate. In this
meeting, Simon Peter recognizes, in a flash, both the divinity of
Jesus and his own misery. Later Jesus is to do many other
miracles even more wonderful and stupefying to human reason.
He will give even more striking proof of His divinity: the raising
of Lazarus for example, in which an already putrefying body is

restored to life. In comparison with this, what is there striking about a miraculous draught of fishes?

And yet, this un-spiritual, we might even say professional or technical, experience was what led Simon Peter to discover the greatness of Jesus and to be frightened by it. We can, indeed, already know in theory, by philosophical reflection, both the greatness of God and human misery, and yet remain untouched by it in our innermost being. We need a first-hand experience, however trivial and limited it may be in appearance, a setback or fulfilment, to produce in us the sudden shock of a personal meeting with God.

From that moment, guilt assumes quite a different aspect. It becomes all-embracing; it no longer exhausts itself in the tangle of our mental discussions and ruminations on what we have or have not done. It concerns our being. In one sense it is more desperate; for all the reasoning which we might enter into on the extent of our guilt, in such and such a circumstance or in such and such a failure, is of a quite different order. But it can reach an issue which all the reasoning could not provide.

However, we do not have direct access to this awareness of the guilt of 'being'; we reach it by the more devious guilt of 'doing'. The concrete remorse of a particular deed, or a particular false attitude, or a failure for which we feel responsible despite all mitigating circumstances, suddenly presents our human misery, not as suffering to be borne, but as a state of guilt before the holiness of God. It is what Paul expresses in the Epistle to the Romans: 'I do not do the good I want, but the evil I do not want is what I do'; and at once, he adds, 'Wretched man that I am!' (Rom. vii. 19, 24). 'I do . . . I am . . .' That is the transition from the guilt of doing to the guilt of being.

We have seen how interminable this critical examination of our actions and thoughts can be and how quickly it can become an obsession; patients with the most delicate scruples give heart-breaking examples of this. So long as the examination develops in the realm of a guilt which I shall call quantitative, that is a search for the exact extent of our objective guilt in any given circumstance, it is for ever inconclusive. But it seems like a schooling, like a necessary path, which leads to the awareness of the guilt of being, a qualitative guilt in which the question of exact limits does not arise, but which utters the cry, 'Wretched man that I am!'

All this is of the utmost interest to the psychologist. For all suggested guilt feelings, all those confused with feelings of inferiority, an infantile dependence on others, on society, on prejudice, on shame, on social judgments—all these guilt feelings stem from the guilt of 'doing'. They comprise moralistic, patho-genic guilt. It is on this plane of 'doing' that all the mutual judg-ments take place which divide men and crush them. What can bring them together is the consciousness of their common misery, and this is to be found on the plane of 'being'. All judgments, all expressions of contempt refer back to a 'that is the done thing . . . that is not done'; they all imply a presumptuous desire to impose on others one's own conception of 'doing'.

As we have seen, this mechanism reproduces itself intermin-ably, catching all men up in an implacable treadmill of guilt and judgment, of revolt and callousness. What is capable of breaking this diabolical enslavement? The transition from the guilt of doing to the guilt of being. What the man of respectability and the bohemian have in common is their humanity, the misery, suffering and slavery of their human condition, of their 'being'. This is what can bring them together, reconcile them, unite them in a common humbling and a common liberation.

So it is an experience of guilt, but of a much more profound, absolute and essential guilt, which will cut the Gordian knot of the lesser guilts, so far described. We have noted the close rela-tionship of the sense of guilt and the sense of inferiority. Now there are two inferiorities, an inferiority of doing and an inferior-ity of being—a quantitative inferiority, arising from mutual judgment and leading men to compare one another, and an absolute inferiority, a qualitative one, a common awareness of human weakness which brings men together in a common repentance.

Chapter XIV

LIBERATION FROM TABOOS

THIS opposition between the guilt of doing and the guilt of being can now help us to a better understanding of the Bible, and to a dissipation of some tragic misunderstandings which often appear to set the experience of psychotherapists up against the biblical message, when in reality the two sides are in profound agreement.

It is, indeed, from the guilt of doing that there arises taboo-guilt and the entire moralistic attitude, the pathogenic effects of which are denounced by modern psychology. Taboo is a magical prohibition: 'This is unclean, do not touch; this is forbidden, do not do it.' Taboos are prohibitions loaded with menacing dread. Moralism follows—the setting up of a rigorous code of prohibitions, a moral code. You will remember Dr. Bovet's account of a young man's comment: 'Religion is what you must not do!'

A majority of people read the Bible in this spirit, as if it were a moral code clothed with sacred authority, a collection of prohibitions and instructions which would lead us, through our strict observance of them, to an existence free of guilt. Utopia indeed! But as it cannot be carried out in every detail, it turns to despair, to neurotic fear of committing some sacrilege, to guilt without release.

We have seen, for instance, that Christ's command 'Judge not', cannot be strictly observed, at any rate for any length of time. It is thus with all Christ's commands. Re-read the Sermon on the Mount: none of its requirements could be fully carried out. Take the simplest, that of giving to others, not only what they claim from us, but twice the amount (Matt. v. 41). Just think of a problem like that which we have mentioned about the use of time; it would be even more insoluble. And the supreme requirement is: 'You must be perfect, as your heavenly Father is perfect' (Matt. v. 48).

It also seems to me that to present the Sermon on the Mount, as is so often done, as the outline of the ethics of Jesus Christ is to go on the wrong track. An ethic claims to be applicable to every-day life. It is limited in scope. It defines a number of precise requirements—taboos, in the language of psychologists—of a kind which would give a good conscience if they were punctiliously followed. Yet in the face of Jesus Christ and His appeal, there is always a lack of something—of a great deal—in our righteousness.

Such is the meaning, for example, of the story of the rich young man who wondered what he must do to inherit eternal life (Mk. x. 17-22). Jesus reminds him of the Mosaic Law, the Decalogue, and the young man can answer truthfully: 'Teacher, all these I have observed from my youth.' We are further told that Jesus, looking at him, loved him. But by a word, He immediately shows this upright young man what he lacks, 'Go, sell what you have . . .'

Notice that in this reminder of the Decalogue, Jesus is careful to omit the Tenth Commandment (Ex. xx. 17), the one condemning covetousness, the source of all greed. Paul Ricoeur[33] notes quite rightly that this Commandment introduces into the Decalogue an unbounded, inapplicable dimension, as we said above. The distinction made by Ricoeur, between the limited and the unlimited in ethical requirements seems of capital importance and to offer to theologians and psychologists today a very fertile meeting-ground.

It must be admitted that, in many respects, the Mosaic Law in the early books of the Old Testament still has a moralistic character, that of a limited code, supposedly applicable to daily life, the meticulous observance of which is supposed to ensure a good conscience and salvation. 'You shall therefore keep my statutes and my ordinances, by doing which a man shall live' (Lev. xviii. 5). In consequence this Law also has the archaic infantile magical qualities of taboo morality, the source of pathological guilt. Thus the notion of uncleanness, of unclean things which must not be touched, a notion which occupies such an important place in the Mosaic legislation, has just the formalistic magical sense of a taboo.

Another result is a neurotic fear since sin may be committed unwittingly, without evil intent: 'If any one touches the carcass of an unclean beast, he has become unclean, he shall be guilty' (Lev. v. 2). Thus, what was meant to dispel guilt, an explicit and exhaustive casuistry designed to give a good conscience, gives rise to a new guilt which is infinitely more distressing because it is unconscious, and impossible to foresee.

Here is a further example. The Ark of the Covenant was invested by the Israelites with this magical taboo quality; it must not be touched. God ordered David to move it to Jerusalem. To this end, it was placed on an ox-wagon. But at Nacon the wagon almost overturned, and Uzzah who was escorting it 'put out his hand to the ark of God and took hold of it, for the oxen stumbled'. Uzzah died there! From what we know of the power of taboos, it is quite understandable that the idea of having touched so holy a thing may have caused death. But the bystanders saw in it a punishment by God who struck Uzzah down for the sin of which he was guilty despite his praiseworthy intention. And the whole people and the king are seized with fear (2 Sam. vi. 6–9).

All through the Bible we can see the clash of the mentalities: the infantile, formalistic, moralistic mentality of taboo, and the prophetic mentality, to use Bergson's term which Ricoeur again takes up. The first offers a limited, defined, explicit morality which localizes the sin in a particular action or a particular unclean thing. It claims to give man a salvation which he can win for himself by strict observance, and in reality it plunges him into irremediable distress. The second places guilt in the heart of man and not in things, in the intention, in being not in doing. It proclaims the unlimited character of God's requirements, and the consequent impossibility for man to wipe out his guilt by the perfection of his moral conduct. The answer, then, comes from God, not from man, in the forgiveness He grants to those who confess their inevitable guilt instead of justifying themselves.

The clash of these two mentalities culminates in the debates which inevitably set Jesus Christ in opposition to the Pharisees and led to the drama of the Cross. The Pharisees represent the moralistic spirit, infinitely sincere and meticulous, which 'strains out a gnat' (Matt. xxiii. 24), such is its anxiety to protect itself from guilt. They are the direct heirs, like so many present-day believers, of the primitive part of the Mosaic Law, which they built up into a crushing casuistry.

Jesus Christ came along with the other solution of the problem of guilt, the solution which springs to life at the very moment when a man despairs utterly of getting right with God through his own efforts, by the observance, however meticulous it may be, of a limited morality. This second solution could already be seen dawning on the Sinai horizon when 'Jewish ethics discovered covetousness,' as Ricoeur[33] says, in other words an unlimited, ineluctable, existential guilt. One by one the prophets are to launch attacks less against open sinners, despised by the righteous, than against the righteous themselves, and to denounce their veiled sin.

It was what Jesus Christ is to proclaim with even greater vigour. The drift of the Sermon on the Mount is not that of a recipe for freedom from guilt by meritorious conduct. Just the opposite—it is the shattering word which convicts of murder a man who has done no killing, of adultery the man who has not committed the act, of perjury one who is not foresworn, of hatred

one who boasted of his love, of hypocrisy the man who was noted
for his piety. As you see, it is just the opposite of a moral code;
it might more readily be likened to a Socratic dialogue about
man's powerlessness to attain genuine virtue and thus to exculpate himself by impeccable conduct.

Words addressed to the Pharisees have the same tenor. By
practising the narrowest moralism, a man falls into a worse guilt,
that of self-satisfaction and the repression of conscience. One
may carefully 'strain out a gnat' and 'swallow a camel'. A man
who seeks to cleanse himself of guilt becomes even more heavily
burdened with it. Those whom God welcomes with open arms
are not the virtuous, but the despised, not those who deny their
guilt, but those who confess it, those who quake with remorse
and impotence. This is the great biblical reversal of which we
have spoken.

Repentance is the door to grace: 'The time is fulfilled, and the
kingdom of God is at hand; repent, and believe in the gospel.'
With these words, Jesus Christ opens His earthly ministry. Those
who considered themselves as first, the wealthy in money or social
position, in virtue, and even in religious experience, will be the
last. For they will have to come down from their social pedestal
before they can find the Kingdom of Heaven. The poor, the
despised, the hopeless, the penitent, those who are weary and
heavy laden (Matt. xi. 28) will be the first; Christ opens His arms
to them and receives them in grace. Such is the purport of the
Beatitudes (Matt. v. 1–12), those promises of happiness to all the
despised, to the humble and the persecuted, promises made
without conditions. And the following part of the Sermon on the
Mount (Matt. v.–vii.) denounces the hypocrisy of those who despised them, in order that they too may humble themselves and
find the same happiness.

You can see how profoundly Jesus Christ is opposed to the
primitive taboo mentality and the moralism of a casuistic law.
The prophets had earlier attacked these outlooks by constantly
denouncing the sin of virtuous people and the vanity of ritual as
a way of ensuring a good conscience. And Jesus Christ gives the
final blow, by convicting of guilt the moral and scrupulous people,
by proclaiming that all men are equally sinful despite all their
efforts, so that not by showing off their vaunted impeccability,
but by confessing their guilt, by repentance, will they find the
grace which erases it.

It is the great answer to the infantile fear of taboo which
modern psychologists see as the source of all pathological guilt
feelings. You will remember, for instance, that it was characterized by the idea of uncleanness: the uncleanness was in some

object, or animal, or man which it was forbidden to touch, under pain of becoming guilty.

Now, at Joppa, in the course of his first missionary journey, St. Peter was praying on the roof of the house. He had a vision. God showed him all the animals which the Mosaic Law declared to be unclean, and said to him, 'Kill and eat'. 'No, Lord,' replied the Apostle, 'for I have never eaten anything that is common or unclean.' But the vision was repeated three times. And immediately afterwards three men came along. They came on behalf of a foreigner, Cornelius of Caesarea, who, four days earlier, had also had a vision in which God had told him to have St. Peter brought to him, in order to hear his preaching and receive baptism (Acts x).

We have in this story the most striking contrast between the two guilts—the infantile guilt of prejudice and taboo, the guilt which, by the Mosaic Law, would have forbidden the Apostle, as he said to Cornelius, 'to associate with or to visit any one of another nation' (Acts x. 28); and the true guilt, the new vision of guilt, which would have been for him to refuse a call by God, through fear of a taboo. And he exclaims: 'God has shown me that I should not call any man common or unclean.' The Apostle Paul later echoed his words when he said, 'Everything is indeed clean' (Rom. xiv. 20); and 'to the pure all things are pure' (Titus i. 15).

A strong wind of liberty has blown, the wind needed by all those neurotics who are paralysed by the taboos inculcated in them by their upbringing. The sense of guilt is not erased, it is shifted from its false infantile object to the real problem: dependence on God and on God alone. This adult consciousness of responsibility before God gives release from moralism and false guilt feelings.

To the Romans, St. Paul writes: 'One believes he may eat anything, while the weak man eats only vegetables. Let not him who eats despise him who abstains, and let not him who abstains pass judgment on him who eats; for God has welcomed him. Who are you to pass judgment on the servant of another? . . . One man esteems one day as better than another, while another man esteems all days alike. Let every one be fully convinced in his own mind' (Rom. xiv. 2–5). And he adds later, 'Whatever does not proceed from faith is sin' (Rom. xiv. 23).

I am emphasizing this point, for the analogy with psycho-analysis is striking. What brings release in psychoanalytical treat-ment? It is the shift from infantile to adult guilt. It is the rejection of moralism, the tracking-down of taboos and fears of human judg-ment so that the patient can discover his genuine convictions, his own individuality, harmony with himself and his inward call.

For neurosis is not simply the effect of false guilt; it is more complex than that. It is a conflict between the true and the false. A penetrating word on neurosis by Dr. A. Stocker[43] comes readily to mind; he considers it as a division of the mind 'between right intuition and false suggestion'. Yes, false guilt, taboo, is a human suggestion which is opposed to the divine call of which every man is to some extent intuitively aware. And the sin, or true guilt, of which St. Paul speaks is precisely a divided life which lacks conviction.

I emphasize this because there is hot debate about it today; to so many of our contemporaries this debate seems to set depth psychology in radical opposition to biblical revelation. You will find it publicized everywhere, in books by psychologists and theologians, in novels and films, in conversation. Yet it is the expression of a tragic misunderstanding.

All the indictments of the psychologists against the Christian Churches are in reality aimed, not at the biblical revelation but at moralism—that moralism which is radically opposed to it, the moralism which tried to stone Jesus, as the Mosaic Law prescribed (Num. xv. 35), for violation of the Sabbath when He cured a man on that day (Mk. iii. 1–6); a moralism which crucified Him. For, in their turn, psychotherapists are daily discovering in their patients the crushing weight of moralism and of social conformism and its taboos.

But it must be honestly admitted that this moralism is so widespread today among all the Christian Churches that confusion is excusable. So much so that the term 'ecclesiogenic neurosis' has gained currency in Germany. Dr. Klaus Thomas of Berlin recently spoke of this in a lecture about the remarkable clinic which he founded, which gives help by telephone to desperate people. See then the mission which we Christian doctors have to fulfil within our Churches, to struggle for the health of souls against a moralistic deformation of the Christian message, which is the negation of it. But it is important that we should be quite clear in our own minds what we are about. A recent experience struck me very forcibly in this connection and I will tell it to you in order to show the importance of this unity of view within our own fraternity.

During our cruise to the North Cape last year I was leaning on the rail one day watching the wonderful Norwegian landscape slip by, with its incredibly green islands and shores contrasting with the great glaciers which come down almost to the sea. A doctor passed in silence, and stood leaning against the same rail beside me, studying the same spectacle. After a moment or two he said, 'I'm quite upset. I have just been told that one of our colleagues here has been divorced and remarried. Is it true?' 'Yes,' I said. After a further silence he went on, 'How is it possible? How can you agree to his taking his place among us Christian doctors?'

I said nothing for the moment. Then my friend added, 'Do you not believe that divorce is disobedience to God? a sin?'— 'Certainly,' I said, 'but if we could have only sinless men among us, there would be no one here; at any rate, I should not be here. We are all alike, we are all forgiven sinners.' A long silence followed. My friend went away. Later he returned. 'You are right,' he said briefly, 'now I know what grace means.'

There you are; he is a zealous Christian, whom I like and esteem highly, very sincere, very reasonable with his faith, keen in evangelizing and in no way pharisaical. The Church proclaims the grace of God. And moralism which is the negation of it, always creeps into its bosom, most particularly among those people who have the most praiseworthy care to uphold their faith by the rectitude of their moral conduct.

Periodically in history, spiritual revivals burst upon the world. Religious movements arise, orders are founded, old Churches reawaken. St. Augustine, St. Francis of Assisi, St. Benedict, the Reformers, Wesley and so many others. The Spirit breathes, charity spreads. The greatness of God and His love are rediscovered and human pettiness is pushed aside. At the same time, the unlimited nature of God's requirements is re-discovered, and the boundlessness of His grace. It is proclaimed. Men feel called, welcomed and not judged. They are overwhelmed, their conduct and way of life are changed, they become fervent, practising Christians.

And then gradually, inevitably, in that more virtuous, more austere environment, a new conformity emerges. Grace becomes conditional. Judgment appears. Anyone who does not subscribe to certain standards is suspected of infidelity and hypocrisy. And that is what awakens hypocrisy, for everyone, in an attempt to live up to his faith, seeks to appear better than he is and begins to hide his faults instead of confessing them. He wants his children to set a good example, as is fitting in a pious family.

Moralism has returned, and with it the breath of the Holy Spirit is stifled. In order to ensure the lost treasure people cling all the more to certain 'principles' inherited from the heroic period, to a new limited morality. What was a spontaneous impulse, free and joyful obedience to God, responding to His wonderful grace, becomes constraint, legalistic obligation and fear of criticism; pathological dread of taboos reappears. Above all, people begin

to pretend to be more virtuous than they are. That was the fault
of Ananias and Sapphira, which the Apostle Peter reproved so
sternly (Acts v. 1–11).

This moralistic deformation has nothing to do with the
debates on dogma which set the different branches of the Christian
Church in opposition. It is not peculiar to the Eastern Church
nor to the Roman, nor to Protestantism, nor to any other communion. It strikes them all. It is not specifically religious, for we
can find it in any society. Born out of revulsion from a stifling
conformity, it gradually crystallizes into a new conformity. Thus,
even revolutions gradually institute an established order which must
in its turn defend itself against new revolt, as A. Camus[5] has shown.

Such is the bourgeois formalism; it sprang from the liberating
outburst of the French Revolution and reached its climax a century later in the hypocrisy of a society which psychoanalysts,
Communists and existentialists have vied with one another in
denouncing. But already there is emerging a Communist conformity with its doctrines of deviationism, and an existentialist
conformity. As soon as the most revolutionary doctrine is repeated by thousands of adepts, it takes on the ring of a well-
learned catechism. Psychoanalysis itself does not escape, with its
divisions and rivalries between different schools; so much so
that, in the disputes, there appears a word that is indeed theological—the word 'orthodoxy'.

As for me, I came into its garden involuntarily, by a back door,
without an admission ticket of any colour and without an official
badge. I stroll about off the beaten tracks. I find it very touching
therefore that qualified psychologists tolerate my presence politely
and that some even give me a friendly welcome. And according to
my humour, I can take the silence of the others as respect rather
than contempt.

It is true that sometimes I stray into the flowerbeds of men of
letters or theologians; this makes me seem like one of those
'enfants terribles' to whom so much is forgiven. Similarly, in
olden times, in the courts of kings, the fool had the right to utter
incongruities, even some truths at times, to the mighty of this
world without reprimand.

And I have done this sort of thing all my life, and I realize that
it is not unconnected with our problem of guilt and our need to
exorcise it. For if a man specializes deeply in one field, he is not
excused for making a mistake in it. Whilst an amateur, a Jack-of-
all-trades, enjoys a benevolent indulgence.

If then moralistic deviation is so widespread, it is because it
stems from human nature itself; so it concerns us doctors as
much as the theologians, us who study human nature as naturalists.

It stems from psychological mechanisms more than from dogmatic concepts. I also believe that it stems from the sense of guilt which is so intolerable that men feel an overpowering need to preserve themselves from it. So there arises the question of paying lip-service to convention, of proving one's good conscience by conforming to the standards of one's environment, to some principles of a limited morality.

It is thus that moralism is incessantly reborn, in all environments, but most particularly, it must be admitted, in religious environments, because of their keener sensitivity to the gnawing of guilt. Like all psychoanalysts I see every day its ravages in families belonging to all the Christian Churches.

But as a theologian has shown, [41] contemporary moralism is especially due to an influence foreign to the Church, to the influence of Kant. His famous 'categorical imperative' claimed to institute an autonomous ethic and attributed to man a capacity to judge for himself between good and evil without the help of biblical revelation.

The result was the morality of 'principles' and 'duties' which is currently taken in our religious environment as the Christian life, and the dangers of which are denounced by psychoanalysts, but the tendency of which is quite contrary to the biblical message because it affirms the salvation of man by himself, by his reason, his own virtue, his own pretence of living guiltlessly.

But it can happen, naturally enough, in the very bosom of the Church, that men burdened with great psychological difficulties, with emotional complexes and morbid dread, contribute to the reintroduction of taboo-morality. Then our role as doctors in the service of the Church is to show the situation clearly in order to preserve the Church from an ever-renascent moralism.

Thus Dr. Nodet [28] made a penetrating analysis of St. Jerome's psychology, in the 'Carmelite Studies' series. The theological authority of the great translator is not in question here. But even saintliness is no protection from disease. And he had with regard to sexuality an anxiety-aversion which was truly unhealthy. His violent diatribes against marriage itself, referred to by Dr. Nodet, bear witness to this. It can be well understood that a saint, rightly enjoying such high prestige in the Church, may by the projection of his own taboos, have largely contributed to the spreading of a contempt for sexuality and marriage, although these were instituted by God. A similar puritanical deviation arose later in Protestantism. It can be seen that a fertile dialogue between theologians and doctors is possible. And as a believer it is a deep concern of mine to help forward such a rapprochement for which many psychoanalysts have in recent years worked so assiduously.

Chapter XV

PSYCHOANALYSIS AND GUILT

IT is a very common idea that the two camps are opposed most especially on the question of guilt. I must therefore attempt to elucidate this issue. I have just shown that the psychoanalysts' objections are aimed at moralism and not at the Christian revelation as such. But from their side, theologians often accuse psychologists of denying sin and guilt and thereby of undermining the foundations of morality and of Christian doctrine.

This view seems to me to be untenable. True enough, I have seen many patients who have told me that their psychoanalyst has advised them to take a mistress or a lover, and some women have even been initiated into the sexual life by their analyst. But it is only true to say that from careful discussion with such women I have never yet had proof that such conduct by an analyst, however regrettable it may have been, was ever dictated by personal interest and not by therapeutic concern. Indeed, it would contravene psychoanalytic doctrine, which recommends abstention from all moral advice, and it only goes to show how difficult it is to follow this out in practice.

But I have heard quite as many stories from the mouths of patients about priests or pastors and of advice just as peculiar which they have given, or of conduct just as regrettable in which some of them have indulged. But in neither group of instances can we ever be quite sure of the objectivity of what we are told. A patient may tell us in all good faith that his analyst advised him to have 'sexual experience' when, in fact, he himself, in the course of analysis, has come to realize that what has hitherto held him back from it is not his moral ideals, as he used to flatter himself it was, but a hypocritically camouflaged fear of the responsibilities involved.

But we cannot remain on the level of such *ad hominem* arguments if we wish to examine so important a question with the full seriousness it deserves. It is inevitable that there should be instances of the regrettable treatment of sufferers, both by doctors and ecclesiastics, but they cannot be decisive in our discussion. Indeed, it happens frequently that the fact that a man has considerable psychological difficulties of his own awakens him to a vital interest in human problems and turns him towards a career in psychiatry or the Church. Such a vocation can have therapeutic value for him.

The essential problem is to determine whether psychoanalysis by itself deadens the moral sense, the awareness of genuine guilt, or on the contrary makes it more acute. That it destroys it is the chief lament of the theologians; but the same mistaken idea is also found amongst psychoanalysts. A colleague converted to psychoanalysis, wrote to me saying, 'Guilt must be "eliminated"!'

However, it does not seem to me in the least that psychoanalysis 'eliminates' guilt. It does not eliminate it but shifts it. Thus, for example, a man is no longer ashamed of his sexual instinct, but he is ashamed of having been ashamed of it. This means that the former guilt was concerned with a taboo, while the second was far more genuine, for it involved sincerity in regard to himself. The guilt no longer has the same content, but it is always there. Another man will be no more ashamed to assert himself, but ashamed rather of the cowardice which has held him back so long, which he has most conveniently interpreted as Christian love. Yet another will be no longer ashamed of his aggressiveness, but rather of the sentimental gentleness under which he has always hidden it.

But above all, and without the analysed person perhaps realizing it, guilt is the driving force towards healing, the decisive power which determines the result of the struggle. It is easy to unburden oneself up to a point to someone who is neutral and kindly disposed. Sooner or later, however, the analysis of dreams or the free-association of ideas brings into consciousness memories of feelings the acknowledgment of which seems almost impossible.

At that point, any loophole of escape or deception can decisively jeopardize the cure; while on the other hand, the courage to retain absolute frankness even to the bitter end, will open the door to a great deliverance. The inward struggle is terrible. What is it that determines the issue? Two forms of guilt are at stake, engaged in mortal combat: one which creates a sense of terrible shame at giving expression to the memory or the feeling, and the other which urges the patient to keep silent, to create a diversion or to take cowardly flight from this difficult task. When the latter form of guilt appears even less tolerable than the former, then the turning point of the cure is passed.

Some years ago I took part at Bossey in a conference of theologians and psychotherapists. My most vivid memory of the occasion is a conversation at table with one of the best known of psychoanalysts. He told me of the overwhelming emotion he had experienced in the course of his own didactic analysis on the day when he became aware that the virtues and acts of his life of which he had been most proud were motivated by infantile behaviour patterns quite unacceptable to him. His voice trembled again as he recollected this and told me of it. What a dreadful humiliation!

Here was a sane man of strong personality, extremely intelligent, a convinced and practising Catholic, unquestionably clear about the Christian doctrine of salvation and perdition, and certainly also faithful in admitting his sins with contrition at the confessional in order to receive there an absolution. But it was in the way of psychoanalysis that he came to the narrow door spoken of by Jesus Christ, who said that it led to life, though there were few who found it (Matt. vii. 14).

It can be seen that we are far from an 'elimination' of guilt. On the contrary, there is a sensitizing of the conscience. It is the end of the naïve mythical view in which the problem of evil was envisaged in a childish and pallid way, as in a fairy tale, with two distinct groups, the good and the bad, the good practising virtue and the wicked devoted to evil.

No; the high drama of evil is that it cannot be localized, that it penetrates into the virtues so that there is some evil within the good, so that at least in a great measure it is pride which makes us virtuous. Thus, for example, very diverse motives are involved in our most sincere efforts to obey God; on the one hand, no doubt, our love for Him, but still more our vanity, a wholly infantile desire to win the admiration of those who are dear to us, and a fear no less infantile of losing the affection of God or of being criticized by others.

There is therefore no way of being genuinely righteous. We are face to face with biblical revelation. Paul Ricoeur[33] rightly stresses the fact that the guilt denounced by the Bible, and to which it gives the only possible reply, is less the guilt of the 'wicked' than the 'sin of the righteous'.

The psychological view is parallel with this. Dr. Jean de Rougemont[34] says 'there are people who in popular slang are called "first-rate" and others "dirty dogs". But the classification is superficial, and valueless for us who would penetrate to the secret attitudes of people. . . . A person's moral stature (he adds) is like the silhouette of a giraffe, lofty in front and far lower behind. A doctor has the privilege of observing men inside and out, so that he can detect defects on the hidden side which do not appear outwardly.'

Recollection in the presence of God can lead to discoveries fully parallel with those of psychoanalytic technique and quite as disturbing. 'What genuine content remains in my life?' a man has sometimes asked me, after working through the hidden motives which he has found for acts of which he had been particularly proud. Even his religious zeal and his work in the Church, appear to him in a fresh and disconcerting light. What remains of genuineness to our life is what comes from God and not from ourselves, from His grace and not from our own merits. This may be the appropriate but humiliating return to oneself to which He leads us by psychoanalysis. God has dealings with us; He speaks to us; He acts within us and lays hold of us. When this is experienced we know that there is genuineness, the sole genuine content, which alone is of value and is sufficient for us, and that we can now abandon all those values by which we thought to gain merit before Him.

I think of a certain Protestant patient who was deeply upset at the end of a long course of analysis by one of my colleagues. Her Christian education had been the elementary kind which narrows sin down to a list of specific actions, abstinence from which is sufficient to give a good conscience. Through psychoanalysis a bottomless abyss opened before her, a wholly new dimension of evil, an evil penetrating even our best intention and best deeds. She was dazed by it.

'It seems to me', she said, 'that grace is too small to contain the whole, infinite guilt of man as I now see it.' I had to help to enlarge her vision of the infinite immensity of grace, in proportion to the measure of guilt which analysis had revealed to her.

Psychoanalysists compare the human mind with an iceberg; the greater part is submerged, hidden, below the threshold of consciousness. Our idea of personality, thanks to them, is enlarged by the dimension of the unconscious. To the same degree our awareness of guilt is also increased. Dr. Sarano[35] writes that psychoanalysis, in spite of its 'enterprise of exoneration' . . . 'lays bare a hidden guilt behind the least slip'. Conscious guilt, which moralists preach about, and in a general sense the Churches also, can be hunted down, however exhausting the chase. But this unconscious guilt, guilt for one knows not what, has something of the character of an hallucination, unless it is realized at the same time that the grace of God has already preceded us into the depths where analysis would lead us.

Before the analysts suggested it, the Bible confidently affirmed that dreams had a divine meaning for guiding this investigation in depth, and also that one dream could assist the interpretation of another, as we so often see in psychotherapy. Thus it was by a dream that Daniel discovered the 'secret' of Nebuchadnezzar's dream, and he attributed the revelation to God 'to whom belong wisdom and might. . . . He reveals deep and mysterious things; he knows what is in the darkness, and the light dwells with him' (Dan. ii. 20, 22).

This light of God which dawns by reading the Bible, by listening to a preacher, by recollection, or by examining a dream with an analyst, always leads to a refining of the sense of guilt. So Dr. Durand, of the Rives de Prangins Clinic, speaks of 'psychological ethics' as promulgated by psychoanalysis.

What does he mean by that? No doubt the extremely rigorous honesty with oneself which psychoanalysis involves. But neither he himself, nor any Christian analyst, would be likely to hold that this demand could by itself suffice for the erection of an entire system of ethics, thereby making the light of revelation unnecessary for us. A simple morality of sincerity inevitably leads to an impasse, as is shown, for example, by a man like André Gide[14] who firmly believed in it and genuinely tried to follow it, but who in the end only came to doubt his own sincerity!

Yet honesty with oneself as laid down by psychoanalysis is the condition of man in which biblical revelation touches him, in which the sense of guilt, the very mainspring of morality, matures. Thus, if we avoid theoretical and doctrinal controversy, we are in agreement with the analysts, even the unbelieving ones. We belong to the same moral family because of this pitiless severity towards ourselves.

The popularization of psychoanalysis has contributed to the collapse of the self-satisfied bourgeois morality in which the older generation was brought up, and as Christians we can only rejoice because in this way an uneasiness is aroused which is very suitable for opening the heart to the message of grace. 'Modern man', says J. Lacroix, 'is continually under judgment.'[21]

Psychoanalysis shifts the accent of guilt from the formal level of the act to the deeper level of its 'motivation'. In my book *Technique et foi* I have shown how this displacement from formal morals to a more profound morality is in harmony with the spirit of the Bible. This idea of 'motivation' is opposed to moralism in two directions. First of all, because a good action can have bad motives. St. Paul says the same thing, when he tells the Philippians about men who 'proclaim Christ out of partisanship, not sincerely' (Phil. i. 17). But it is the idea which matters more than explicit statements, and this is met with throughout the Bible, reflected in the words of the prophets and of Christ Himself. Thus, for example, He says: 'Beware of practising your piety before men in order to be seen by them' (Matt. vi. 1).

Conversely, an action which is condemned by religious formalism can be justified by reason of its motive. So when the Pharisees reproached Jesus with having healed a sick woman on the Sabbath day, the day when the Law forbade all work He justified Himself by appealing to the love which is the motive of His conduct: 'Ought not this woman, a daughter of Abraham whom

Satan bound for eighteen years, be loosed from this bond on the sabbath day?' (Lk. xiii. 16).

It has just been shown that the entire Sermon on the Mount (Matt. v–vii) makes this same displacement of guilt from acts themselves as they appear, to the secret motives which inspire them. In the same way, in the discussion about meat sacrificed to idols (1 Cor. viii), St. Paul strongly opposes the legalism which has penetrated into the Corinthian Church. He shows that what matters is the motives which inspire anyone's conduct. If a person refrains from eating such food out of a concern to cause no offence to a brother Christian, out of a loving concern for him, then it is good. But not so if he is restrained from fear of the judgment of others, or fear of defiling himself, as the early Jews understood defilement.

This assertion, that it is the intention which matters, is an important development. Ancient Jewish legalism led to a meticulous casuistry, which engendered scruples and anxiety. When what has to be done is predetermined down to the last detail one is quickly obsessed by the fear that something has been overlooked, and that is the start of a vicious circle.

Against this legalism, Christ took His stand as liberator. Yet at the same time, He threw a relentless beam upon the secret depths of human personality. He located guilt, not in the outward deeds, but in the heart of man: 'What comes out of the mouth proceeds from the heart, and this defiles a man. For out of the heart come evil thoughts, murder, adultery, fornication, theft, false witness, slander. These are what defile a man; but to eat with unwashed hands [in accord with the moralism of the Pharisees] does not defile a man' (Matt. xv. 18–20).

Elsewhere He also says to them: 'Now you Pharisees cleanse the outside of the cup and of the dish, but inside you are full of extortion and wickedness' (Lk. xi. 39). In this way He removes guilt from the formal level, unprofitable anxiety about taboos, to the deep and productive realm of the conduct's motivation. This is exactly the shift made by psychoanalysis. It frees us from an anxiety about taboos, but it also destroys the pleasant illusion that we can bask sheltered from guilt.

Further, we recognize with the Bible the fearful universality of evil: 'None is righteous, no, not one. . . . All have turned aside, together they have gone wrong; no one does good, not even one' (Rom. iii. 10–12). 'Man . . . drinks iniquity like water' (Job xv. 16). And in this same book of Job there is a curious passage which refers to faults that God can find even with the angels— 'His angels he charges with error' (Job iv. 18). None escape guilt; all thirst for salvation and pardon.

Chapter XVI

REPRESSION OF THE CONSCIENCE

THE righteous! Men free from guilt! This is the utopian dream which is for ever recurring in the human heart. For there are no such people. We need only observe other folk to convince ourselves of that. Although in the romance of a honeymoon the wife adorns her husband with all the virtues; although the little child can believe for some time that his parents are perfect; although the convert in the enthusiasm of his conversion may endow his spiritual father with a halo, the day will dawn when these beautiful illusions are dispelled.

We should have to close our eyes in order to remain optimistic about man today. To be sure, there are bursts of generosity, wonderful deeds of devotion, acts of courageous loyalty. These are the more striking as they stand out against a background of innumerable iniquities and hidden immorality. It is this contrast which is perhaps the most disturbing thing, and it is understandable that Dr. Hesnard[16] speaks of the check to vital morality, and of the flagrant contrast between the wonderful moral exhortations that have filled the centuries and the actual deeds of men.

Dr. Fanti[11] has published the moving reflections of one of his patients on this universal public and private iniquity. Certainly it is a patient who is speaking, but this gives to his exposure an added poignancy. It comes from a man who, from his high international position, is well placed to observe society as it is. Who dare dispute the picture he paints, with its cynicism, the power of evil forces threatening to engulf humanity in a catastrophe more terrible than anything it has previously experienced, and the complete absence of true humility in a world where it is unceasingly proclaimed?

We are less clear-sighted about ourselves than about other people. The righteous of whom Jesus speaks are those who think themselves to be righteous, who endeavour to give themselves that image of themselves, and who banish guilt from the field of consciousness. I know no one who can bear the awareness of his guilt continuously. At rare and fugitive intervals we tremble at it and then we at once fall back again upon false solutions by the repression of this consciousness. Yet, surely, these are the most vital moments in our life. They are the moments of truth;

moments when the truth is plain, freed from the disguises and side-tracking and special pleading and the alibis behind which we seek to hide, from ourselves and from others, our heavy burden of guilt.

Left to himself, man is lost. His own efforts, his good will and good intentions, his own virtues cannot banish his 'dis-ease'. He is aware that even his most sincere efforts to banish the evil bring new ones in their train. There is a poison within himself, given with life itself, and present throughout its duration, which contaminates everything in advance.

He perceives the solidarity of evil, a fatal link binding all men and all generations together, a fundamental blemish, an original sin—'Who can bring a clean thing out of an unclean?' cries Job (xiv. 4). The evil is within and not merely outside, in the way the Apostle James suggests when he speaks of the tongue as 'an unrighteous world among our members, staining the whole body, setting on fire the cycle of nature [or 'the wheel of birth', i.e. heredity], and set on fire by hell' (Jas. iii. 6).

There are none righteous; all are guilty, as they know and feel more or less clearly. Guilt is no invention of the Bible or of the Church. It is present universally in the human soul. Modern psychology confirms this Christian dogma without any reservations. So it does the Church justice. 'Far from cultivating guilt,' writes the psychoanalyst Mme Choisy,[7] 'the Church, like psycho-analysis, brings it to consciousness, and this is a way of dispelling it.'

This is the broad picture our study paints. I have only sketched it incompletely, with touches here and there in harmony with my own temperament. I am no more than an idler in the garden of humanity, like a botanist out on a walk who picks a little bunch of flowers, a mere token of the inexhaustible richness of nature which escapes him. Someone with a more orderly mind than mine might demonstrate more rigorously the universality of guilt and the weight with which it presses inexorably on all men.

The weight of this guilt is so intolerable that everyone shows this self-justificatory reflex which modern psychology speaks of as the 'repression of conscience', that is to say the repression of guilt into the unconscious, out of the field of consciousness. The Evangelist tells us that when Jesus spoke the Parable of the Pharisee and the Publican He 'told this parable to some who trusted in themselves that they were righteous' (Lk. xviii. 9). And there are other texts with the same purport: 'A wicked man puts on a bold face' (Prov. xxi. 29). 'Every way of a man is right in his own eyes' (Prov. xxi. 2). 'This is the way of an adulteress: she eats, and wipes her mouth, and says, "I have done no wrong" ' (Prov. xxx. 20).

Think how many things we say, often very cleverly and dis-creetly, which have no other object than the justification of our-selves in the face of criticisms which may be made of us. Even Bible quotations can be used for that purpose. A pastor, in all good faith, has given me in a letter a complete theological justi-fication of adultery. A husband who is deceiving his wife will often say to her, to pacify his own conscience: 'It's in your own interest to let me do it; for I'm much nicer to you if you don't hold it against me.' And when a married couple facing divorce savagely fight for the guardianship of the children, it is often because this may serve them as a certificate of innocency.

A man makes himself hard and inflexible in order to escape his guiltiness. The strange paradox present on every page of the Gospels and which we can verify any day, is that it is not guilt which is the obstacle to grace, as moralism supposes. On the contrary, it is the repression of guilt, self-justification, genuine self-righteousness and smugness which is the obstacle. I have a patient in my consulting-room. The conversation is heavy, life-less, oppressive, and I catch myself glancing at the clock which will put an end to it. I feel there is just nothing I can do—for it is a man who is satisfied with himself. He enjoys excellent health; but the situation is tragic.

A precisely opposite picture is presented by a patient steeped in self-reproach. Such weight of guilt is clearly pathological. Furthermore, the faults of which he accuses himself are those we all of us commit. One question then haunts me: 'Is health paid for by some degree of repression of guilt? Might we not all be depressed if a measure of superficiality and unconcern, just as much as grace, did not help to reassure us?'

I am not going to try to answer that question now. No doubt it is a mystery known only to God. But it seems to me that Paul Ricoeur[33] is right when he suggests that we should regard neurosis as a 'failure to exonerate oneself of guilt.' Then good health would be the visible success of the process of exculpation, per-fect vigilance of the reflex of self-justification.

The psychoanalyst, Dr. Nodet,[27] with similar care poses a kindred question: 'The sense of sin, like the conquest of virtue, presupposes a measure of spiritual disquiet. The neurotic perverts the sense of sin by infecting this healthy disquiet with a morbid anguish. But a quite uncommon force of personality may be necessary to recognize and retain a vital disquietude without any assistance from neurotic anguish. Then is neurosis necessary for salvation? Let us be frank enough to admit that sometimes it helps, and usually without our knowing it.'

All this is very subtle and delicate. Morbid and healthy

components are constantly fused in the behaviour of people who are well, as of people who are ill, without it being possible to define their limits precisely. You may have had my experience of sending a schizophrenic to the psychiatric clinic for shock treatment. It was a necessity; psychotherapy was impossible, and even dangerous, because it would arouse a torrent of problems enough to overwhelm him, without a chance to resolve any of them.

But then, when the patient returns·cured, he has forgotten his problems; he is at peace now because his life is smooth, commonplace and without an object. Were then the torments he suffered merely produced by his illness, and without any genuine human significance? I cannot think so. The pathological feature was the obsessional and catastrophic character of the flood of problems, but in themselves the problems were the genuine human problems which agitate all of us, though in tolerable doses, so to say. After the cure they have disappeared as if by magic. Yet I now no longer have real contact with this all-too-well-pacified patient; previously he seemed far more human than he is now.

What happens in an exaggerated way with patients also occurs on a smaller scale with healthy people, who are all, as Dr. Knock so truly remarks, unwitting invalids. A certain degree at least of disquiet, of exactly the same disquiet which we have to fight when with those who are sick it assumes too large proportions, seems to be indispensable for human experience, for vital development, and for the recognition of grace. The natural reaction of people in good health is to run away from this dis-ease instead of facing up to it. But it is a false solution, because it involves a measure of self-deception. And it is a false solution above all because, as everyone knows today, a feeling repressed into the unconscious is far more injurious than when it is conscious.

But it is a universal reaction, as old as man, and it involves in particular the discharging or projection of one's guilt upon someone else. It is already described for us in the first pages of the Bible in connection with the first act of human disobedience. God asked Adam, hiding among the trees of the Garden of Eden: 'Have you eaten of the tree of which I commanded you not to eat?' (Gen. iii. 11).

You remember Adam's reply? He blamed his wife. And Eve, in her turn, said it was the serpent's fault. It was the first domestic conflict. And throughout history all married couples in conflict have thrown the same accusation each at the other: it is not my fault, but yours. It is precisely this which envenoms discussions, because each in turn needs to free himself from guilt by accusing the other. With married couples the dispute is endless when each partner discharges his guilt upon the other, instead of shouldering it and recognizing his proper measure of blame.

It is the same in all such conflicts. There are two ways always open to both parties; the projection of responsibility upon the other, or the conscious acceptance of his own due responsibility. The first way keeps the conflict going endlessly; the second may lead to its genuine resolution. The former may provide periods of armistice, but the second alone can give assured peace.

Then again, there is the conflict between the two generations, referred to earlier on, when the parents are possessive in an authoritarian or a sentimental way. A 'strong' child revolts and wins his freedom by a conflict, the scars of which he continues to bear, and which influences his behaviour in innumerable circumstances of his life. A 'weak' child submits. But the submission is a mere façade which hides suppressed rebellion. Both of these, in the depths of their being, project the responsibility upon their parents, which from an objective point of view is not far wrong.

But the other way, the truly creative way, is typified by the young woman who said to me: 'I myself am responsible. It is not my mother who has crushed me, but I who have let myself be crushed and who have effaced myself out of a sentimental weakness for my mother.' This way of looking at it, even if from an objective point of view it may be disputed, leads to far greater freedom.

For even if rebellion, as A. Camus[5] has shown, is a desire for freedom, which endows it with nobility and humanity, nevertheless, it is not freedom. One can be a slave to one's rebelliousness, which may be open or muffled, expressed or repressed. Psychology has to pass from the hidden revolt to the more healthy and authentic revolt which is lived-out. Only a spiritual experience can liberate from both a false submission and rebelliousness, by means of an awareness of one's own responsibilities.

In the same way, for example, a married couple both still retain a measure of remorse for having had sexual intercourse before their marriage, even if consciously they maintain that it was legitimate. Half unconsciously they throw the responsibility for this upon each other—the wife on her husband, for having constrained her to this premature offering of herself for fear of losing him; and the husband, in a more subtle way, upon his wife, for not having resisted him. This can be the source of all kinds of mutually aggressive acts, and even of unconscious aggression towards the child born out of wedlock, as though it were its fault.

Another example is as follows. A woman in conflict with her husband denounces his stupid extravagance. Her feelings have driven her to become a veritable detective; she has caught her husband in the flagrant offence of twisting his accounts, and she brings to us the definite proofs she has accumulated. But why is the husband driven to dissipation in this way?

Our wife or husband becomes what we make them. Their faults confirm our own failure, because we could not preserve them from those faults. It was precisely in order to rid herself of an obscure feeling of guilt that this woman triumphantly brandished the proofs of her husband's faults. She showed the strength of her need to demonstrate that it was not her fault that the marriage was a failure.

This is the spontaneous cry of children when father suddenly intervenes in a squabble. Each shouts against the other: 'It's not my fault.' In this respect all of us remain children our life long, and our first movement is always to the excuse: 'It is not my fault.' This psychological mechanism operates without limit, in all societies, all undertakings, between social groups and between nations.

Every country calls its spy network 'counter-espionage'. Recourse to arms is always thought of as an act of legitimate defence. Even Christians cannot resolve the dilemma and are caught between two forms of guilt—that of learning to kill, if they are soldiers, or, on the other hand, of being traitors, if they refuse to do this for the land which gives them security.

There are so many unrestrained passions in the world, so many irrefutable and sincere accusations of other people, ceaselessly aggravating the conflicts between men, just because every man carries feelings of guilt within himself against which he has the urgent need to protect himself by projecting his responsibilities upon other people. The pleasure in gossip and scandal answers to this need of feeling oneself less isolated and alone with one's own repressed guilt by emphasizing other people's guilt.

If that is true on the large scale it is also true in the details of daily life. When we are discontented with ourselves we complain about others. It is like the party game hunt-the-slipper. The players are in a circle, and each hands on quickly to his neighbour the slipper he has received. The one in possession of the slipper when the game is suddenly stopped is out. Taken together, humanity is like these players; guilt is handed on from one to another.

Unfortunately there is a difference between the game and guilt. A player who passes the slipper to his neighbour no longer has it in his own hands: whilst we do not rid ourselves of our own personal guilt by putting it upon others. Camus[6] writes: 'I know without any doubt that everyone is a bearer of the plague, for absolutely no one in the world is without the marks of it.'

If we do not project our responsibilities upon our wife, our parents, our friends or supporters, we project them upon society, upon the economic system, or perhaps, as Dr. Bovet has shown us at a recent congress, upon certain groups of people who are looked upon as responsible for all the ills of the world—Jews, capitalists, atheists, etc. We may also project our responsibilities upon heredity, or upon our own body, regarded as a thing outside ourselves for which we may not be responsible. It seems even that contempt for the body and for sexuality which lies at the source of so much false shame and neurosis answers to this general need to ease ourselves of personal responsibility. The development of insurance also answers to the need to shift responsibility, and so the point is reached that someone guilty of an accident is heard to say, 'It doesn't matter, I'm insured'.

Finally, responsibility is projected even upon God. Many who do not dare to confess it openly carry hidden within themselves a grudge against God for all their suffering and all their faults. So Adam says to God: 'The woman whom thou gavest to be with me, she gave me fruit of the tree, and I ate' (Gen. iii. 12); and thereby he insinuates subtly that the final blame rests with God who has given him his wife.

At the call of God the Israelites set out to conquer the land of Canaan which God had given to them. But intoxicated by their victory at Jericho they gave themselves over to pillage, which was forbidden, and then in over-confidence they advanced unwisely against the men of Ai, who soundly defeated them. Then Joshua their leader reproached God: 'Alas, O Lord God, why hast thou brought this people over the Jordan at all, to give us into the hands of the Amorites, to destroy us?' (Jos. vii. 7). Previously, in the wilderness under Moses' leadership, the Israelites blamed God for every misfortune which their own disobedience had brought upon them. So just prior to his death Moses exclaimed: 'A God of faithfulness and without iniquity, just and right is he. They have dealt corruptly with him. . . . Do you thus requite the Lord, you foolish and senseless people?' (Dt. xxxii. 4–6).

Nevertheless, I am always glad when a man is bold enough to tell me his complaints against God. Often it is someone who calls himself an unbeliever because, so he thinks, there is too much evil in the world for him to be able to believe in God. He may tell me God does not exist, or perhaps that He is not an omnipotent, just and good God. It seems to me such a man honours God more truly than many believers who accept the drama of human life too superficially. He takes the omnipotence and holiness of God seriously; and he also indirectly reveals the sensitivity of his conscience and his own personal feeling of guilt, because he experiences the need to project it upon God.

All unawares, such a person is in agreement with the most genuine believers. 'Behold, these are the wicked; always at ease, they increase in riches. All in vain have I kept my heart clean and washed my hands in innocence,' the Psalmist cries. And he continues: 'But when I thought how to understand this, it seemed to me a wearisome task' (Ps. lxxiii. 12, 13, 16).

It is natural for man to project his guilt upon other people and upon God. But he does not thereby get rid of it, and the rebellion against others and against God which results becomes in its turn a source of fresh impulses to evil, and therefore of more guilt.

Chapter XVII

THE AWAKENING OF GUILT

THE repression of conscience, the reflex of self-justification, and the projection of guilt upon others, are only false solutions to the problem of guilt. They constitute a natural and automatic tendency towards healing, but they solve nothing and they are indeed a hindrance to a true solution since they strengthen self-righteousness. The only true solution, both from the psychological standpoint and in the light of the Bible is the reverse of this, namely, the acceptance of our responsibilities, genuine recognition of our guilt, and repentance and the receiving of God's forgiveness in response to this repentance.

To tear men from this impossible situation and to make them capable once more of receiving grace, God must therefore first of all reawaken within them the repressed guilt. This is the positive significance of the sombre, severe and threatening pages of the Bible. The great reversal of outlook in the Bible, which we have mentioned in connection with the narrative of the woman taken in adultery, reminds us that it was not only the removal of the woman's guilt, with which she was overwhelmed, but also the awakening of a sense of guilt in her accusers which was involved. There is not only the rehabilitation of the scorned, but the humiliation of the scornful.

To the latter the Bible, and Jesus Christ Himself, speaks with an implacable severity which is the source of much misunderstanding, because it seems to be contrary to the love of God. This severity can only be understood if we are aware of its ultimate aim. It aims, not to suppress the arrogant sinner, but to arouse his sense of guilt, and so to humble him, thereby opening for him the way to grace.

Many doctors have difficulty in accepting the very many passages in the Bible which speak of the wrath of God (Num. xii. 9), His threats (Is. xvii. 13), His punishments (Job xxxi. 23), of the fire and brimstone He rains down (Gen. xix. 24), the illnesses he sends (2 Kgs. v. 27), and of eternal punishment (Mk. ix. 43). It is certain that there is here a great obstacle to faith, and I freely confess that I quite understand such people. It seems to them that orthodox theologians speak too glibly of these things, whilst on the other hand modernist theologians get rid of them too easily, selecting from the Bible what pleases them and turning a blind eye to the remainder.

It is what I will call the dramatic character of the Bible which seems to me to point the way to understanding. The Bible depicts the relation between God and man, not as something static, defined and dogmatic, but as a dynamic relationship, an historical process with all its vicissitudes and uncertainties, with the prospect of the ultimate goal, salvation. Nowadays psychologists are particularly sensitive to this approach, since psychology has become dynamic, no more regarding man as a fixed entity, but with an eye to what he is to become, his evolution, and the dramatic forces operating within him.

This is like the attitude of the Bible. It places man in history, not in the abstract realm of essences. The God of the Bible is a God who enters history, who acts, speaks and strives. He wages a severe struggle with man, to deliver him from his Fall, with a view to his final salvation. Here, by analogy, we may call the doctor to witness that all medical treatment is a hard struggle. In particular, he knows the severity, sometimes almost brutality, in wrestling for a cure in psychotherapy. It is no easy matter to overcome the resistance of the psychological censor and to guide a patient to understanding and awareness against which all the powers of the soul are deployed with bitter and often astute opposition.

It is from such an angle that we can better understand some of those passages in the Bible which may offend us by their brutality. If God smites vigorously it is because man also resists vigorously, and because God wishes to save him in spite of himself, and even against himself.

Reconsider in this light, for example, the passage in Leviticus xxvi. 14–39. Its dramatic character is very obvious: 'And if by this discipline you are not turned to me [says God] but walk contrary to me, then I also will walk contrary to you, and I myself will smite you sevenfold' (vv. 23, 24).

So the Bible depicts the relationship between God and man as a struggle, a conflict, in which God's action is the more vigorous the more man hardens himself, in order to rescue him from the curse of his own hardness. This is the meaning of the violent assertions made by the prophets, who quite often compare the dialogue between God and His people with the conflict that arises between a loving husband and the wife who is unfaithful to him (e.g. Jer. iii. 20).

I know very well the objections which may be made against this: does not such a presentation of a God who is shaken by passion, bear the mark of puerile, primitive, anthropomorphism which modern intellectuals like ourselves ought definitely to spurn? To be sure, some biblical expressions may make us smile. H. Michaud[26] gives an example of this. Biblical writers had seen that a man's nose dilates when he is angry. So when they mean that a man becomes angry they say that 'his nose burns'. The same expression is used with reference to the wrath of God: 'Yahweh's nose burned against Moses' (Ex. iv. 14).

Naturally, we must not take literally such descriptions of God in human terms. Yet we must take care not to reject, along with the form of the expression, the profound truth it implies. We must beware of robbing God of His humanity under the pretext of ridding ourselves of a naïve anthropomorphism, for then we should be left with no more than a remote, frigid, immutable God, inhabiting eternity, a stranger to life, to history and to existence as we know it, a God of the philosophers and not the living God of the Bible. If we may dare to say so, a God without passions would be a God without a soul, a dead God, even more dead than the God of Nietzsche.

A theologian such as Karl Barth[2] has struggled for a long time, with salutary vigour, against a too human, sentimental and facile view of God; he has made us take notice once again of God's sovereign grandeur, so that it is now more striking to find him speaking of His humanity. He quotes the German proverb, 'When you look at the moon, you never see more than half of it'. We must attempt to see, if not simultaneously then successively, these two aspects of God: His eternity and His actuality, His transcendence and His nearness, His immutable purposes and the shifting, varying historical vicissitudes in which they are embodied day by day.

A God without wrath would also be a God without pity. He would be a mere concept of perfection and not a God who saves and suffers, who speaks and is moved. He would not be a God who passionately challenges men: 'You have burdened me with your sins' (Is. xliii. 24). He would not then be the God who intervenes in the destiny of every man—our own and that of each of our patients.

So we must, I think, take the anthropomorphic expressions of the Bible for what they are, namely, a way of evoking a God who is dynamic, active, alive, which could not be suggested in any other way than by using terms like passion, jealousy, anger, repentance drawn from the psychology of man. Without holding to the words literally, we must preserve the personalistic conception of God they embody, under pain of having no more than an abstract God, an object for intellectual speculations but not of spiritual experience.

The Bible therefore sometimes speaks of God repenting: 'And it repented the Lord that he had made man on the earth' (Gen. vi. 6, AV, RV). The prophet Amos in his visions begs the Lord to abandon the scourge with which He is punishing His people, that is, the locusts which devour the growth, and the fire which devastates the fields. His prayer is heard, and 'the Lord repented concerning this' (Amos vii. 3, 6). The prophet Joel affirmed that the Lord 'repenteth him of the evil' which He sends (Joel ii. 13). The expression is indeed naïve. But the truth which it contains is vital: the God of the Bible is a God on the move, a God who may be appealed to and with whom one can speak, a God who may be moved and who responds.

From the poignant intercession of Abraham for the city of Sodom (Gen. xviii. 22–33), to the parable of Jesus Christ about the unjust judge and the importunate widow (Lk. xviii. 1–8), the Bible is penetrated throughout with this dramatic dialogue with God, with a God who hears and who may change His mind. If you deprive God of this characteristic vitality you make Him into an inflexible, implacable, unforgiving and inaccessible God. And at the same time, you deprive man of prayer, of personal contact with God, of hope, repentance and access to grace. For the spiritual life is not a state, but an active process. The penitence of a man is no stable state, but a movement, a conversion; and God's pardon is not a static attribute, but a movement, a drive.

Our relationship with God is a dramatic engagement, something like a bout of fencing, with its succession of offensives, retreats, feints and rallies. Every man is plunged into it, believer or unbeliever, by the simple fact that he exists and that he lives a human life with all that this implies of contradictions, risks, successes and failures, guilt, aspirations, evasions and resistances.

An immutable, indifferent God might be of interest to philosophy, but not to the doctor or the psychologist, for He would play no part in human development. Even the God archetype with which Professor C. G. Jung[20] presents us is not as impersonal, immanent and inert as He has been reproached for being. He is a God who acts, for as Jung says, 'When I say as a psychologist that God is an archetype, I mean by that the "type" in the psyche. The word "type" is, as we know, derived from *tupos*, "blow" or "imprint"; thus an archetype presupposes an imprinter.'

For a man crushed by the consciousness of his guilt, the Bible offers the certainty of pardon and grace. But to one who denies this it bears terrible threats in order to make him introspect himself: 'Behold, I will bring you to judgment [says God] for saying, "I have not sinned" ' (Jer. ii. 35). This striking contrast is expressed in many biblical texts, as for example in the one cited by James: 'God opposes the proud, but gives grace to the humble' (Jas. iv. 6).

Therefore I venture to say that the aim of 'operation severity' is not the crushing of the sinner, but, on the contrary, his salvation. For that, God must pull him out of the vicious circle of his natural attempts at self-justification. We have seen that these reactions lead to rebellion, so that the sequence of events is that wrongdoing produces guilt, guilt produces rebellion, and rebellion leads to more wrongdoing.

There is no end to the sequence and the way it enters into human affairs. If I have behaved badly towards my wife, I am irritated with her, and this irritation leads me to commit other faults. The same vicious circle enters into man's relations with God. Irritation against God, conflict with Him, and bitter despair over guilt, lead quite fatally in their turn towards evil in still graver forms, and so the vicious circle closes in upon itself.

This can be seen clearly in the story of Cain (Gen. iv. 1–15). We are told that Cain was very angry with God because God regarded the offerings of his brother Abel more favourably than his own. Why? We are not told. But we are told that Abel was a shepherd and Cain a husbandman. Abel symbolizes, therefore, primitive man who lives off the products of nature, while Cain is the civilized man who, by his labour, forces nature to yield him greater riches. We can imagine then that Cain shows the typical malaise of civilized man, which we find still today in an exaggerated form when the scientist is afraid of the atomic power which his science has unleashed.

Whatever the reason may be Cain is angry with God. He throws the responsibility of the drama upon God, because the reason for his irritation is precisely the injustice he attributes to God. But God knows of this vicious circle of guilt and anger which we have been speaking about; He knows that Cain's feet are on a dangerous road; He knows that irritation will lead to temptation, to wickedness, and then to the murder of his brother Abel. He seeks to deliver Cain from the toils of his anger.

In this passage God in no way shows Himself as the judge, the accusing God, the implacable God, as some people have imagined. On the contrary, He speaks very lovingly to Cain. He does not accuse him, but he questions him in a kindly way: 'Why are you angry, and why has your countenance fallen?' A psychotherapist would behave no differently in presence of an aggressive patient. He questions him to help him to gain clearer insight into himself, since it is by entering into himself that he will escape the blind allurement of anger.

To that end, God warns Cain of his danger: 'If you do ill, sin is couching at the door; its desire is for you.' He invites Cain to become aware of his personal responsibility to control the situation instead of submitting to it. We see perfectly clearly already in this old story a saving God, not one who overwhelms the guilty but one who shows him kindness in order to break the vicious circle of his guilt and anger. This is the God who will say to Ezekiel: 'As I live, I have no pleasure in the death of the wicked, but that the wicked turn from his way and live' (Ezek. xxxiii. 11).

I have made no attempt to establish accurately whether the guilt from which Cain was suffering was genuine or false guilt. Indeed, the text does not allow us to know. Had Cain truly behaved in such a way as to merit divine disgrace? Or had he merely feelings of inferiority with respect to Abel? But indeed anyone with a feeling of inferiority towards his brother thinks himself less loved and less appreciated by God than his brother. But it makes no difference whether the guilt were genuine or false guilt, it would equally involve resentment, anger and revolt against God.

The mechanism is set in motion, with all its terrible power. God Himself, in spite of His kindly efforts, is checked by the passionate outburst which closes Cain's ears to His appeal. Far from bringing Cain back to himself, the questions of God inflame his fury still more, so that when he meets his brother he challenges him, the quarrel becomes acrimonious, and he kills him.

The dialogue with God then takes a different turn, so some would think, and now God speaks menacingly: 'Now you are cursed . . . you shall be a fugitive and a wanderer.' But this is not how I understand it. This new dialogue also opens with some questions by God: 'Where is Abel your brother? . . . What have you done?' Again the questions invite Cain to turn within himself and to acknowledge his guilt in order to find grace. But again they come up against his obstinacy: 'Am I my brother's keeper?' and then his rebelliousness, 'My punishment is greater than I can bear'.

His punishment is precisely his intolerable guilt, the unconfessed guilt, bitter, repressed, provoking revolt which seems in his eyes to be a curse and an act of abandonment. He feels himself placed under a curse, repulsed and driven far away from God. This is the law of guilt. God does not say: 'I curse you.' He says: 'And now you are cursed from the ground.' God knows that the sequence guilt-anger-crime-guilt can lead only to despair.

The proof is that God, far from crushing Cain, comes again to protect him against the ultimate consequences of this vicious circle, and puts a sign on Cain to prevent anyone killing him (Gen. iv. 15). A final result of the law of guilt is insecurity. As crime provokes crime, so guilt produces fear; consciousness of having killed leads to the fear of being killed: 'Whoever finds me will slay me,' Cain cries. By the protective device He gives him, God makes thereby what would now be called in psychology a security gesture.

The relationship between guilt and fear may be found also already in the story of the Garden of Eden, in the dialogue between God and Adam after the Fall, when God asks, 'Where are you?' 'I was afraid and I hid myself,' Adam replies (Gen. iii. 10). The dialogue which ensued is familiar enough—the misfortunes, pains and sufferings which God announced to the serpent, the woman and her husband (Gen. iii. 14–19). And this also is generally taken as a sentence pronounced by God, a punishment with which he strikes the guilty.

With an interpretation like that, it might seem that God had drawn Adam into a trap. He had forbidden him to eat from the tree of the knowledge of good and evil. This prohibition is looked upon as an arbitrary order, a capricious act of divine authority to beguile Adam into the temptation of disobedience and then crush him with the punishment. This common way of understanding the text seems to me quite untenable.

It is clear, on the contrary, that God knows to what calamities, even to death itself, Adam will expose himself if he eats of that tree, if he aspires to be his own God, judging for himself what is good and evil. It is not out of caprice, but in order to protect him against these consequences that God forbids him to eat of the tree. When he does eat, he brings upon himself, just as Cain does later, the calamities which flow from his act according to the law of guilt we are studying here.

At this juncture I opened the last book of Suzanne de Diétrich[9] and found the same interpretation there of these old stories in Genesis. When God says to man: 'Cursed is the ground because of you; in toil you shall eat of it . . .' this is no punishment inflicted by God in rage but rather a natural law which God knows and proclaims, in the same way that a physicist foresees that a stone left to itself will inevitably fall to the earth which is attracting it.

Similarly, as Dr. P. Waardenburg[45] has shown, when in another place the Bible says that God visits 'the iniquity of the fathers upon the children' (Ex. xx. 5), it is showing acquaintance with the natural laws of heredity.

The proof is, as in the case of Cain, that God does not completely abandon Adam to his misfortune and his fear. 'I was afraid, because I was naked,' said Adam (Gen. iii. 10). In that way he was expressing the feeling of insecurity which is associated with guilt. 'Naked' signifies without protection. So we are told later that God made Adam and his wife garments of skins (Gen. iii. 21). It was a gesture which gave security, a symbol of the divine protection which still accompanied man along the dolorous road on which he had set his feet.

The psychological insight shown in these old stories is very striking. They express things we can observe any day. Guilt—true or false, the guilt of remorse or the guilt of inferiority—leads to anger, rebelliousness and fear, and these in their turn lead on to evil. Evil consummated, in its turn, produces guilt. We might say that guilt is the villain of the piece. The dialogue with God, His questions and His prohibitions, are so many efforts made by God to prevent man from being caught in the toils of this vicious circle, and then to awaken him to repentance and grace through his consciousness of guilt.

The stories also testify to the incredible power of this bondage, which can readily be confirmed; for neither the law of God, His questions, nor the misfortunes and sufferings which come upon man as a result of his disobedience, are able to tear open the sinister vicious circle. It is shown already from these early pages of the Bible that a further intervention of God is necessary, namely His incarnation in Jesus Christ, the death upon the Cross, the resurrection and the gift of the Holy Spirit, in order to save man from the inexorable sequences of the law of guilt.

It is a matter of daily experience that the worst thoughts spontaneously leap forth in anger. It is the same with anger as with the complexes and temptations of which we spoke at the beginning. At one and the same time it acts in some degree as an excuse and as an expression of guilt. A person may say: 'Don't pay any attention to what I said yesterday; I was under the influence of anger.' In such a case it is as though someone not ourselves, and unfamiliar to ourselves, did the speaking on that occasion, and had thought and planned even to the extent of a crime. Yet at the same time, we do not feel that these thoughts were entirely foreign to us; we know they were hatched in our brain.

We recognize that there is no smoke without fire; and in some respects anger is like the liberation of a part of ourselves which slumbered under the watchful eye of a psychological censor. Other people are not utterly deceived, and they cannot believe that what was thought and said in anger was completely false. It is like the revelation of another self which was there all the time but was normally concealed. Hence we can understand what Christ means when He states that there is no clear dividing line between anger and crime! (Matt. v. 21–22).

As is the case with complexes and temptations, we feel that we are responsible, if not for the words spoken in anger, then at least for the anger itself, for the personal defeat, the inability to be master of ourselves and to keep our personal integrity. We are conscious of the divorce within ourselves between the rational and well-disposed part of ourselves, and the passionate part, on the hunt for something to smash or someone to hurt. The terrible power of these hidden forces is plain. So if, indeed, any guilt sets in operation mechanisms for secrecy, self-justification, accusations directed against others, and bitterness and rebellion against God, all this springs to life in anger, and anger in its turn leads on to wickedness and guilt.

My wife and I were leaving Marseilles. We were in very good humour. We had been present at the wonderful inaugural lecture of Professor Jacques Dor[10] on human surgery; and we had attended a lecture there given by Professor Jean de Rougemont of the University on the subject 'Is man a robot?' We had been most agreeably welcomed by the doctors and students whom Professor Pierre Granjon had brought together over a number of years in groups for the study of integrative medical treatment.

We were driving to Spain. 'Are you taking the motorway?' asked my wife.—'Of course not! The motorway goes to Aix and we want to go through Salon.'—'But isn't there a branch to Salon?'—'No, indeed!' Just imagine! my wife thinks she can give me directions in an area I know so well. Instead of stopping and looking at the map, I push on through interminable suburbs. No more signposts; I branch off, turn back again, and lose still more time; I become irritable, and still more stubborn.

In the end we rediscover our bearings on the motorway. I am abashed. We have lost half an hour and our good humour into the bargain. The sciatica I had been suffering from for two days suddenly comes on much worse. A very trivial fault—my presumption—had released the mechanism of obstinacy and yet graver faults, because I had not recognized it. To err is human, to persist in error is diabolical, the ancients used to say. True enough, the devil is mixed up in it. Error and guilt are human. It is obduracy which inflames them. Happily, we quickly recovered our good humour, although my sciatica persisted.

Irritation, obduracy, aggressiveness: this is the law of unconscious and repressed guilt. Conversely, pardon and grace produce joy, relaxation and security, the atmosphere in which guilt can become conscious, mature, be openly acknowledged, and in its turn lead on to pardon and grace. So the enemy, guilt, becomes a friend, because it leads to the experience of grace.

But at this point a new and most powerful vicious circle comes into operation, arising from the fact that the feeling of guilt inhibits confession. It is like a mouse entering a mousetrap and releasing the mechanism which will entrap it. Here, for example, is an intelligent, idealistic man, and we examine the conditions of his infancy which have perverted his attitude to sex. It is just because of the fear and shame which have been associated with sex for him that he has not sought normal marriage, and his sexual life has found expression in a connection with a married woman.

It is understandable that such an outlet, far from reconciling him to sex, has only aggravated his inhibition, because adultery has aroused in him very strong guilt feelings.—'You are a fervent Roman Catholic,' I say to him. 'Why hasn't the practice of confession freed you from the baleful consequences of your guilt?'—'That's just the irony of it,' he replies, 'up till then I was most faithful at confession, but afterwards I no longer dared to go because I was too ashamed of a fault which I knew I was not strong enough to abandon.'

After some years he began making his confession again, but never with the zest and faithfulness of his youthful days. The intervening years had been laden with a new guilt, namely his flight from his religious duties. This new guilt is now interfering with the blossoming of his life and jeopardizing his psychological recovery. The majority of Roman Catholics who criticize their Church discover, when they have been helped to become entirely sincere with themselves, that their criticisms are a screen for a feeling of guilt at having avoided confession.

Chapter XVIII

THE CONDITION OF MAN

IT is abundantly clear that no man lives free of guilt. Guilt is universal. But according as it is repressed or recognized, so it sets in motion one of two contradictory processes: repressed, it leads to anger, rebellion, fear and anxiety, a deadening of conscience, an increasing inability to recognize one's faults, and a growing dominance of aggressive tendencies. But consciously recognized, it leads to repentance, to the peace and security of divine pardon, and in that way to a progressive refinement of conscience and a steady weakening of aggressive impulses.

From these grounds the dual character of religion, which any doctor can prove from his daily encounter with men, is understandable. Religion may liberate or suppress; it may increase guilt or remove guilt. A moralistic religion, a deformation of religion saturated with the idea of taboos and picturing God as a threatening being, awakens fear, and sets in motion the sinister mechanism of obduracy, revolt and wickedness. A religion of grace breaks in to this vicious circle, and leads to repentance and thus to freedom from guilt.

There is no connection here with the theological discussions between the various Christian denominations. It is purely a psychological matter. Within all the Churches and all Christian groups there are those who are of a moralistic nature, censorious and showing morbid guilt, while there are also generous spirited people, messengers of a God who pardons, who themselves alleviate guilt. Both can glean from the Bible passages which support their attitude, for it contains both assurances of grace and severe threats. We have noticed in the incident of the woman taken in adultery that Jesus speaks quite differently to the woman and to her accusers.

Unfortunately, people pick out precisely those passages in the Bible which are not addressed to them! Psychologists ought to show the Churches clearly that this is the case; it is a daily observation with them, and it is the source of numerous catastrophes. Those who flaunt their self-satisfaction, at the cost of a repression of their guilt, who scorn and pass judgment upon other people and flatter themselves on their virtues, are the ones who notice the assurances of grace which really concern the people they condemn; while the latter worry themselves by reading the divine warnings which are really directed to the former.

It is as though there were two people in quite contrary circumstances, the one in sorrow and the other glad with the joy of the birth of a child. I may despatch at the same time two telegrams to them, one expressing sympathy and the other congratulations. But the postal authorities mix them up, so that the one containing congratulations is delivered to the person in grief, and the happy father receives the one with condolences. It would be immediately obvious that there had been a mistake!

The misfortune is that our patients make the same mistake without noticing it. Those who are depressed, anxious, rejected and ashamed show this most clearly; instead of drawing from the Bible the marvellous consolation which is there precisely for them, they have a morbid passion for hunting out texts on the severity of God, His wrath, curses and punishments. They torment themselves in this way with Bible references not directed at them, and increase their distress by the implacable condemnations which do not concern them at all.

They imagine they have committed the sin against the Holy Spirit, and they quote to us the words of Jesus: 'Whoever blasphemes against the Holy Spirit never has forgiveness, but is guilty of an eternal sin' (Mk. iii. 29). Then, ironically enough, the uncontrollable and irresponsible mechanism of the association of ideas leads them to blasphemous thoughts; for as we well know, we only have to want to avoid a thought for that thought to become irresistible. But in truth, this saying of Christ is not addressed to anyone in distress who is just the one who is afraid of blaspheming, and who may for that very reason give way to a blasphemous thought; but on the contrary, it is for someone full of self-satisfaction and with no conviction of guilt who scorns salvation and the gift of the Holy Spirit. So we may say with certainty that anyone who is worried with having committed the sin against the Holy Spirit has not committed it, precisely because he is worried.

Another patient comes to me with the text from the Epistle to the Hebrews: 'It is impossible to restore again to repentance those who have once been enlightened . . . and have tasted the goodness of the word of God . . . if they then commit apostasy' (Heb. vi. 4–6). A spiritual experience had delivered this man from sin. Then he has fallen back into it again and thinks himself finally damned. I can only assure him that I myself constantly fall back into the sins from which God had delivered me. And yet others quote from the same Epistle the passage which refers to Esau who 'found no chance to repent, though he sought it with tears' (Heb. xii. 15–17).

It is well to recall at this point the dramatic character of the Bible. The Epistle to the Hebrews was written in a time of persecution, to arouse the tenacity of believers, which had been shaken by the apparent triumph of the enemies of the faith. It is to such circumstances that we owe the stern note of some of its pages. Still other patients quote St. John, the apostle of love: 'There is sin which is mortal' (1 John v. 16).

What may trouble us most is to find in the mouth of Jesus Christ Himself numerous allusions to eternal punishment. Yet we must observe that the majority of these are found in the parables, that is to say, in narratives which are made up and which are told as such, and which therefore must not be regarded as descriptions of a concrete reality. Thus there is the parable of the poor man Lazarus (Lk. xvi. 24), of the tares thrown into the fire (Matt. xiii. 40), and of the sorting out of the fish (Matt. xiii. 48); there are the talents (Matt. xxv. 30), and also the curious ending to the parable of the marriage feast (Matt. xxii. 13). The story of the Last Judgment (Matt. xxv. 41) we have already looked upon as a parable.

Furthermore, we must remember that the language of the Bible taken as a whole is very different from our language today with its fondness for clearly defined precision and objective description. Bible language is always poetic, full of images, deliberately suggestive and not descriptive, evocative and not argumentative.

It is in the light of this that we must read the four other passages in which Jesus Christ speaks of punishment. In two of them (Lk. xiii. 28; Matt. viii. 12), Jesus challenges the comfortable assumption of the Jews of His day that they were sure of salvation regardless of their conduct, merely because they were Jews, descendants of Abraham, and belonging to the chosen people (Jn. viii. 33–44). This assumption constituted a kind of protection against guilt, so that the purpose of the threatening words of Jesus was to arouse in these Jews a sense of guilt and of personal responsibility which would open the way to grace. This is the theme of the early chapters of St. Paul's Epistle to the Romans.

The remaining two passages, which are a doublet, are found in St. Matthew's Gospel: 'If your hand or your foot causes you to sin, cut it off and throw it from you; it is better for you to enter life maimed or lame than with two hands or two feet to be thrown into the eternal fire'* (Matt. xviii. 8; cf. v. 29–30). No one, I think, would contest the figurative nature of these texts.

---

* Some manuscripts read 'the Gehenna of fire'; v. 29–30 mentions only 'Gehenna' —Ed.

The position I would uphold, then, is that Christ's references to punishment make no claim to describe a precise and definite reality, but are to strike the imagination of men who are so inclined to repress their guilt and reassure themselves with trust in their own merits. These texts, along with all those to which allusion has been made, about the wrath and vengeance of God, are meant to stress the sharpness of the human drama, and to save men from a facile and deceptive solution concerning guilt. They remind us that 'God is not mocked' (Gal. vi. 7). His grace, which is promised to one who seeks it by repentance, cannot be given to someone who would defy it with impunity.

You know the remark of the Abbé Mugnier, who, when he was asked whether he believed in hell, replied: 'Certainly I believe in it; but I also believe that there is no one there.' This seems to me to be more than a flash of wit. It is a view which is inherent in the entire outlook of the Bible, that the severity and the threats of God—or what men in their remorse attribute to God—are aimed at nothing less than their salvation and at keeping them out of the abyss.

Those of us who are doctors can say frankly that the Christian Churches of all confessions, and many of the sects, have all too often abused this bogy of hell. Theologians, but above all poets and painters, in their pious emotion have outdone the Bible in their fantastic descriptions of eternal sufferings. I am not denying that their purpose was good, and that it was precisely intended to lead men to repentance and salvation.

But it seems to me, as I have already said, that care must be taken as to who is being addressed.

It is a tactless approach to speak of eternal punishment, with all the force of impressive details, to one who is ill, or to young men or young women making a retreat, who are as untutored as choirboys and who have not got beyond an infantile or Freudian idea of guilt. Much harm can be done. Like myself, you have no doubt seen many souls who are still disturbed and fearful from a moral trauma suffered in their early years.

'Gospel' means 'good news': it is good news of the grace of God. Yet there has been freely cultivated in Christendom a fear of eternal punishment. I do not think we can measure exactly the part it plays in the fear of death. Nevertheless, it seems that the fear of death is greater in the Christian West than in the Far East.

The fear of hell can assume incredible proportions with some patients. They can find no language sufficient to express it. One such, a colleague of mine, said to me: 'My damnation is cosmic, atomic.' The words are meaningless, but no extravagance of language could match the depths of his despair. Naturally I am not asserting that the preaching of the Churches is the cause of such illnesses. But the illness lays hold of it and is nourished by it; whilst, on the other hand, preaching of the most dour kind most often runs up against the imperturbable equanimity of those it is intended to shake.

Then again, I have often seen souls tormented, not on account of their own damnation, but of that of others, say of deceased relatives whose conduct is judged as more culpable than that of other folk from a superficial moralistic viewpoint; or there may be disquiet over the fate of the innumerable people who have died without ever having heard of Jesus Christ.

There are plenty of other Bible passages, connected with the problem of guilt, which are disturbing. For example, there are those which attribute to God the hardening of men: God sent Moses to Pharaoh and gave him the power to work miracles able to move the Pharaoh. Yet He adds: 'But I will harden his heart' (Ex. iv. 21). There are many analogous verses, like that of Isaiah quoted later by St. John: 'He has blinded their eyes and hardened their heart, lest they should see with their eyes and perceive with their heart' (Jn. xii. 40).

The sharpness of the problem did not escape St. Paul, who writes: 'So then he has mercy upon whomever he wills, and he hardens the heart of whomever he wills. You will say to me then, "Why does he still find fault? For who can resist his will?" But, who are you, a man, to answer back to God?' (Rom. ix. 18–20). This text agrees with what we have said on the subjectivity of guilt, and the impossibility of discussing it objectively and rationally.

But we are also aware that there is a profound and mysterious truth hidden here; namely, that God's plan of salvation is not only accomplished by men's obedience, but even through their resistances and disobediences. This is the answer to all those people who cannot forgive themselves for their past faults. I see many such. Very often it is not a question of moral failures properly so-called, but of a decision or a direction of living, or a choice which after the event proves to have been erroneous.

I always remember a man who came to see me one day with a most depressed air. 'I have come to the conclusion,' he said, 'by reading one of your books, that all the principal decisions of my life, which I believed I had freely made, were in fact no more than evasions. So my entire life has been false; I have lost a sense of God's plan, and I shall not find it again.' Just think how guilty I felt at that statement! I attempted to reassure him: 'You are still within God's plan. He reigns over our lives, and our flight cannot prevent Him reigning. And He also guides us, in a mysterious way, even through our evasions; otherwise the whole world would be lost, for everyone is evasive, myself included on scores of occasions.'

These inexhaustible reproaches which so many people direct against their own past conduct—even when they had chosen in good faith and believing themselves inspired by God—arise from a view which is too naïve about God's plan, as though the slightest error of direction would wreck completely the whole success of a life! What does place the plan in jeopardy is precisely this false and naïve notion, with the despair and guilt it arouses.

Fulfilment of God's plan is happily not dependent upon the faultless obedience of men! That God does indeed make use of the obedience of those who give heed to Him is obvious enough. What is amazing is that He also uses their faults and their hardness of heart. So Joseph can say to his brothers: 'Now do not be distressed, or angry with yourselves, because you sold me here; for God sent me before you to preserve life' (Gen. xlv. 5). This covers a very great mystery, which I do not seek to unravel, because it completely passes beyond the scheme of rational explanations and belongs to the realm of faith. So, if I meet with a check in my ministry one natural question arises in my mind: whose fault is it? mine or the other man's? But perhaps it is neither the one nor the other; perhaps it is simply that the time is not ripe. Very often we encounter in the Bible this idea that God has His hour, and we must wait for it. My guilt is perhaps simply my impatience.

But it is often that of leaping to conclusions about the will of God. His plan infinitely exceeds my vision. Possibly my check has a meaning in His plan which escapes me completely. My tendency is to identify my cause with God's, my success with His success, my frustration with a frustration to Him. If God shows me my responsibility for this frustration, then I have indeed to recognize my fault, but not to wear myself out because of it. Above all, I must not fall into the spirit of judgment by attributing my check to the obduracy of the man I am wishing to aid. I must in faith discern the will of God even in the resistances which this man opposes to my ministrations.

This is the way, for example, to understand the hardening of Pharaoh's heart, for he gave God an opportunity of showing gloriously His saving power towards His people. St. Paul looks in the same way at the resistance of the Jews to the preaching of Christ: 'Their trespass means riches for the world' (Rom. xi. 12). By that he is saying that if the Jews had not rejected Christ, Christ would have remained a merely national figure, to some extent; He would have been only the Messiah they were awaiting for the attainment of their own national salvation. So the mysterious conception of a divine plan which includes even our faults, reaches its climax with the Cross of Golgotha, which is both the supreme manifestation of man's guilt and also the supreme act of salvation by God.

We who are practitioners are called upon to help men, and particularly the sick, by all the means in our power, by science, by technique, by our humanity and our faith. If they are tormented by guilt feelings then we must show them that the Bible, as a whole and in spite of obscurities, offers them the assurance that God removes the guilt of anyone who suffers from it, and that by His severity He arouses guilt in others so as to lead them in their turn to the same experience of repentance and grace.

To speak with more precision, all of us are at the same time guilty and obdurate. We all experience guilt feelings, and we also continually seek to escape from them, not by the pardon of God but by the mechanism of self-justification and the repression of conscience. Therefore we ourselves have need at one and the same time of both aspects of the biblical inversion. We need the assurance of grace to meet our conviction of guilt, and we need the severity of God to drive us back upon ourselves, to the recognition of our guilt and misery, and to make us entrust ourselves still more ardently to the divine grace.

This is the meaning of the traditional Christian *felix culpa*. It is a happy fault, happy guilt, for it has led us and continually leads us, through begging for grace, to bow before God that we may receive it. The salutary saying of George Fox, the founder of the Quakers, is well known, that the light which shows us our sins is the light which heals.

It follows that what we have distinguished in order to clarify the discussion, is in fact integrated into one experience; we have both at the same time a sharp sense of guilt and a sharp awareness of grace. The more acute, penetrating and refined our sense of guilt, so much the more acute, far-reaching and joyous is our awareness of grace.

In the Epistle to the Romans chapters seven and eight, St. Paul gives a most moving description of our human lot. I have already alluded to it, but here it deserves more careful attention. There seems to be a striking contrast between vii. 1–24 on the one hand, and the last verse of that chapter (vii. 25) together with the whole of the following chapter, on the other. There appears to be a break in the thread of the argument which has worried translators.

In the first section the apostle depicts man's inescapable guilt and despair: 'I do not do the good I want, but the evil I do not want is what I do. . . . Wretched man that I am!' (Rom. vii. 19, 24).

But in the second part this despair is swept away to give place to a paean of triumph: 'Thanks be to God through Jesus Christ our Lord!... There is therefore now no condemnation for those who are in Christ Jesus' (Rom. vii. 25; viii. 1).

The contrast is so sharp that the explanation has been sought by supposing that St. Paul may have been describing in succession man's condition in two distinct phases of his life—in chapter seven, before his conversion, and in chapter eight, after it. This simple interpretation is entirely contradicted by experience, as I have already abundantly proved. Those who think that conversion gives shelter from sin and guilt are grossly deceived, and they fall into a repression of conscience. I have seen many instances of this, especially with various sects in which it is said that converts no longer commit sin and where scandals are rife.

The fact is that the Christian is still accompanied by guilt after his conversion, and it even becomes more acute, as we have seen. The condition described in Romans chapter seven is the state of everyman, converted or not. There is no 'before' or 'after' in it.

Some translators of the Bible have been deceived over this. They have carefully inserted three dots between verses twenty-four and twenty-five. Not all translations have this pious emendation, of course; but the intention of the translators who have inserted them is clear. They assume that St. Paul had snapped the thread of his argument, and after describing what man is like before conversion, oppressed by the consciousness of guilt, he has then taken a leap into the future and described the same man long afterwards, converted and sure of forgiveness, without saying how he passed from the one state to the other.

Recently I met a theologian friend of mine who said to me: 'I have long asked myself what was concealed by these three dots, and what happens between the condition of man in chapter seven and his condition in chapter eight, and whether it happens once for all or whether it recurs time and again throughout life. Then one day I realized that the three dots mean nothing at all, and that a man is at the same time such as is described in chapter seven and also in chapter eight.' That is correct; the dots represent nothing at all, because they have simply been invented by the translator, and they pervert St. Paul's message.

We have the sharp consciousness of guilt of chapter seven and the vivid certainty of grace of chapter eight simultaneously! This can be seen in history; for believers who are most desperate about themselves are the ones who express most forcefully their confidence in grace. There is a St. Paul, as I have just shown; and a St. Francis of Assisi, who affirmed that he was the greatest sinner of all men; and a Calvin, who asserted that man was incapable of doing good and of knowing God by his own power. The same thing can be seen in the consulting-room. Those who are most pessimistic about man are the most optimistic about God; those who are the most severe with themselves are the ones who have the most serene confidence in divine forgiveness.

To separate consciousness of guilt and consciousness of forgiveness is to doom oneself to a misunderstanding of man. To imagine that after conversion one is sheltered from sin and guilt is to beguile oneself with a dangerous illusion. It is even to prepare the way to profound despair on the day when it is realized that, in spite of an entirely sincere conversion, one has fallen back into sin, and guilt is experienced once again in an even more vivid form.

But perhaps it is necessary to experience such disillusionment in order to discover the incredible scope of God's grace. How many of us have not experienced successive phases in conversion? In the first flush, our soul is irradiated with light and purified, and obedience seems easy and joyous; love is given to us for those whom we used not to love; we feel ourselves to be sheltered from temptations, which have lost all their attractions. At the same time our faith is somewhat over-simple in that the contrast between our old life and our new life is seen in black-and-white, but we witness to the new life with power and sincerity.

Then with time the grey colouring returns; the tones fuse; even crude temptations arise afresh; obedience becomes an effort; and we discover, even more sadly than before, the ineradicable nature of sin. But above all, slowly we apprehend better both ourselves and God—God's holiness, and over against it, our misery. And we become aware of a guiltiness of which we had no conception previously.

It is then that we understand more profoundly how vast the grace is which receives us just as we are, with all our despair, all our weaknesses and all our relapses. By degrees the awareness of our guilt and of God's love increase side by side. 'It is the saints who have a sense of sin', as Father Daniélou says,[8] 'the sense of sin is the measure of a soul's awareness of God.'

A patient of great shrewdness, who had become very sensitive to human problems through his illness and the trials of his own life, wrote: 'I know what it is. We are destined to remain suspended between sin and grace, between heaven and the abyss.'

What grace removes is not guilt, but condemnation. St. Paul is quite clear: 'There is therefore now no condemnation.' And paradoxical as it may appear, we have seen that the condition for such absolution is contrition and a conviction of guilt—the very opposite of an absence of guilt.

Quite recently I have had some wonderful conversations with a Roman Catholic priest, severely tested by inner conflicts, a restless, tormented man, incredibly clear-sighted about himself and fully conscious of his doubts, his rebelliousness and hesitations, and of the profound gloom into which he has been plunged. 'Yet all of that,' he says, 'nevertheless in no way shakes my calm certainty of faith and of grace.'

I feel myself closely akin to that man, in a deep community of spirit. I completely understand him. For though less tried by life, I also for my part am both heavy and light-hearted, sad and joyous, utterly sad and utterly joyous, weak and strong, tormented by guilt for innumerable things and yet confident of the grace of God, not for later on but now in the present, in the midst of my anguish and weakness, my guilt and my doubts, and even because of them. 'I came not to call the righteous, but sinners', Jesus said (Matt. ix. 13).

Part Four

THE RESPONSE

Chapter XIX

DIVINE INSPIRATION

IN the first part of the book we have determined the extent of human guilt. In the second part we have attended to the danger of discussing guilt objectively and of imagining that we can judge who is guilty and who is not. In the third part we have seen Christ welcoming with the word of forgiveness those whom the world despises and who are conscious of their guilt, and, on the other hand, speaking with severity to those who are self-satisfied and who repress any sense of guilt.

But we have just seen that in practice these two attitudes are less distinct than might be thought, and that both of them are present to us at the same time, so that we therefore run the risk of deviating either to the one side or the other—either into the morbid scrupulosity of moralism, or into a life of obduracy and without scruples. What we seek, then, is some guiding thread which will lead us towards a true solution and away from either excess.

We seek this, not only for ourselves, but also for our patients, for we see such a number of them oppressed by scruples through this moral formalism which is so constantly at work, particularly in the circles of the pious and notably in the sects. But we must not urge them to reject all moral obligation, under the pretext that it is only motives that count. The over-scrupulous awaken our pity; but in reality those who lack scruples are no more to be envied.

It is a delicate matter. I am no more recommending here some simple subjective morality of good intentions, than the 'psychological ethics' of Dr. Durand discussed in Chapter 15 claimed to reduce moral principles to sincerity. The Church has received the deposit of a divine revelation and it has to formulate it so as to guide men in their conduct and to enlighten them concerning the demands of God. So Jesus Christ Himself declared: 'Think not that I have come to abolish the law and the prophets; I have come not to abolish them but to fulfil them' (Matt. v. 17).

It is also quite well known to what catastrophes laxity of conduct and licence can lead, and the claim to be responsible only to oneself and to be free to behave as one wishes so long as one is sincere. Children of divorced parents come under our care who are reduced to a sad life of neurosis because their father or mother justified adultery in this way and so brought about the collapse of the family. Any doctor will have attended the wife who is suffering from gynaecological, digestive or cardiac disturbance because her husband was being unfaithful. And, to crown all, the husband was sometimes taking revenge on the over-strict education under which he had suffered, and claimed to be liberating himself from outworn prejudices; and he may have justified his conduct with reference to some antinomian texts in the Bible. We doctors are involved daily in moral problems of this kind touching the family life of those who consult us. It follows that we must be fully alert if we are to guide them between the besetting dangers of legalism, on the one hand, and licence, on the other.

The stakes are high. So few people seem to be able to escape one extreme or the other; either the anxiety of leading a moral life, with a haunting burden of scruples, taboos and fears about what they must not do; or an affirmation of freedom, and the pretence of being more sincere through giving way to their instincts and capricious desires, in spite of the suffering they entail. Some try to find a way out with the help of a philosophy of mediocrity and compromise. They shun the worst depths, less by any inner power than by fear of the police, or of what 'people might say', or from fear of the consequences; while they try not to take the problem of morals too seriously.

It is obvious that in such a realm as this we cannot offer a solution to our patients which we have not tested in our own life. We ourselves must have found the secret of life! This secret is there in the Bible. It is to seek above all other things the Kingdom and the righteousness of God (Matt. vi. 33); not, that is, a moral code, but a living and personal relationship with God.

Some maintain that in order to avoid legalistic scruples it is necessary to consider the will of God only in exceptional circumstances, in some heroic conflict, for instance, or in the choice of a career or of a marriage partner. They think also that God is too high and mighty to enter into the details of our daily life. But where do they draw the line? How do they know if this, which seems to them to be a mere detail, is not very important in the eyes of God?

Experience has taught me differently, that sometimes obedience on a small matter turns the ultimate orientation of a life and the sincerity of its submission to God; moreover, we can hardly determine what His will is in exceptional circumstances if we are not already applying it in small issues. To think otherwise is to depart from the teaching of the Bible, for the Bible shows us a God who is concerned with the smallest details in the lives of His children (Matt. xxv. 21). His sovereign greatness implies just this, that we accept His authority over the whole of life, and not merely over certain privileged areas.

But then again the problem is how to refrain from falling into scruples, casuistry and legalism. St. Paul, who strives so vigorously against all this, and who sets in sharp opposition 'the glorious liberty of the children of God' (Rom. viii. 21) and slavery 'to the elemental spirits of the universe' (Gal. iv. 3), and the perspectives of faith and grace as against those of the Law, does not deny that the Law has a limited function. In his eyes it is not an end but a means; it was 'our custodian until Christ came' (Gal. iii. 24).

What is so narrowing, oppressive and deadly about the Law or about a moral code is that it is a thing. To rest upon it is to rest upon a thing and not upon a person. But the entire message of the Bible is that God is alive, He is a person, and He calls us into a living and personal relationship with Himself. A law commands and prohibits—and prohibits more than it commands. A person speaks, inspires, directs, understands, leads continuously to deeper and more discerning perceptions, and produces a shift from the formal system of acts to the more penetrating system of motivation.

In communion with the living God, just as in psychoanalysis, the sense of guilt, so far from being blunted, is sharpened rather. Its depth and inescapability are revealed still more. But it has nothing moralistic about it. It is not a question of *sins* in a moralistic sense, but of *sin*; of the wretchedness of man over against the holiness of God. It is through such humiliation, through such a conviction of sin, that access is granted to a personal relationship with God, which is the true solution to guilt. This is why the Law was a custodian, a means: 'If it had not been for the law, I should not have known sin,' St. Paul says (Rom. vii. 7). And he adds further that the Law was given so that the 'whole world may be held accountable to God' (Rom. iii. 19).

But instead of petrifying us, this sense of guilt is stimulating and revivifying, because it leads to a true and personal relationship with God. One day a woman entered my consulting-room radiant. She explained that she had arrived before the time of her appointment. In the waiting-room she had said to herself, 'I must really try and collect my thoughts'. Only the previous day she had raised questions about silent communion and this personal encounter with God. Then four words had flashed into her mind, like words of fire: 'Make amends—love—endure.'

'Endure.' You can understand what that meant when I say that she was suffering from a serious nervous disorder of the digestive system, in spite of the sedatives which a foreign colleague was wisely prescribing for her. 'Love'—and the meaning of that is clear when I say that she had come to consult me after a painful marital conflict. And the 'make amends' is intelligible when it is said that during the same time of recollection in the waiting-room she felt herself called to make a most difficult confession before me. While she was debating in her own mind about it, the phrase which came into her mind was: 'Humble yourself, and do not rationalise.'

But how happy she was now! I was astounded. Then she immediately added: 'I can feel and measure the love of God.' Then, after thinking for a moment: 'Fundamentally, I think we cannot really love mankind without having realized the immensity of God's love.'

If I had said to this woman, 'You must . . . ! You must make amends, love, endure', that would have been mere legalism. I should have interposed an impersonal 'must' between herself and God. In the circumstances quite a different thing happened, she had encountered God, and at the same time His law. And His law was therefore no longer a mere law, but an appeal, a living word.

This, then, is the secret: a personal encounter with God. It brings a much greater severity with oneself and at the same time a liberation from morbid scruples. Life becomes a joyous adventure which is endlessly renewed. Everything speaks of God, and God speaks to us through every circumstance. All the narratives of the Bible and all the teaching of the Church lead us to this deeper knowledge of ourselves, and it is God Himself who is speaking to us through them. There is an enlargement of the field of consciousness.

In this intimate contact with God the way in which we judge ourselves is fundamentally transformed. In place of the legalistic concern about what is permissible or may be defended in principle, the stress shifts to the ultimate motives which we bring to bear on our actions. And this is reminiscent of the effect of psychoanalysis upon its patients, as we have seen, leading them to an awareness of their unconscious motives.

So Paul Ricoeur[33] is surprised that Dr. Hesnard[16] claims, against the obvious tendencies of psychoanalysis, to restore an 'external' moral system of principles and actions, as over against an 'interior' moral system of intentions and feelings. It seems to me that there is some confusion due to the terms interior and exterior. 'There is no longer an internal morality,' writes J. Lacroix,[22] 'and an external morality, a morality of intention and a morality of act, but there is a valid inward guiltiness and a false inward guiltiness.'

Notice, moreover, that Dr. Hesnard himself has written: 'We do not by any means condemn all inwardness, of whatever kind it may be ... we do not deny there is a sin of intention, which, when the intention is genuine, is equivalent from a moral point of view to the outward act.'

What in fact he is denouncing is the mental ruminations of the over-scrupulous, which we have taken great care not to confuse with inward communion, with the dialogue with God which delivers us from precisely this state. We have to liberate our patients from exactly this same confusion. Another psycho-analyst, Dr. Nodet, [27] has expressed this very well when he writes that with those who are scrupulous 'the sense of one sin has become a protection for not recognizing some other sin, which is usually a more serious and humiliating one'. So, indeed, it is a kind of alibi, whereby a man appears to accuse himself, but in reality is justifying himself, by flaunting in this way the sensitivity of his conscience. Therefore it is absurd to say that the over-scrupulous have an over-lively sense of sin. The truth is that their sense of sin lacks depth.

Self-recollection will lead such a person, as does psycho-analysis, to penetrate more deeply into himself, and to become aware of unconscious sin. This idea of unconscious guilt is found also in the Bible. 'Who can discern his errors?' the Psalmist asks; 'clear thou me from hidden faults' (Ps. xix. 12). And again: 'Thou hast set our iniquities before thee, our secret sins in the light of thy countenance' (Ps. xc. 8). Innumerable other passages express this experience, that by contact with God our eyes are opened to a more penetrating vision. A false moralistic sense of guilt is effaced by the conscience laying hold of a true sense of guilt.

This new sense of guilt is often of a totally different character, one quite unknown to moralism and legalism, and this is a point which deserves to be stressed here because it has important consequences. It is the discovery that our real failing is to have sought to direct our own affairs—albeit, by good principles, by principles even drawn from the Bible—instead of letting ourselves be directed by God, and opening our eyes and ears to the personal inspiration He grants.

We may notice in this connection the delightful story of Balaam (Num. xxii–xxiv). The prophet, who has a sincere zeal to serve God, lets himself be tempted, after some scruples and hesitation, into a political adventure at the instigation of King Balak, who is intent upon exploiting for his own ends the spiritual authority of the prophet. But God calls the enterprise a 'perverse way', and He sends His angel to bar the prophet's road. But he is pushing on head down and does not see the angel; it is the ass

which sees the angel, and turns aside. Balaam is angry with the
beast and strikes it. And so, indeed, it is often the sign when we
are angry that we are refusing to acknowledge unconscious guilt.

But God accosts Balaam, and then he admits, 'I have sinned, for
I did not know that thou didst stand in the road against me'
(Num. xxii. 34). So God would lead us, yet we are not always
attentive to His warnings. A friend may see something more
clearly than we do ourselves, and in our presumption we are angry
with him or her, as Balaam was with his ass.

We often also find ourselves drawn into an impasse by false
moral problems. We complain that they are insoluble and that the
Christian life and obedience to the ethics of the Gospel are impossible. We may have intended to do right and we protest our
good principles. But it is not a question of doing right, but of
doing what God expects us to do at the given moment, of letting
ourselves be guided by Him. Then, like Balaam, we perceive—
sometimes too late—that God was wanting to spare us difficulties,
but that we took no notice of His warnings.

I have often encountered guilt of this kind; an intuition of being
no longer guided by God, of having, so to say, missed a signpost
and strayed far from the path. This is the sort of guilt we experience when we meet with frustration, as we have seen; the feeling,
indeed, that we might have been spared the frustration if we had
had a more lively awareness of divine inspiration.

I take care not to take a success as the mark of genuine direction by God. That would involve a childish view of the Christian
life, from which the Cross had been eliminated. But Balaam's
question constantly haunts our minds: are we truly within the
plan of God and travelling the road on which He would lead us?
This is no longer the question of morality, or of the law, or of
some distinction of a rational or even spiritual kind between good
and evil. It is the more supple, living and personal question about
our contact with God, and our attention to His inspiration.

It is to be noticed that we are far from moralism. The idea of
God's guidance is found throughout the Bible. Although God
sometimes gives general rules, He more often speaks in a highly
personal and concrete way to men within a given situation. He is
present within us, by the Holy Spirit. 'It is no longer I who live,
but Christ who lives in me,' cries St. Paul (Gal. ii. 20). Yet we
constantly deceive ourselves about the direction God gives; we
frequently catch ourselves acting according to our own lights and
not according to His inspiration, not having sufficiently com-
muned, or in our communing attending to our own ideas rather
than to those of God.

In dealing with the story of Balaam just now, I omitted one

point which very well illustrates the difficulty of this problem of God's guidance. Before setting out on his donkey, the prophet spent two periods of serious recollection. Twice over he delayed his reply to the ambassadors whom Balak, King of Moab, had sent as an escort. He wanted a night to pass, for night favours the manifestation of the unconscious and is propitious for the counsel of God.

During the first night of communing, Balaam received the impression that God did not want him to go; while on the second occasion, when the ambassadors returned with the presents and promises to which Balaam claimed to be insensible, he nevertheless received the impression that God wanted him to accept the invitation and go to King Balak. The first time, the text says: 'God said to Balaam, "You shall not go with them".' The second time: 'God came to Balaam at night and said to him, ". . . rise, go with them".' Then, after having stopped him on the road, in spite of everything God lets him go, though now better armed for resisting the moral pressure of the King.

It may seem strange that I recommend so strongly the quest for God's guidance while I maintain that even the most fervent believer may be mistaken about it. Such a view may appear paradoxical, difficult, illogical. But that is the position; it expresses the difficulty inherent in our human condition. It is still more dangerous to simplify things arbitrarily by setting up some rational moral system which is supposed to spare us from the uncertainties and hesitations of conscience. We can neither suppose that the quest for God's guidance is easy, nor withdraw from the quest and fall back upon some formal and suffocating ethical system which evades the difficulty and degenerates into moralism.

At all events, life is simpler for those who do not believe in divine inspiration or who do not trouble about it; and simpler also for those who believe in it in a naïve way and have no fear of being mistaken. But it is not a question of having an easy life, but one as near as possible to the truth. As a correspondent of mine has said, the depth of our human misery is that we are never completely certain 'whether we are actually obeying or disobeying God'. Nevertheless, it is precisely by such groping, and through many errors, returning upon our tracks and renewed communing, that we come to understand God better, to discern His will better, and to deepen our contact with Him. When we comprehend this biblical idea of God's guidance, our view of guilt is also profoundly altered. It is freed from all legalism, and it becomes more subtle, vibrant and creative. The whole of guilt, is comprised in the fact of losing the guidance of God, shutting one's eyes to it, or refusing it. It is a much more severe and exacting sense of

guilt, but not in the least oppressive. We are seized by a new passion, that of discerning signs from God by which He would
preserve us from faults we might commit even in good faith
and unconsciously.

Another Bible narrative helps us to understand this. It concerns
Abimelech, King of Gerar (Gen. xx). Abraham had lied to him,
because he was afraid that Abimelech would kill him in order to
take Sarah his wife. He had told Abimelech, 'She is my sister'.
It was not entirely false, because she was indeed his half-sister.
But she was also his wife; and Abimelech eloped with her, and
was about to commit sin, all unwittingly. Then, as in psychoanalysis, God revealed by a dream that Sarah was married. 'It was
I who kept you from sinning against me,' God said to him in the
dream. And here we have an element which is contrary to all
moralism: Abraham, who had done the lying, was also the instrument for God's blessing—by a prayer he healed Abimelech's wife
of her sterility (Gen. xx. 17).

It can be seen, then, how the idea of guilt is transformed and
freed from legalism with its taboos. Real life is life directed by
God. Sin means to lose contact with God, and to be guided by
Him no longer. An act can be regarded as right in the light of
moral principles, and yet not be the will of God, and may do
much harm. Such a view as this, which is the perspective of the
Bible, wipes out every hope of erecting a moral code upon man's
natural and rational knowledge of good and evil. 'A genuine
fault is a hidden fault,' says Ricoeur,[33] 'and it requires an external
revealer.'

This revealer is the Word of God, the Word which addresses us
through the Bible and the Church, by the voices of the prophets,
through the word and example of Christ, and by the message of
the Apostles; sometimes through the mouth of a friend, by some
test or blessing, by some humiliating or pleasant circumstance.
But it always leads to an awakening of conscience and to the
uncovering of some hidden guilt.

So far as I am concerned, what has most often opened my eyes
to my own unconscious sin is the witness of friends when they
have told me about their own faults. This, let it be noticed is the
complete opposite of judgment. Instead of denouncing my guilt,
they spoke to me of their own, and an amazing light flashed into
the depths of my heart. An inward voice murmured, 'This is
true of myself, but I have never recognized it'.

Sometimes people speak to us about their faults in order to
teach us and to provoke deliberately this movement of self-
awareness. But then we feel that behind their apparent humility
they are judging us, and that in fact they are boasting of being

better able to recognize their errors than we ourselves are, and we react in the contrary direction by justifying ourselves.

But if their testimony is truly humble, spontaneous, living, without ulterior motives, if it is a genuine word of acknowledgement by those who have found the true solution, who have discovered the grace of God, then it draws us also in turn into the same experience, which is the greatest experience a man can undergo. Thus, St. Paul says to King Agrippa: 'I was not disobedient to the heavenly vision, but declared . . . that they should repent and turn to God' (Acts xxvi. 19, 20). Repentance means the recognition of guilt, and it is the sense of guilt which drives us to God and reveals to us the love and forgiveness of God. It is a psychoanalyst, Dr. Laforgue, who writes:[23] 'The peculiar characteristic of a religion like Christianity is represented by a faith which removes guilt, through belief in Redemption, Pardon and Grace. . . .'

Chapter XX

EVERYTHING MUST BE PAID FOR

FOR twenty centuries the Church has been proclaiming salva-tion, and the grace and forgiveness of God, to a humanity oppressed with guilt. How then is it that even amongst the most fervent believers there are so few free, joyous, confident souls?

It seems to me that this arises, at least to a large extent, from a psychological attitude which I now want to stress, namely, the idea deeply engraved in the heart of all men, that everything must be paid for.

Here is the case of a man in distress. For a long period we have been able to keep to the scientific plane and to disarm his morbid guilt feelings. But there still remains a lively genuine remorse. He looks at me with a despairing glance, and then I speak to him of the grace which effaces all guilt. But he exclaims: 'That would be too easy!'

It seems to him impossible that God should remove his guilt without him having to pay any price. For the notion that every-thing has to be paid for is very deep-seated and active within us, as universal as it is unshakeable by logical argument. So the very people who long most ardently for grace have the greatest difficulty in accepting it. It would be too simple a solution, and a kind of intuition opposes it.

I am not now thinking only of atheists, or of those many believers who are on the fringe of the Churches. We can see practising believers going regularly to confession, to Communion, to the Lord's Supper, without really believing that their guilt is wiped out. Perhaps, indeed, the very frequency of their acts of devotion, and of their pilgrimages, a certain feverishness and meticulous zeal, far from being an outward sign of their faith are indications that in spite of everything this doubt remains in their hearts.

They insist strongly on their past faults, as though these were not liquidated. Yet they are believers who have received individual absolution from a priest at confession, or liturgical absolution in Protestant worship. In a general way, theoretically and as a dogma, they believe in 'the forgiveness of sins', without grasping it for the failings which continue to gnaw within them; or maybe they do not realize that this absolution concerns not only certain sins which are mentioned most particularly in Church, but the sum total of latent, diffuse, vague, distressing guilt of which we are speaking here.

I am not only speaking of our traditionally Christian western world. Think of the innumerable multitudes of Hindus who plunge into the waters of the Ganges to be washed from their guilt. Think of the votive offerings and the gold-leaf which covers statues of the Buddha. Think of all the penitents and pilgrims of all religions who impose upon themselves sacrifices, ascetic practices, or arduous journeys. They experience the need to pay, to expiate. In a more secular sphere, less aware of its religious significance, think of all the privations and all the acts of charity which so many people impose upon themselves, in order to be pardoned for the more or less unfair privileges which they enjoy.

Furthermore, many physiological or psychological troubles are linked with a semi-conscious, confused, vague sense of guilt. So, for example, many men who have deceived their wives suffer from impotence when they marry their mistress after divorce, or even after the death of their first wife.

Numerous illnesses, both physical and nervous, and even accidents, or frustrations in social or professional life are revealed by psychoanalysis to be attempts at the expiation of guilt which is wholly unconscious. It is a form of punishment which the sufferer administers to himself, and it goes on repeating itself indefinitely with a kind of inexorable fatality.

It is objective observation of men which obliges us to make a fresh appraisal of their moral and spiritual life, and also to open our eyes to the extensive repercussions it has on their health. They attempt—vainly, and unconsciously to be sure—to make expiation, to 'pay'. And they do pay, quite literally, with their health. The dreadful agony of this inexhaustible guilt to which the neurotics are martyrs is a kind of expiatory sacrifice which they are rendering.

A doctor had two sons, one of whom suffered a disability. The parents were worried about the feeling of inferiority which might result from it, so they behaved more indulgently towards him. It was a naïve idea! Later on a psychotherapist had to be consulted to help the boy to accept his disability. One day the analyst said to his father: 'You have weighed down the mind of this child while thinking that you were lightening the load. When he acted foolishly he ought to have been punished in order to make recompense; in that way the account would have been settled. But because of your indulgence he has kept within himself the weight of his guilt, even though you have forgiven him.'

Although this was a case of infantile need, in this respect men remain infants all their life long. The need to pay for one's rehabilitation is universal. We can see this in the case of offenders pursued by justice. They do their utmost to obtain the indulgence of the courts. But in so far as they do not undergo the penalty which their crime demands they feel inward distress. After punishment their fellow-citizens also accept their reintegration more readily. They have paid the price.

How can punishment, penalty, sacrifice or an illness efface a crime? It is utterly illogical. The calculations of justice are purely conventional. Yet it is inscribed in the human heart: everything must be paid for! To wash away the past, expiation must be made. This is the meaning of all the rites and sacrifices of all religions. Here we meet all over again the defilement and purification of which we have spoken. The texts of the Mosaic Law, so detailed in their description of the prescribed ritual, answer to this need, the need of assuring by their perfection the purification of the nation and of each individual.

Cultic acts are one way of paying. That is their psychological significance. They are supposed to guarantee freedom from guilt by discharging the debt which gave rise to it. It is from this angle that we have to understand the Law of Moses. We find there, on the one hand, individual atonement offerings and guilt offerings, and, on the other, in the annual Day of Atonement, rites which aim at the collective purification of the nation. Individual sacrifices are differentiated according as to whether they are intended to expiate the sin of a priest, a ruler or an ordinary citizen. And this gradation implies the idea that a sin is the more grave according as the person who has committed it is the more highly placed in the social hierarchy (Lev. iv. 3, 22, 27; v. 15; vii. 1–10; Ex. xxix. 37; Num. xxix. 5).

The idea that illness is defiling—a foreshadowing of the modern concept of infection and contamination—is also prominently implied in the ritual concerning leprosy and the purificatory sacrifices at the healing of a leper, which are expressly called 'guilt offerings' (Lev. xiv).

As a matter of detail, the Law takes into account the financial position of the leper who is healed and allows him easier terms if he is poor. But he has to pay some price for the removal of the ban which made him untouchable. It can be seen how intertwined are the ideas of isolation for health reasons and guilt, such as still brood over the minds of modern patients when they have to go into quarantine, or are sent to a sanatorium or put into an asylum. The sanitary character of the isolation here appears in the fact that persons suffering from gonorrhœa are treated like lepers (Num. v. 2).

But what particularly interests us is the communal ritual of the Day of Atonement (Lev. xvi). This ritual implies the idea of men's solidarity in guilt. In order to feel at ease and reconciled with God, the individual not only needs to be cleansed from his own personal sins, but to live in a social setting which is purified, where the danger of passive contamination from evil is warded off.

An early point which strikes us for its psychological bearing is that the person in charge of the sacrifice must undergo a rite of atonement for his own sins before proceeding to the atoning rites for the people (Lev. xvi. 11). This embodies a spiritual demand the truth of which is well known. I may prescribe digitalis for a patient without taking it myself. This is the technical method. But I cannot be to a patient a messenger of divine grace without having benefited from it myself. This is the spiritual method.

In the same way a priest receiving confessions must make confession himself; and a psychoanalyst must himself have been analysed. This shows that his discipline, however much he may deny it, is not purely technical but belongs to the spiritual order. Dr. Ponsoye's word[32] reminds us of this: 'The doctor of the future will purify himself in order to purify others.'

A second point of interest is that the person sacrificing sprinkles the mercy seat with blood, and this assures its sanctification. The mercy seat is felt to be the place of God's holiness in the midst of His people. How then does it come to need sanctification? This involves an idea deeply planted in the human mind, the idea that man soils and contaminates everything he touches, and that the evil with which he is infected can rebound even upon God Himself. This is the origin of the belief that holy things must not be touched. It is the same idea as taboo, which denotes at the same time what is holy and what is forbidden.

We find the same idea pushed to the point of obsession amongst our patients. Through their feeling of being accursed they have the impression that they defile everything they touch, and that in the case of holy things this constitutes sacrilege. I recall, for example, a Protestant who enveloped his Bible in a number of covers, and who only opened it after a series of complicated rites, for fear of poisoning the spring from which he desperately and vainly sought purification.

The idea that man defiles and degrades everything he touches, although it does not reach such intensity in healthy people, none the less exists in every one. It is a measure of the existential guilt which every man bears vaguely within himself, the Promethean sense of man's curse. It is present even in the idea of respect, which implies restraint and discretion in approaching a revered person.

It suddenly shows itself in the unexpected timidity which seizes a man who is normally free and easy, coarse and jaunty, when he enters a Church, or comes into high society, or goes to court or to a hospital, when he is present at a funeral service, meets a person of high rank or comes into contact with great sorrow. It can suddenly appear in the strange uneasiness which may be shown, in the presence of a simple ingenuous girl, by a man who is usually bold in his approach to women, and who will defend her vigorously against a less reserved friend.

But to return to the Mosaic Law. After the officiating priest has purified himself and sanctified the mercy seat, the sacrifice of a scapegoat is prescribed for the purification of the people. The entire rite has great psychological significance. In fact, there are two scapegoats, not one, between which the lot is cast (Lev. xvi. 8). The duality expresses the ambivalence which marks the whole of this problem of evil and guilt. One of the goats is to be sacrificed to the Lord, and the other, laden with the sins of the people by the laying-on of hands, is to be sent away into the wilderness. The wilderness is the place where evil spirits reign, and the devil himself.

Thus, the removal of evil and guilt has two interdependent aspects: its obliteration from before God, and its expulsion and return to the devil to whom it belongs. In biblical thought there is no question of two sacrifices, one to the good power and one to the evil power. A dualism of this kind would be inconceivable to the Mosaic mentality. Yet although its outlook is profoundly monotheistic and affirms the total sovereignty of God, it nevertheless does not underestimate the active power of evil.

This power is personified by Satan and the evil spirits associated with him, who have a strategy of their own and, as one might say, like matter and energy, their own principle of conservation. There is profound truth in this, namely that evil must go somewhere. Just after the war C. G. Jung[19] made reference to the two demoniacs whom Jesus healed by driving the demons out of them into a herd of pigs (Matt. viii. 28–34). He was warning the world to be on guard against the danger of a reincarnation of the demon of Nazism.

This means that under earthly conditions the exorcism of evil is for ever an uncertain affair. The scapegoat continually roams the desert in company with the evil spirits, ready to reappear on the horizon. Some words of Christ have an odd relevance: 'When the unclean spirit has gone out of a man, he passes through waterless places seeking rest, but he finds none. Then he says, "I will return to my house from which I came". And when he comes he finds it empty, swept, and put in order. Then he goes and brings with him seven other spirits more evil than himself, and they enter and dwell there; and the last state of that man becomes worse than the first' (Matt. xii. 43–45). The dramatic complexity of the problem of evil could not be expressed in a more realistic and disturbing way.

Dr. Baruk[3] has stressed the profound truth, and the universality, of this psychological de-tensioning by means of a scapegoat. For example, when a wife suffers from the faults of her husband and yet at the same time is attached to him, she begins to excuse him by saying that it is not his fault he was so badly brought up. In that way the wife transfers the guilt to her mother-in-law in order to exonerate her husband. She makes the mother-in-law his scapegoat.

The device can work quite well, and the wife is able to live in harmony with her husband and patiently to endure his faults. But the scapegoat—the mother-in-law—prowls in the background; in a thousand ways the wife suspects her of dark and treacherous acts, and ends by being obsessed with her. She ceases even to be aware of her own guiltiness towards her, the wrong she does her with an energy which is explained by the panic fear of this threatening enemy against whom she continually erects fresh barriers.

This mechanism is extremely powerful and widespread. Every class in school has its scapegoat, either a pupil or, often, a master; in every workshop and office, in every assembly or family there are scapegoats who give rise to a measure of harmony through the fact that guilt and reconciliation is unloaded upon them.

In my opinion the same mechanism also plays a salutary part, for instance, in bull-fighting, so that in the countries which hold it in honour there is less neurosis. Bull-fights are, in fact, much more than spectacles; they are rites. This is shown by the strictness of the traditions which control the sequence of events. There is proof of it in the resistance encountered by those who demand the abolition of the killing of the bull. For this doubtless possesses the value of an atoning sacrifice. The same is perhaps true of the death penalty, the elimination of which from the penal code is met by an instinctive opposition in many countries.

Duelling, the ceremonial for which has its traditional pattern, offers another magical method for the discharge of guilt. As soon as blood has flowed, honour is satisfied, and the opponents embrace each other. The one who has been offended himself affirms that he is satisfied and thereby pronounces the absolution of the one who has wronged him, even if it is the former who has been wounded and not the one who has done the wrong! All these are modern survivals of a primitive, magical mentality, the mentality of taboos, which was naturally still dominant among the early Israelites. As an example of it we have the idea of 'putting to the ban'; this has moral significance, yet it is permeated as we shall see by a magical element. Through an error in spying, Joshua's forces were defeated by the people of Ai, and left behind them thirty-six dead (Jos. vii). The misjudgment of the spies was the objective, or historical, or one might say, the scientific, cause of the defeat. But a magical cause was sought for it.

One Israelite, Achan, was guilty. He had taken spoil and hidden it in his tent. Now looting had been forbidden by the Lord's command—it was the first step in humanizing warfare, a remote anticipation of the Red Cross! All the people were involved in the consequences of its defiance. The curse must be lifted, and the guilty party found. The procedure was by the drawing of lots by tribes, by families, then by households; and Achan was indicated. He confessed; his loot was discovered; he himself was stoned and his possessions were burned.

And so we see that all rites and sacrifices answer to the idea that payment must be made for everything. They are an expression of psychological laws which modern studies, such as those of Dr. Baruk or Dr. C. G. Jung, help us to understand better. But they are also permeated by the spirit of magic which belongs to primitive mentality. They possess genuine efficacy, but only in so far as people still retain an infantile idea of guilt. In that way they may be freed from guilt, because they believe that it is paid for by the duly completed ritual.

But in so far as moral consciousness becomes more sensitive and man attains to a sense of personal responsibility, confidence in the efficacy of the rite will be destroyed. Ritual, however meticulously carried out, no longer seems sufficient to bring peace of conscience. A more certain form of atonement is needed.

Chapter XXI

IT IS GOD WHO HAS PAID

IT is true that from the earliest Bible times the surmise thrusts itself into the minds of inspired men that what God wants is righteousness, and not that men should give themselves up to iniquity with the confidence that they can square their conscience by certain rituals. Already in the early Law the idea appears that an individual guilt offering does not dispense with the need for making reparation for the wrong done (Lev. vi. 1–7). In the case of theft, fraud, or perjury the guilty party must restore to the injured party the value of the object plus one-fifth, and at the same time make a guilt offering to God. But even this deterrent did not keep men from the slippery slope of their natural inclination to make an immoral use of ritual, by hiding the remorse for their wrong-doing under the cover of a good conscience at having carried out the sacrifices.

So the protestations of the prophets are raised with an ever increasing vigour against those people who devote themselves at the same time to iniquity and to ritualistic piety. Numerous passages might be cited of their proclamations on this theme. From Isaiah (i. 11–17) we have:

'What to me is the multitude of your sacrifices? says the Lord;
I have had enough of burnt offerings of rams
and the fat of fed beasts;
I do not delight in the blood of bulls,
or of lambs, or of he-goats.
When you come to appear before me,
who requires of you this trampling of my courts?
Bring no more vain offerings;
incense is an abomination to me.
New moon and sabbath and the calling of assemblies—
I cannot endure iniquity and solemn assembly . . .
your hands are full of blood.
Wash yourselves; make yourselves clean;
remove the evil of your doings from before my eyes;
cease to do evil, learn to do good;
seek justice, correct oppression;
defend the fatherless, plead for the widow.'

Or from Jeremiah (vii. 8–11):

> 'Behold, you trust in deceptive words to no avail. Will you steal, murder, commit adultery, swear falsely, burn incense to Baal, and go after other gods that you have not known, and then come and stand before me in this house, which is called by my name, and say, "We are delivered!" '

All the other prophets could be quoted, for they were all raised up by God, to denounce injustice and iniquity with the same severity, in order to awaken guilt in those who repressed it behind the smugness of men of piety. There is no moralism here—let me stress that there is no trace of moralism with the prophets. What we have is invective and appeal, something extremely personal. Moralism and its casuistry means, as we have seen, submission to a thing, submission to the Law in fact. But the prophets live in the atmosphere of an entirely personal dialogue between God and man.

So, in their succession, the prophets all present their demands over against the false securities of the atoning ritual. They re-awaken the guilt these rites have stifled. For in their wholly personal relationship with God they have experienced another solution diametrically opposed to this one, namely, that it is God Himself who wipes away human guilt, and He does so precisely when a man acknowledges it instead of imagining that he has paid the price of it by some ritual act. Only then is guilt truly obliterated and a man freed from his past.

Such, for example, is the moving narrative of Isaiah's vision (vi. 1–7): 'In the year that King Uzziah died I saw the Lord sitting upon a throne, high and lifted up; and his train filled the temple. Above him stood the seraphim. . . . And one called to another and said: "Holy, holy, holy is the Lord of hosts." Then Isaiah cried: "Woe is me! For I am lost; for I am a man of unclean lips, and I dwell in the midst of a people of unclean lips; for my eyes have seen the King, the Lord of hosts!" Then flew one of the seraphim to me, having in his hand a burning coal which he had taken with tongs from the altar. And he touched my mouth, and said: "Behold, this has touched your lips; your guilt is taken away, and your sin forgiven." '

There could be no more moving expression of genuine atonement, the complete atonement freely granted by God to a man who repents. At once Isaiah is a new man, ready to take up the vocation of a prophet. He has passed through 'metanoia'. We can link with this the call of Moses at the burning bush in the wilderness of Horeb (Ex. iii). You remember why Moses was in exile, far from his people. He had fled because of guilt: he had committed a murder. He was a hot-headed man, eager for justice. He had seen an Egyptian striking a Hebrew, had intervened and killed the Egyptian (Ex. ii. 11–15). The next day he intervened again between two Hebrews who were quarrelling, but the one exclaimed: ' "Who made you a prince and a judge over us? Do you mean to kill me as you killed the Egyptian?" Then Moses was afraid, and thought, "Surely the thing is known". When Pharaoh heard of it, he sought to kill Moses. But Moses fled from Pharaoh, and stayed in the land of Midian.'

We can appreciate the inward struggle which had taken place in the mind of this exile during the long hours spent in watching his father-in-law's sheep. His motive, indeed, had been excellent. It had been love for his people, for justice, and indeed for God, which had fired him. His genuine zeal had taken him too far, and his life lay broken, weighed down both with remorse and with the fear of judgment by the people he had hoped to succour.

And then God raises him to life again and renews his vocation. He makes Moses undergo 'metanoia'. Out of the hunted murderer He makes His servant the most mighty leader and spiritual guide of His people. But Moses undergoes the transformation only by passing through a terrible inward crisis, for God demands, in fact, that he return to Egypt, the scene of his crime. This is the exact opposite of his flight away from human judgment in which Moses had sought his salvation.

Moses protests. He piles one objection upon another. He pleads his feeling of inferiority: 'Who am I that I should go to Pharaoh, and bring the sons of Israel out of Egypt?' (Ex. iii. 11). What's more, he cannot express himself well: 'Oh, my Lord, I am not eloquent' (Ex. iv. 10). He has doubts and is afraid the Hebrews will not believe him: 'They will say, "The Lord did not appear to you" ' (Ex. iv. 1). He is afraid they will pose theological questions which he cannot answer: 'If they ask me, "What is his name?" what shall I say to them?' (Ex. iii. 13). He tries yet again to resist: ' "Oh, my Lord, send, I pray, some other person." Then the anger of the Lord was kindled against Moses' (Ex. iv. 13–14).

We notice here again the wrath of God about which we have spoken and which expresses the dramatic character of the dialogue between God and man. The resistances put up by Moses were hard to break. We can see behind the parade of doubts and feelings of inferiority another anxiety of a much more powerful kind, namely the fear of judgment by men who might recognize him as a murderer and reject his right to speak in the name of God. And so a false guilt, the guilt of inferiority, which other men's judgments may create, is closely intertwined with genuine guilt. But, as with Isaiah's vision, there is a fire kindled by God, a burning bush, which purifies everything and liberates both from guilt and from feelings of inferiority.

In a sense, Moses had expiated his guilt by his exile. But it was an expiation without hope and without termination like all human expiations. God was going to ask him to pay in his own person a much more costly price—victory over himself, his doubts, and fears, and timidity; and then the terrible struggle against Pharaoh, the bitter disillusionments he was going to cause his people, the forty years in the wilderness, hunger, thirst, and then death before his mission was complete. But all this will not now be expiatory. It will be a positive vocation. The expiation is over and done with, there at the burning bush. God Himself completed that when Moses recognized his own wretchedness in His presence: 'And Moses hid his face, for he was afraid to look at God' (Ex. iii. 6).

This may have reminded you of another narrative about a man tortured by the feeling of guilt—the Apostle Peter. Under the impulse of fear, he had denied his Lord, and then after the resurrection he found himself face to face with Him, in a conversation which changed his life (Jn. xxi. 15–19); it was a facing inward, an experience of 'metanoia'. Out of the man bruised by guilt Jesus was going to make the bold spokesman of the Day of Pentecost, the inflexible witness who would face persecution, the leader of the Church.

At the same time, Jesus told him the price of this vocation and the suffering which he would have to undergo, even in his case also death on a cross. But this will not be expiation. St. Peter had started to live out mere human expiation by the dark despair which had settled upon him from the time of his denial. It was precisely from this false expiation that Jesus delivered him. By a word, Jesus Himself blotted out the past, and further, He placed His full confidence in Peter: 'Feed my sheep,' He said to him three times.

So from one end of the Bible to the other, we constantly witness the same paradoxical happening. The guilt that men are never able to efface, in spite of sacrifices, penance, remorse and vain regrets, God Himself wipes away; and men are at once freed from their past and transformed. The most fearful become bold, the most cowardly become courageous, and they face the judgment of their fellows without fear. The most timid of men, a Jeremiah who continually longs to keep silent (Jer. xx. 9), dares to speak out in such a way as to give grounds for one of the worst accusations to be levelled at a patriot, that of defeatism.

Throughout the Bible we are therefore faced with two opposite views, two opposite solutions for the problem of guilt, two divergent ways for reconciliation between man and God: a false solution, which nevertheless contains an element of truth, by means of atoning sacrifices, and also by moral effort, though for ever inadequate; and the true solution, atonement through God Himself.

No price can be paid to God great enough for what He deserves (Ps. l. 10–12):

> 'For every beast of the forest is mine, the cattle on a thousand hills.
> I know all the birds of the air, and all that moves in the field is mine.
> If I were hungry, I would not tell you; for the world and all that is in it is mine.'

In the Psalm which follows, the opposite solution is expressed most movingly (Ps. li. 2, 3, 7):

> 'Wash me throughly from my iniquity, and cleanse me from my sin!
> For I know my transgressions, and my sin is ever before me.
> Purge me with hyssop, and I shall be clean; wash me, and I shall be whiter than snow.'

But the wonderful announcement of God's free grace, which effaces guilt, runs up against the intuition which every man has, that a price must be paid. The reply which comes is the supreme message of the Bible, its supreme revelation; it is God Himself who pays, God Himself has paid the price once for all, and the most costly that could be paid—His own death, in Jesus Christ, on the Cross. The obliteration of our guilt is free for us because God has paid the price.

Jesus Christ has come 'to save that which was lost' (Matt. xviii. 11). One who existed 'in the form of God' has identified Himself with us 'being born in the likeness of men. And being found in human form he humbled himself and became obedient unto death, even death on a cross' (Phil. ii. 6–8). The prophet Isaiah had already glimpsed this great mystery (Is. liii. 2–5):

> 'For he grew up before him like a young plant,
>   and like a root out of dry ground;
>   he had no form or comeliness that we should look at him,
>   and no beauty that we should desire him.

He was despised and rejected of men;
    a man of sorrows, and acquainted with grief;
and as one from whom men hide their faces
    he was despised, and we esteemed him not.
Surely he has borne our griefs
    and carried our sorrows;
yet we esteemed him stricken,
    smitten by God, and afflicted.
But he was wounded for our transgressions,
    he was bruised for our iniquities;
upon him was the chastisement that made us whole,
    and with his stripes we are healed.'

It was announced by an angel of the Lord to St. Joseph, while the Virgin Mary awaited the birth of Christ: 'You shall call his name Jesus [i.e. 'saviour'] for he will save his people from their sins' (Matt. i. 21). It was proclaimed by Jesus Himself on the eve of the crucifixion. He took a cup, and gave it to His disciples, saying: 'Drink of it, all of you; for this is my blood of the covenant, which is poured out for many for the forgiveness of sins' (Matt. xxvi. 27, 28).

It is proclaimed again by all the apostles. By St. John: 'The blood of Jesus his Son cleanses us from all sin' (1 Jn. i. 7); and again: 'He is the expiation for our sins, and not for ours only but also for the sins of the whole world' (1 Jn. ii. 2). By St. Paul; 'In him we have redemption through his blood, the forgiveness of our trespasses' (Eph. i. 7). By St. Peter: 'Christ also died for sins once for all, the righteous for the unrighteous' (1 Pet. iii. 18). By the author of the Epistle to the Hebrews: 'The blood of Christ shall . . . purify your conscience from dead works' (Heb. ix. 14).

Recently my wife made a study of this question of the atoning death of Jesus Christ. I was amazed at the impressive number of Bible quotations which she accumulated one after another on her list, in harmony with each other and drawn from the whole Bible. They all expressed the certainty that the removal of our guilt is assured to us by Jesus Christ, and that 'we were reconciled to God by the death of his Son . . . justified by his blood' (Rom. v. 9, 10). And let us remember that in biblical thought blood is sacred because it is regarded as the seat of the soul (Lev. xvii. 11), and it is the symbol for life, for the living person. That is why the Israelites were ordered to bleed animals before eating them. All the passages where the blood of Christ is mentioned mean that we are saved by His life, by the gift of His own person.

Consequently the ancient ritual sacrifices of the Mosaic Law appear as a foreshadowing of the atoning sacrifice of Jesus Christ.

This theme is developed at length in the Epistle to the Hebrews, which was addressed particularly to Jews instructed in the Law. The contrast is stressed between the provisional character of the old sacrifices and the definitive character of the sacrifice of the Cross: 'And every priest stands daily at his service, offering repeatedly the same sacrifices, which can never take away sins. But when Christ had offered for all time a single sacrifice for sins, he sat down at the right hand of God. . . . For by a single offering he has perfected for all time those who are sanctified' (Heb. x. 11–14).

Salvation is not an idea; it is a person. It is Jesus Himself—God Himself—who yields Himself up. In His presence all the interminable debates which arouse within us the feeling of guilt, all moralistic hair-splitting and our defences against the judgments of others, all these fall away. We see it happening in the story of Zacchaeus, who enriched himself, so popular report had it, at the expense of the people. He tried to justify himself and to demonstrate his good conscience; but Jesus cut him short with the words: 'Today salvation has come to this house' (Lk. xix. 9).

Salvation is no longer some remote ideal of perfection, for ever inaccessible, it is a person, Jesus Christ, who comes to us, comes to be with us, in our homes and in our hearts. Remorse is silenced by His absolution. He substitutes for it one other single question, the one He put to the Apostle Peter: 'Do you love me?' (Jn. xxi. 15). We must answer that question, and find in our personal attachment to Jesus Christ peace for our souls.

All men benefit from this unique atonement; all men, indeed, 'the whole world' as we have just been told by St. John (1 Jn. ii. 2). Jesus Christ died for all men without any distinction, for the men of every age and clime, for Brahmins, Buddhists, Mohammedans, pagans and atheists, for those who had died before He lived, and all who will live in the ages yet to come.

He Himself said: 'I have other sheep, that are not of this fold; I must bring them also, and they will heed my voice. So there shall be one flock, one shepherd' (Jn. x. 16). And again: 'Men will come from east and west, and from north and south, and sit at table in the kingdom of God' (Lk. xiii. 29). For the rest, His word to Zacchaeus is sufficient: 'The Son of man came to seek and to save the lost.' We have demonstrated clearly enough the universality of guilt, the solidarity of mankind in the state of perdition, so that the universality of salvation, that all men are reconciled to God by His sacrifice, may be clearly recognized. 'Since all have sinned and fall short of the glory of God, they are justified by his grace as a gift, through the redemption which is in Christ Jesus' (Rom. iii. 23–24).

Our privilege as Christians is to know that we are forgiven, and that forgiveness reaches us through Jesus Christ. The order to His disciples to go 'into all the world', was simply to proclaim the 'good news' (Mk. xvi. 15), to convince all men and to multiply the visible signs of God's grace by mighty works and healings. It was to propagate 'metanoia', this radical transformation, the arousal of a consciousness of guilt and effacement of the guilt, humiliation of the proud and restoration of the distressed. But this was not the procuring of salvation. Salvation was already there, offered and assured for all men. Everything was accomplished.

Chapter XXII

LOVE WITH NO CONDITIONS

THIS is what Jesus expressed in His Parable of the Prodigal Son. When the son returns, the father is waiting for him. He has already forgiven him. He sees him afar off; and it is the father himself who runs to meet him and who fervently embraces him before the son is able to say anything. The gesture is spontaneous and unconditional.

During his exile, racked by suffering and remorse, the son pictured his father as angry with him. He asked himself how he could move him to mercy, and he thought out a servile confession for obtaining his father's forgiveness. He never dreamt of a full pardon which would reinstate him with the honour of a son, but merely of his toleration as a servant. What happened was the precise opposite of this. He made his confession, but his father had already welcomed him with open arms, so that the confession was turned into his reply to the kiss, instead of being its precondition.

The proclamation of Jesus Christ is about the love of God, a love which is all-inclusive and unconditional. And here we impinge upon one of the most important themes of modern psychology. Freud has shown us, it may be remembered, that guilt is awakened in the infant's mind by the fear of losing the love of his parents; and also that all the traumas of his mental life are connected with this doubt about being loved. The infant feels that he is being rejected and no longer loved. The anxiety of guilt is just this anxiety of being loved no longer. The child has the impression that his parents' love is conditional; that they will love him only on condition that he is good.

The truth is, that because of their zeal to train him up and to keep him away from wrongdoing, the parents give him the impression that this is the case. They even go so far as to say, 'I shan't love you any more because you've been a bad boy.' But it is not true. They love their child even if he is naughty, and their care to keep him away from wrongdoing is itself a guarantee of their love. Yet even if parents refrain from a lie of this kind, children attribute the idea to them, and imagine that their parents love them on condition that they are good.

In every age, men have projected precisely the same idea on

God. They picture God as one who loves them only on condition that they are good, and who refuses them His love if they become guilty. Fear of losing the love of God—this is the essence of our human problem and of psychology. Even a person who does not believe in God, trembles to lose his love. This false idea of God, still so widespread among His people, is just what Jesus came to remove. He shows us that God loves us unconditionally, loves us not for our goodness or our virtues but because of our misery and guilt.

Yet how many people remain burdened and oppressed, even within the Christian Churches! 'What a wilderness it is,' writes aul Ricoeur,[33] 'or rather, what a castle of Kafka it is, when a Christian man has lost the sense of forgiveness whilst retaining his sense of sin.' No psychotherapist will contradict this saying of the philosopher. Alas! we must frankly admit that this is the state in which the majority of Christians appear to be today.

And do not objections arise in your mind, you who read this? Do you accept without any reservation this assurance of God's unconditional love, and His unconditional forgiveness? Is not repentance a condition?

I do not think that in the mouth of Jesus Christ repentance has the force of a condition, but rather of a route. Jesus seems to me to be a penetrating and realistic observer of men, who describes things as they take place. Certainly, in the Parable of the Prodigal Son what happened was that the son repented and as a sequel to his repentance he returned home; he then found that his father had already forgiven him in advance, and without any conditions. You see the difference. The father did not make the repentance of his son a condition for his love. He did not tell him that he had forgiven him because he had fulfilled the condition of forgiveness, that he had merited pardon by his repentance. Forgiveness leapt spontaneously from the father's heart, for indeed it had never been absent from it.

Consider another parable, that of the Pharisee and the Publican in the Temple (Lk. xviii. 9–14). The Pharisee makes a display of his virtues. But he does not do so in any arrogant way, as is often thought; he does not speak of his good works as though they were personal merits, but as 'graces' received from God. The publican strikes his breast. Jesus concludes: 'I tell you, this man went down to his house justified rather than the other.' These words can be understood also in the way I have just indicated. 'I tell you . . .' is the comment of an observer, in other words: 'This is how it happens.'

The same thing can be said about forgiveness of one's fellows. In the Lord's Prayer Jesus has taught us to ask God to forgive us

'as we also have forgiven our debtors' (Matt. vi. 12). And He
clearly adds: 'If you forgive men their trespasses, your heavenly
Father also will forgive you: but if you do not forgive men their
trespasses, neither will your Father forgive your trespasses'
(Matt. vi. 14–15). These words could therefore be taken in the
sense of a 'condition', a right, a meritorious demand, for a forgiveness which we gain by the forgiveness which we ourselves
grant to others.

How tragic that would be for us! What a burden would press
upon us! One has to be a psychotherapist to know how rare the
forgiveness of others is, and how aggressiveness can be repressed
behind false forgiveness. Here we have all the drama of moralism
again. For if forgiveness of others is the condition for God's
love, then we must appear to forgive, we must do our utmost to
forgive, we must camouflage or repress our aggressiveness under
friendly words, and the repressed aggressiveness eats within the
soul, becomes the source of false guilt and morbid anxiety, and
bars the way to salvation.

The very thought of it makes me shudder. What a drama is
there! For what false love, what false forgivenesses between men
—and particularly in the Churches and in religious families—and
for what anxieties these repressions are responsible, anxieties of
which we are the secret witnesses! And all this happens because
that piece of Christ's teaching has been taken in an infantile way,
and God has been credited with a conditional love, which places
the condition of salvation back upon our own shoulders; because
we try hard to fulfil the condition, and when we are not able we
feign it.

But these words of Christ can be understood as a factual
description of the way things happen, of the route that is followed.
It was our infantile fear of not being loved which made us
aggressive and which prevented us, in spite of all our moral
resolution, from truly forgiving others. Freed from this fear,
when we grasp that God's love is unconditional, we find the
power to forgive others; for God does not love us because we
love Him and obey Him, and in that way fulfil some condition,
but, as St. John says, 'because he first loved us' (1 Jn. iv. 19).

When repentance, 'metanoia', and the forgiveness of others is
in question we can present these as a condition laid down by
God; or, on the contrary, as a map of the route, a kind of signpost which Jesus, in His wisdom and psychological insight and
love, erects to show us where the road lies by which we can
forsake our despair. The same preaching about repentance may
seem oppressive or liberating according to the sense in which it
is understood—whether as a condition imposed by God, which

indeed, we can never completely fulfil and by which God may then refuse the grace to which He calls us, or whether, on the contrary it is taken as the outstretching of His hand to lead us there.

Between these two interpretations is the same difference which legal writers observe between the expressions *de jure* and *de facto*. *De jure* has a legal sound to it, implying an established rule, a set condition. *De facto* denotes the simple recognition of what takes place or of the way in which it takes place. There is always an element of blackmail about 'condition', the sort of blackmail that parents sometimes use with their children, or which the children attribute to them. The temptation is similarly great for those who serve God, and in quite good faith we can all fall into it without even being aware of the fact, by making this unique treasure which we hold—the assurance of God's grace—into a means of exerting pressure upon men in order to keep them from immorality. A kind of blackmail involving salvation can at any time insinuate itself into the most sincere exhortations about good behaviour, the fulfilment of religious duties, or conversion.

Other people make a distinction between God's love and His forgiveness, as though He always loved us and without any conditions, but that He laid down certain conditions for forgiveness. The distinction is subtle; it is an intellectual one, which does not hold in the presence of the human heart as we know it, or in the face of Scripture.

So far as a human being is concerned, caught up in this drama of guilt, a God who does not forgive can no longer be regarded as a God who loves unconditionally; and a God who lays down conditions for His forgiveness does the same for His love. From the point of view of Scripture, He would be a God who denied Himself: 'If we are faithless, he remains faithful—for he cannot deny himself,' writes St. Paul (2 Tim. ii. 13). It is not because of us but because of Himself that God forgives us. This is what the prophet Isaiah once expressed so vigorously when he heard God say to him: 'I, I am He who blots out your transgressions for my own sake, and I will not remember your sins' (Is. xliii. 25).

I insist therefore upon this word 'unconditionally' because it seems to me very important in practice. Most people admit that if there is a God He ought to love us. But there is a decisive step between great love or very great love or very very great love, and a love which is unconditional. It is the distance between what is finite, be it as large as possible, and what is infinite.

See what happens with our patients. Often they are urged by a strong inner impulse to increase their aggressiveness towards us, or the insistence of their doubts and their negativism, as if to put us to the test. They have found in us a kind, understanding attitude, full of the love they so vitally need. But how far does it reach? It is natural we should love them, in so far as they show themselves confiding, frank and pleasant. But will it change if they become insolent, uncommunicative, sceptical; if they are rude, if they overstep the line, if they prolong the interview after it should have ended?

It is like a defiance which they hurl at us, and they push it further and further as though to see whether ultimately they do not indeed run into a barrier, whether we shall not lose our temper, grumble at them, pass judgment on them, and lose patience. It must be realized that the stakes are enormously high. They have to know if the bridge over which they venture their life is firm. In the same way, to test a new bridge, a line of large wagons is sent over. When a patient asks: 'Will you forgive me if I commit suicide?' that means: 'Have you a never-failing love for me?'

To be sure, such is not the case. No man can love unconditionally as God loves. Anyone who claims to love without limit does not know what love is; for one who knows it truly admits that he is incapable of it. But this behaviour of patients shows the vital need we all have of finding something absolute upon which we can count absolutely, something unfailing which gives the lie to all the relativities life teaches us through its many sufferings, wherein every trust has its limits, every hope its disappointments, every friendship its eclipse. This absolute is God; and what our patients are looking for when they put us to the test in this way, is at least some reflection of God, of a love which goes beyond mere convention; and it is a proof that they all seek God, even without knowing it.

We also, without having suffered as much as they, have learnt that there is no light without shadow, and no treasure for which in one way or another the price does not have to be paid. Then suddenly there dawns upon us the vast, entire endowment of God's free love and forgiveness, and of the reconciliation He offers us in Jesus Christ. It is this which bowls us over, frees us from the burden of guilt, transforms us, provokes 'metanoia'. This is the discovery which has always, in spite of the preaching of the Churches, to be made anew. It is this discovery which periodically in history gives rise to an outburst of infectious faith, mass conversions and irrepressible joy.

It happened in the early Church. The Apostle Peter announced this assurance of salvation at Pentecost: 'For the promise is to you and to your children and to all that are far off, every one whom the Lord our God calls to him' (Acts ii. 39). The Apostle

Paul unceasingly returned to it with haunting insistence: 'For by grace you have been saved through faith; and this is not your own doing, it is the gift of God' (Eph. ii. 8). He states it more definitely: a grace-gift is not reckoned as a due or merited as a payment (Rom. iv. 4). 'Since all have sinned and fall short of the glory of God, they are justified by his grace as a gift, through the redemption which is in Christ Jesus' (Rom. iii. 23–24).

But periodically in the Church this prodigious news of free salvation becomes indistinct because of the very efforts the Church makes in exhorting men to obey, to be virtuous and to do good works, so that little by little these appear to be the condition for salvation. Then the anxiety about damnation rises once more on the horizon. Yet periodically, also, the Church is renewed by men who discover afresh the free gift of God and cry it out. Of such are St. Augustine, St. Francis of Assisi and many others.

Such a one was Luther. Nothing illustrates better this periodic oscillation of outlook than the history of Protestantism. Luther, an impetuous man, driven to despair by the feeling of guilt, after vainly plunging into penances and mortifications, discovered afresh in his turn that salvation is not earned, but is a gift of God, free and offered in advance to the sinner, and that it is sufficient to accept it by faith. From his cry of relief, the Reformation was born, like an explosion, at a time when the Church was insisting on works, merits and indulgences, all of which laid the cost of salvation upon men's own souls.

Thanks to God, in spite of schism the Reformation profoundly influenced the Catholic Church itself, and it is in its turn reformed in this respect. But as time passed, moralism, the religion of good works, gradually re-entered the heart of Protestantism. It crept in and for a long time was not noticed, but now it reigns in the majority of the Churches which sprang from the Reformation.

It is significant that a Protestant patient of mine could say to me: 'Protestantism seems to me to be an immense effort to earn grace by good conduct, whilst Catholicism freely dispenses this grace to any who seek it from a priest.' The patient was not wrong. Moralism has re-established the idea of merit, of a grace which is conditional. And in some Protestant circles these conditions so proliferate and harden down as to be oppressive. I know a young lady the authorities of whose Church disapproved because she had spoken to a woman wearing a red jumper; such clothing was regarded as a sign of frivolity and it was blameworthy to have anything to do with so worldly a person.

In one of the Catholic intellectual circles a theologian, Jean Guitton,[13] stresses that 'one of the implications of the Christian doctrine of grace' is the 'gratuitous nature of the gifts which are made to us'. I am pleasantly surprised to find him adding that this is 'an implication which Protestants think about perhaps more often than we do'. Alas, I fear that this homage to Protestantism is unjustifiable. Today, in fact, this is no longer a confessional question, but a psychological one. At the heart of all the Churches there are moralistically minded men who wish to impose upon others conditions for salvation, and there are others who live joyously by the marvellous assurance of free salvation.

It is a psychological matter because it concerns a tendency inherent in the human mind, the mechanism in fact for covering up guilt which I have described, which makes a show of one's merits, virtues and abstinences for self-justification, and eagerly presents them to others as the conditions for grace.

Here is a patient who comes to visit me every week for some years. In greeting her in my room I say to her in a jocular way: 'Here you are, on your little pilgrimage to Geneva, your weekly reward!' She immediately replies: 'A reward I have not merited!' 'But,' I retort, 'we merit nothing in this world.' This is precisely what bowls us over and drives us to our knees—that God bestows favours which we do not merit. If we did deserve them where would be the gift and where would be our joy?

But my patient continues her reflection. 'In the last resort,' she says to me after a while, 'this wounds our self-love, this receiving of what we do not deserve. And this is why we have difficulty in accepting it. We would prefer to have merited it; we contend with God for the merit.' Yes, we cannot hide from ourselves the fact that this tremendous affirmation of free salvation runs up against very strong resistances within each one of us. It is paradoxical, because we yearn for it with all our heart—God offers it to us—and we are reluctant to accept it! Yet even with believers, who proclaim it in their hymns, liturgies and missals, there are inward protests more or less unconscious, more or less avowed. For the affirmation offends our reason and our logical conception of justice.

It is not just. The people who have made the greatest and most sincere moral effort to be faithful to God in their conduct, are the very ones who have the greatest difficulty in admitting that God also generously accords His grace to others who have deprived themselves of no whim or pleasure, whether in lying, cheating or harming their fellow men.

It's not just! That is the reaction of the elder brother of the prodigal, who stands aloof from the festivities and thus excludes himself from the great divine joy (Lk. xv. 24–32). A tragic reversal of things, when the profligate son enjoys fellowship with the

father he has wronged, whilst the one who had been wisely submissive comes into conflict with him for the first time and breaks
out in anger. We meet with the same spiteful reaction amongst
the vineyard workers in the parable, who grumble at their employer when they see that he pays their fellow-workers, who have
only worked one hour in the cool of the evening, the same wage
as themselves who have borne the heat of the day (Matt. xx.
1–16). How Jesus Christ understands the human heart!

God's greatest servants are not proof against a similar tendency to revolt. Jonah is a most likeable prophet! In a time of
recollection he realized that God was calling him to go and preach
repentance in Nineveh, a city consumed with immorality, a great
city 'in which there are more than a hundred and twenty thousand
persons who do not know their right hand from their left, and
also much cattle' (Jonah iv. 11). Having a presentiment that God
in His goodness may pardon Nineveh, Jonah attempts to dodge
so thankless a task, and runs away by ship.

But he lacks neither faith, nor courage, nor humility, and when
the tempest arises he admits outright both his faith and his fault
in having wished to fly from the face of God. He said to his
shipmates: 'Take me up and throw me into the sea; then the sea
will quiet down for you' (Jonah i. 12). Everyone knows how a
great fish saved Jonah by swallowing him in order to vomit him
up on the shore the third day. A splendid symbol, which Jesus
Himself interpreted like a Jungian analyst, seeing it as prefiguring
His own death and resurrection (Lk. xi. 29–32).

Jonah then decides to be obedient, and God even turns his
disobedience to good account, since the miracle of which he had
been the object impresses the Ninevites who see it as a 'sign' from
God, as Jesus speaks of it. Jonah walks in the streets and cries
out: 'Yet forty days, and Nineveh shall be overthrown!' (Jonah
iii. 4). But Nineveh was not overthrown; it repented, and a fast
was declared, from the king down to the herds and flocks! And
God forgave it.

But Jonah is not able to forgive God for His goodness, a goodness which gives the lie to the threats he had been charged to
utter. Jonah falls into a fit of nervous depression; he flees from
the world, and sits down in solitude. 'Now, O Lord,' he says,
'take my life from me, I beseech thee, for it is better for me to die
than to live' (Jonah iv. 3). Fortunately, God was able to revive
his spirits. He made to shoot forth a castor-oil plant, and then
He made it wither away. Jonah's annoyance reaches a climax, and
God says to him: 'You pity the plant . . . and should not I pity
Nineveh?'

We of the Reformed Church have great need today to recover

the spirit which drew from Calvin the passionate cry: 'To God alone be the glory!' These four centuries later we find ourselves in a sombre period of history, when the Church contributes rather to the oppressing than to the liberating of souls. We were plunged into this situation at least by the beginning of the century, and this time it was the psychologists who raised the cry of alarm. And already theologians—Protestant as well as Catholic and Orthodox—struggle vigorously against a moralistic and activistic perversion of the Church.

Yet I notice a larger proportion of people oppressed by this deviation amongst Protestants, even when their Church connection is slender, than amongst Catholics. The fulfilment of duty, the renunciation of all pleasure, good resolutions, the daily attempt to conquer one's faults, shame at one's instincts, the fear of being found fault with, judged, misunderstood—all this is substituted for the zest of a love towards God. And on all these points one remains continually at fault, ever more hopeless, with defeat after defeat, constantly and increasingly fretted by guilt.

This moralism itself multiplies defeats, because despair leads on to defeat by sapping the vital forces of the soul, and defeat leads to despair. It is precisely from this inexorable and vicious circle that God would deliver us by His unconditional forgiveness, and it is tragic to see those who believe in Him and who seek to serve Him living lives crushed by these sinister coils even more than unbelievers, until they are no longer even able to love a God who seems to them so hard and so cruel.

You see our task, its sacredness, and its urgency. Like the prophet Isaiah, we have need to cry aloud for grace (Is. xl. 1–2):

> 'Comfort, comfort my people,
>   says your God.
> Speak tenderly to Jerusalem,
>   and cry to her
> that her warfare is ended,
>   that her iniquity is pardoned,
> that she has received from the Lord's hand
>   double for all her sins.'

Dr. Baruk[3] has quoted another passage from the same prophet (Is. lxi. 1) which seems to him to define the vocation of the doctor:

> 'The Lord has anointed me
> to bring good tidings to the afflicted;
> he has sent me to bind up the brokenhearted,
> to proclaim liberty to the captives.'

Chapter XXIII

THE WAY OF CONFESSION

WE are the instruments of healing grace when we prescribe the remedies God has given us, when we handle the lancet, when we use the forces of nature over which He has given man dominion (Gen. i . 28), and when we work for the development of science to which He Himself has called man (Gen. ii. 19). We are again the instruments of His grace when the sick in mind find release through our psychological techniques.

But should we remain silent when it is a question of man's supreme malady, his great human anguish, his existential sickness—when it is a question of the sense of guilt, with which all our unbelieving colleagues are concerned today, moved as they are by their compassion and their great pity for human suffering? Should we conceal God's great answer because theologians accuse us of exceeding our role as doctors and of encroaching upon their territory?[39] No! if we did we should resemble a practitioner hesitating about lancing a very advanced boil because the surgeon has more experience with the lancet than he has.

You have seen that we cannot enter the field of psychology without sooner or later coming imperceptibly and inexorably, even before we have realized it, upon human problems, those concerning the meaning of life, perdition and salvation, despair and hope, the sense of moral guilt and the forgiveness of God. There is no frontier. Dr. Maeder[24] has particularly brought to light the inevitable transition from psychotherapy to the cure of souls. Suddenly during a consultation we feel in the patient's accent, in a pause, or even without any clear sign, that in reality he is now at confession, that he is experiencing 'metanoia', that he is aware of his sense of guilt, and that he trembles at his wretchedness and needs an answer.

This answer comes from God who has entrusted it to the Church. It is not a question of interfering with the value of the sacraments, but rather of making our patients aware of them again. Let the Catholics go to confession and receive absolution from the priest; let the members of the Orthodox Church confess more freely and receive absolution in communion; let the Protestants confess to their pastor and take part in public worship, in the confession of sin and in solemn absolution. But as for the assurance of God's grace and the message of God's forgiveness, it behoves everyone to proclaim them, and more particularly us doctors, as so many distressed souls come to us.

A certain clerical tendency is seen in the bosom of Protestantism as well as in the bosom of the Catholic Church. For example, a theologian[44] who strives very successfully to restore auricular confession to honour in the Protestant Church, according to the guiding rules of the Reformers themselves, nevertheless adds that such confession can be made only to a clergyman.

It is not my business to discuss this matter on theological grounds, although I can find no biblical text that justifies such an affirmation and although it seems to me to contradict the teaching of the Reformers about the priesthood of all believers. It seems quite simply that the theologians envisage the question too theoretically and formally. It is practically impossible to cut a man short who in the course of a consultation or a mere conversation goes on from confidences to confession, still less from the confession of false, morbid guilt to that of real guilt.

I have amply shown that false and true guilt are inextricably entwined and that there is 'continuity' between them, as Dr. Sarano[35] affirms. Now, no one questions the fact that the doctor is qualified to hear morbid confessions and to try to unburden the patient of them by a deeper sense of awareness; but this is precisely to enter the field of genuine guilt, for which the false guilt acted as a covering and at the same time a sign. We have seen that classification or demarcation was impossible, and certainly impossible if it had to be done before the patient spoke, in order to be able to send him back to the cleric in time, if the latter alone were qualified to hear him.

The heart of the matter is, I think, that the word 'confession' denotes for the doctor a psychological event and for the cleric an act of piety. We doctors consider that confession occurs each time there is that intense shudder of shame and humiliation implied by the avowal of what a man knows he is guilty of, and which he concealed up to that time with the greatest determination. And so what characterizes confession is a state of mind.

For the cleric confession is a ceremony, an occasion set aside precisely for that purpose, in which the penitent as well as the cleric know that they are proceeding to a solemn act. I take care not to disown the religious and even psychological value of this solemnity, which many Church-people need—I mean Protestants, for it is a matter of course for Catholics—in order to be assured of God's forgiveness.

But the theologians agree with us about the importance of the state of mind. Contrition may be absent from a confession proper,

made in the confessional or to a priest or pastor, and may yet
move a man in my consulting-room without his even realizing
that he is in fact making confession. This is particularly striking
among practising Catholics who go regularly to ritual confession,
quite sincerely, faithfully and with all the humility and contrition
possible yet without even having felt—or but rarely—as upset as
they do in my office.

That is because the course of the interview has suddenly
aroused in them a deeper sense of awareness and an admission
which they never thought of making during confession, without
there having been on their part any intention of evading the
sincerity and honesty of confession. They prepared themselves
conscientiously for the confessional without there occurring in
their minds what leaps up so spontaneously when they are in my
room.

I will go further: an unbelieving patient in the consulting room
of an equally unbelieving psychotherapist may go through
exactly the same experience, through the same emotion at
confessing what he knows he is guilty of, and may feel the same
relief. That is what Jesus Christ Himself, in His Parable of the
Pharisee and the Publican, expresses in quite a general way when
He says that the latter 'went down to his house justified rather
than the other' (Lk. xviii. 14). Jesus makes no appeal to any
ceremonial or ritual here. There is not even a confessor. It is the
publican's state of mind which counts. And Jesus adds the general
comment that 'every one who exalts himself will be humbled,
but he who humbles himself will be exalted'. Whether we know
it or not, it is always God who justifies. Thus, it is God who
blessed the services of the unbelieving psychoanalyst I mentioned
and who made him the instrument of His grace for his unbelieving
patient.

Conversely, it may happen that a man talks to me about his
faults, thinking he is confessing, but does so in a calm, neutral
tone which takes from his words all nature of confession. The
important thing is not what one has said but one's state of mind.
In a silence, a sigh or a glance there may be a more authentic
confession than in long speeches.

But the same question that we have examined in connection
with repentance and the forgiveness of others arises again:
whether confession is the condition for God's forgiveness. Again
my reply is that it is rather the way to it. To discuss conditions
would, at bottom, be to claim that we can enclose the sovereign
freedom of God within our human formulas; and it is in any case
to raise a religious problem in a rational spirit which is alien to
the Bible. For the Bible recounts events which have been

experienced, just as we doctors relate case-histories as actually experienced and of which we are witnesses: that is how it took place.

The Bible shows us a way, not in theory, but through the example of those who have lived. It shows us kings who make confession; for example, King David, to whom God sent the prophet Nathan to move him by a parable (2 Sam. xii. 1–14). At his words David became aware of his guilt and cried: 'I have sinned against the Lord.' Then Nathan said to David: 'The Lord also has put away your sin.' The Bible shows us King Hezekiah to whom God sent the prophet Isaiah to cure him. But instead of being grateful, the King boasted of it! And so he incurred the anger of the Almighty. 'But Hezekiah humbled himself for the pride of his heart. . . .' (2 Chron. xxxii. 24–26).

The Bible shows us an entire people becoming aware of its guilt as it rediscovers the law of God and which confesses its sins for a quarter of a day (Neh. ix. 3). It shows us Ezra, who could indeed be proud of the great deeds he had done at God's inspiration, identifying himself with his people and groaning: 'O my God, I am ashamed and blush to lift my face to thee. . . . From the days of our fathers to this day we have been in great guilt. . . .' (Ezra ix. 6–7).

The Psalter gives us, in trembling accents, the experiences of King David and of many believers. As he comes into my consulting room a man tells me that it was reading Psalm xxxii which made him decide to come and confess (Ps. xxxii. 1, 3, 5):

'Blessed is he whose transgression is forgiven,
    whose sin is covered . . .
When I declared not my sin, my body wasted away
    through my groaning all day long . . .
I acknowledge my sin to thee,
    and I did not hide my iniquity;
I said, "I will confess my transgressions to the Lord";
    then thou didst forgive the guilt of my sin.'

The Bible is alive. And it is above all through the example of those who have found the way to forgiveness that it makes us in our turn follow in their footsteps. It shows us the crowds which ran to John the Baptist 'confessing their sins' (Matt. iii. 6), and it sees in this great movement of repentance the sign heralding the ministry of Jesus Christ who was approaching.

The Apostle James writes: 'Confess your sins to one another, and pray for one another, that you may be healed. The prayer of a righteous man has great power in its effects' (Jas. v. 16). These last words well indicate the entirely practical meaning of his

exhortation, practical relevance which characterizes his entire
Epistle. He therefore does not claim to formulate a condition for
forgiveness and cure, so much as to express a truth of experience
which was quite spontaneous and very common in the early
Church. Dr. Bovet has quoted us also a whole series of biblical
accounts in which there is experience of repentance without
confession.

But if confession is not a condition, it is a path which innumerable men have followed in their turn, and always with the same
result. I myself had for a long time a religious life which was
rather intellectual and theoretical; I was a militant Church mem-
ber; I truly believed not only in God and in Jesus Christ, but also
in the Holy Spirit, the communion of saints, the forgiveness of
sins, and the holy Catholic Church. But that, for me, was a belief
rather than a living experience until the day when I met men who
simply and honestly confessed their sins.

Those men showed me the way, not by exhortation but by their
example in my presence. I threw myself wholeheartedly into the
regular practice of confession, moved by an inner impetus and
not in order to fulfil a legalistic condition. The whole climate of
my life changed. I was at last experiencing what I had known for
a long time. 'Now I understand', I said, 'what the action of the
Holy Spirit, the conviction of sin and the experience of grace
really are.'

And immediately a spiritual ministry opened before me. I have
seen men come to me in large numbers and find true freedom as
the result of an absolutely concrete confession of their faults.
Certainly, we all know 'that we are not better than others' as is
commonly said. But an expression as vague as that has no nature
of confession about it; it serves rather to excuse us for our guilt
and to hide it from us than to face us with it. To speak in general
terms of our lack of honesty or love, or of our impurity, is by no
means to go so far as to experience confession.

These are still only vague rubrics, a sort of table of contents,
whereas it is the book itself which counts, the detailed account of
what we have thought, said and done in such and such a circumstance. It is even very often in the rigorous accuracy of a particular word which we should like to avoid and conceal beneath a
more veiled expression, that the sincerity of a confession and its
effect are involved.

But we all feel a formidable inner resistance to entering thus
into true confession, the sort which really humbles. It costs us a
good deal, and we can understand the saying of Leviticus which
presents it as a way of paying for one's iniquities (Lev. xxvi. 41).
And so many conversations are a subtle game played by men torn

between their intense need to make confession and their inner resistance. One man talks to me for a long time about a little pain of his. I should be wrong to be surprised that he returns to the subject so insistently. In reality, by prolonging his consultation with me he is trying to overcome his resistance. The pain was only an excuse for coming; he will tell me so shortly. His real aim in coming is a confession he does not know how to begin to make and which he puts off as long as possible.

Another declares from the start that he is of a reticent nature, and he talks and talks without stopping, in a flood of words, of all the circumstances of his life, of all he has suffered, and even of many of his faults. I end up by telling him: 'It seems to me that for a reticent man you open up singularly well!' Then he bursts out: 'That's because I've not said the most important thing!' And there and then he embarks upon a real confession. A woman talks to me for hours about the suspicions she entertains about her husband before she dares suddenly to speak of the wrongs she does him.

Never stop patients in the middle of their confidences, even if they appear harmless. They are like the sprint the athlete throws himself into in order, at the end, to be able to make a particularly difficult jump. Neither should you break the poignant silence which may suddenly hold up the conversation. At that moment a great struggle is being waged in his soul, and you may compromise the issue by giving him the opportunity for a digression. Sometimes I have had to wait nearly an hour for the result.

Perhaps you can sometimes help someone to enter into confession by exhorting him to confess; but I am not made that way. I do not think I have ever said to anyone: 'Confess!' If I hear so many confessions it is even perhaps because I do not expect them, because I do not suspect their imminence, because they always take me by surprise, so to speak, as if I had never heard any before, as if I did not know how much all men need confession. And very often, after his confession, a man has told me that for months he had himself been astonished that I had never invited him to make confession.

But what astonishes me still more is the prodigious effect a real confession can have. Very often it is not only the decisive religious experience of freedom from guilt, but, 'as well' as that (Matt. vi. 33), the sudden cure of a physical or psychological illness. Sometimes in less than an hour there occurs in a patient, whom I am seeing for the first time and to whom I have spoken but a few words, a release from psychological tension which I should have been very proud to obtain after months of therapy. But at any rate, this always and to the highest degree facilitates a

personal contact which is the most decisive factor in every psychotherapeutic cure.

Much has been written about the relationship between psychological confession and religious confession. People have been
careful to establish their theoretical reciprocal limits, and to pick
out specific criteria to distinguish them. The one aims at a cure,
the other at reconciliation with God. I do not dispute it. All
these learned studies are just and judicious.

But in practice, every psychological confession has religious
significance, and every religious confession, whether ritual and
sacramental or free, its psychological effects. It is perhaps in this
fact that we perceive most clearly the unity of the human being,
and how impossible it is to dissociate the physical, psychological
and religious aspects of his life. Every doctor, even without
specializing in psychotherapy, in so far as he has understanding of
what is human and likes contact with human beings, may suddenly find himself promoted to a confessor's priesthood without
having sought it.

This immediately poses a problem which is much more delicate
still, namely, that of absolution. It is obvious that a Roman
Catholic cannot be satisfied with lay absolution without being
guilty in relation to his Church, and therefore in relation to God.
A practising Catholic who in my consulting room becomes aware
of a deeper sense of guilt, spontaneously hastens to return to his
confessor. Others who had abandoned the confessional return of
their own accord. But we can never fail to recommend that
Roman Catholics, for psychological reasons as much as out of
respect for their Church, should go and ask for sacramental
absolution.

Even with Protestants I admit to having behaved for a long
time a little timidly and indirectly in my embarrassment, and it
was undoubtedly because of a survival of the spirit of the taboo
which makes us laymen hesitate to have anything to do with
sacred things which would be reserved for those who have been
officially ordained. I felt clearly that an authentic confession
necessarily calls for a response, for an absolution, which yet I
dared not pronounce explicitly. I got out of it by recalling some
biblical promise about God's faithfulness in forgiving whosoever
admits his faults; or else by suggesting to the man who had
spoken out so loyally that I should pray with him in order to
express through prayer our gratitude to Jesus Christ for His
atoning work.

I have become more simple, more true and more bold, and
that from motives both religious and psychological. General
affirmations about the forgiveness of God have not at all the

effect of a categorical, personal, individualized word pronounced with conviction on behalf of God and addressed to the man who has confessed his sin. Truly, the will of God produces assuagement and the sure personal conviction that the sin confessed is wiped away. If, out of timidity, I evade this office, it is I who make myself guilty before God for eluding the mission He entrusts to me and the responsibility with which He has charged me in inducing this man to take me as a witness of his confession.

A pastor recently told me that after a public lecture he had given, a Jesuit father asked him in private this question: 'Who, in your opinion, Pastor, is entitled to administer absolution?' My friend replied by opening the Gospel. After His resurrection Jesus appeared to His disciples and said to them: ' "Peace be with you. As the Father hath sent me, even so I send you." And when he had said this, he breathed on them, and said to them, "Receive the Holy Spirit. If you forgive the sins of any, they are forgiven; if you retain the sins of any, they are retained" ' (Jn. xx. 21–23).

Thus, in a Church which professes to have no other rule than biblical revelation, it is obvious that it is the Holy Spirit who entitles men to give absolution in the name of God. All those to whom Jesus has given His peace are sent in their turn by Him to transmit it to men; those to whom He has given the Holy Spirit He invests with this priesthood. But the Holy Spirit is not the monopoly of clerics. On the day of Pentecost it was bestowed upon hundreds of people without any distinction (Acts ii. 33). A little later, the Apostle Peter saw the Spirit bestowed upon foreigners—upon Samaritans (Acts viii. 17), and then upon a Roman officer, Cornelius, and all his household (Acts xi. 15). It was the fulfilment of the promises indicated by the prophets: 'I will pour out my spirit on all flesh' (Joel ii. 28), as St. Peter himself asserted (Acts ii. 16).

Chapter XXIV

THE ORDER OF MELCHIZEDEK

I SHOULD like to arouse in you a wider vision both of the human problem and of our task as doctors in the face of this problem; a deeply biblical vision of the universality of guilt and the universality of divine forgiveness. I should like to encourage you to think and act on a universal scale beyond all the particularities of Church rites and dogmas. St. Paul writes that God our Saviour 'desires all men to be saved and to come to the knowledge of the truth. For there is one God, and there is one mediator between God and men, the man Christ Jesus, who gave himself as a ransom for all' (1 Tim. ii. 4–6).

The clergy see especially the members of their respective Churches coming to them; but sometimes there are people who are more or less unconnected, who nevertheless bear witness, by approaching the clergy, to a certain respect for the Church which the latter represent, and its institutions and rites. It is obvious that the clergy must reply to them in the precise terms prescribed by their Church and offer salvation according to the rites it has instituted.

But we doctors welcome distressed folk indiscriminately and in all their diversity. Some are devout, and we must respect their form of piety whether they are Catholics, Orthodox, Protestants, Jews, Mohammedans or Buddhists. There are many who are religious without being devout, who are not at all clear about their own attitude, baffled perhaps by the arguments which divide the Churches. There are some whose spiritual life hangs on the mere recollection of a reading or a conversation which has struck them, or of a prayer their mother used to say when they were children.

There are some who say they cannot pray and yet who utter sighs which are more authentic prayers than any prayers they may have learnt (Rom. viii. 26). There are some who do not know what they are searching for and yet who search for it passionately. There are some too who claim to be indifferent and they are precisely the most anxious, hiding their anxiety beneath their indifference. There are some who say they are bereft of all belief and who suddenly reveal a deeply religious soul; and there are some who are aggressive towards the Church and God and who prove precisely by their aggressiveness that they take them seriously.

But however diverse they may be, they are also extraordinarily similar. They all suffer. They all bear in their lives problems, disappointments, aspirations and hopes. Even when they commit suicide, as Dr. Plügge[30] has shown, their action still betrays a supreme hope in something else, when everything on earth has disillusioned them. They are an innumerable crowd, a tormented crowd, a crowd seeking an answer and an assurance, dragging their past heavily along and wanting to lay down their load.

They tell us about their illnesses, their symptoms, their conflicts; in fact, everything they can describe clearly. But they all expect from us something more than our technical attention: not only our sympathy, our personal solicitude or our encouragement but also, in whatever form it may be and perhaps quite unobtrusively, a beam of the divine grace which alone can efface guilt.

Here life takes precedence of form. The Churches instituted forms, dogmas and rites, afterwards to make concrete and to solemnize this great reconciliation with God. They have their full value, but their value lies exactly in expressing in definite form a primary reality, a universal truth, namely the help of God in human misery, the reconciliation He offers and the blessing which He has bestowed upon us and which He asks us to transmit to all men on His behalf. It is a spiritual priesthood to which He calls us; in practising it we are not competitors with the Church, but rather her collaborators.

This is not an ecclesiastical priesthood. It is not our job to teach universal truth in particular theological formulas. We do not have to preside over any rites. Sooner or later, those whom we have helped to draw nearer to God will feel the need to integrate themselves into a Church or a community and to express their devotion according to the dogmas and rites it prescribes, which it is the job of the clergy and not ours to teach them.

If I may say so, we are like a lodge-keeper posted at the gateway of the garden of God to welcome those who seek admittance. In the garden there are many paths and guides to conduct the visitors. But first they must have passed through the gateway and we must have been faithful in showing them that that indeed was the issue they sought to their wandering lives, and that it is indeed in this garden where they would find the answer to their problem.

But many doctors are embarrassed at this intermediary function for which they have been prepared neither at the university nor by the Church; they do not know how to define or practise this spiritual ministry which is not enfeoffed to a particular Church. The tragedy is that it is precisely the believing doctors who are often the most timid. Whereas atheist colleagues are not embarrassed to discuss religion with their patients, they on the other hand show themselves to be prudent and reserved, out of a sort of excessive respect for the sacred or some fear of being accused of usurping a priesthood which is not theirs.

But the clergy too are often held back by a similar anxiety not to exceed the limits of their function or to ape the doctor and the psychologist which they are not. Thus a common sphere, like that of guilt, which belongs at one and the same time to psychology and to religion, resembles in some ways a no-man's-land, an evacuated zone respected by both camps so as to avoid entering into conflict.

The comparison is doubtless too military, for if doctors and theologians are a little afraid of each other, they do respect and admire each other and rarely fight! Let us say rather that they stand on opposite sides of the street and from a distance raise their hats very courteously to one another. But the fear of encroaching upon the others' territory prevents them from going into the roadway, so to speak, and from mingling with the other people there, from entering life, life as it is lived, the reality of life, which constantly raises spiritual problems but not in dogmatic or ritual terms. The huge and forsaken crowd passes along the street between these two well-intentioned groups of observers, who consider it each from his particular point of view, either psychological or ecclesiastical. It therefore seems to me important to fix a meeting place, a universal spiritual ministry exempt from all denominational peculiarities and from any cliquish spirit. And this, I believe has a biblical basis.

In certain aspects the Old Testament seems impregnated with a Jewish nationalism which monopolizes salvation for a single chosen people. And yet already in the Old Testament there appears the vision of the universal nature of salvation. Well before the special covenant which God concluded with Abraham and his offspring, it tells of a first covenant proclaimed by God to all men after the Flood, a perpetual covenant, not only with all men 'for all future generations', but also with 'every living creature of all flesh' (Gen. ix. 8–17).

From then on the covenant of God with Abraham and the chosen people is set within the framework of a universal covenant. The later covenant does not contradict it, it does not restrict salvation, but focuses it, and maps out a way to its full implementation in Jesus Christ. So before the grace of God becomes incarnate in a people, in a Church, in forms and particular rites, it is addressed to all men, and it becomes incarnate only the better to prove itself to the benefit of all.

Such is also the impressive message of Melchizedek, King of

Salem (Gen. xiv. 18–20). Abraham was already the man chosen by God for the realization of His plan. He was already the man to whom God spoke personally, and had called to leave the paradise of bureaucracy which was Ur of the Chaldees and to adventure forth under divine guidance. He was already a believer, the father of believers, who had obeyed and had left his country without knowing where God would lead him.

And yet, it was a stranger, Melchizedek, whom God sent to him to bless him. Melchizedek brought bread and wine, the symbols of the covenant which Jesus Christ later took again to found His Church. And Abraham, after being blessed, gave the tenth of all he possessed to the 'priest of God Most High'. Thus Melchizedek appears as a symbol—our Jungian friends would say 'archetype'—of the messenger of universal salvation, of the universal saviour who outstrips in time and space Abraham and the special covenant which God soon after sealed with him and his descendants.

You see that this sequence has a meaning: before the special covenant of God with Abraham and his descendants there was already the more general affirmation of His blessing, which was administered by this strange character Melchizedek. His name means 'king of righteousness', and he is King of Salem, 'salem' meaning 'peace', 'salvation'. Melchizedek prefigures Christ, the Prince of Peace. That comes out very clearly in the Psalm where King David refers prophetically to Jesus Christ, his 'Lord', who sits at the right hand of God, and affirms that God has consecrated him by an oath (Ps. cx):

> 'The Lord has sworn . . .
> "You are a priest for ever
> after the order of Melchizedek".'

Jesus Christ Himself, expressly identifies Himself with David's 'Lord', the 'priest after the order of Melchizedek', when He quotes this Psalm of David, and applies it to Himself, thereby proclaiming Himself the Christ announced in the Psalm (Matt. xxii. 41–45). Why this reference to Melchizedek? It is a reference to the universal covenant of God, the one which precedes the special covenant with the chosen people and which embraces the latter. It is an affirmation of the fulfilment by Jesus Christ both of the promises made by God to His people and of the universal promises made to the whole of His creation.

Thus a bond joins the first pages of the Bible to the last; it is a bond of universality passing through what is particular in order finally to achieve universality. That is what the author of

the Epistle to the Hebrews stresses when he refers to this Psalm
of David three times (Heb. vi. 20; vii. 1, 17, 21): 'Thou art a
priest for ever, after the order of Melchizedek.'

The author of the Epistle certainly regards Melchizedek as a
symbolic figure, since he says of him that he is 'without father
or mother or genealogy, and has neither beginning of days nor
end of life' (Heb. vii. 3). By this he proclaims the symbol of the
universality of the salvation incarnate in Jesus Christ.

Thus, there is an 'order of Melchizedek', a universal order,
which contains and exceeds all particular orders and all special
covenants. Our Churches individualize salvation. Each one of
them has its place in God's plan for the fulfilment of universal
salvation. Their particularism does not therefore contradict His
universalism, but it does not limit it either. What each of them
offers to its members in various forms is the same living, universal
reality—reconciliation between God and man.

So I ask my colleagues: We all who for ten years have been
seeking together ways to a spiritual revival of medicine and a
clarification of our universal spiritual task, can we not appeal
to 'the order of Melchizedek'? We call ourselves doctors of
the whole personality. From the medical point of view, the
expression 'integrative medicine' is a good one for it signifies that
we envisage man in his entirety, in his unity, as a spiritual being
as well as an animal.

But this necessarily means that we affirm our spiritual vocation.
It means that we affirm that we are called to assist our patients
not only in their physical or psychological difficulties, but also
in their spiritual ones, yet without any proselytizing of them.
We belong to the most diverse Churches—Orthodox, Catholic
and Protestant of all denominations. We are submissive sons of
our respective Churches, but we have a common spiritual
ministry. If we need a biblical reference for this ministry of ours,
we can call ourselves doctors according to the order of
Melchizedek.

Does the name sound barbarous to you? Come now! At a time
when new worlds are opening up, we must certainly get familiar
with many names more difficult to pronounce than this! Does it
perhaps strike you as proud? as if it were a matter of a super-
Church which claims to be more universal than particular
Churches, called to embrace them or to supplant them so as to
distribute apart from them salvation to all men?

No! It is rather a matter of a *sub*-structure; and it is in that
respect that it concerns us doctors. It is a question of this human
terrain, this human problem we are studying, the universal
problem of guilt, and the universal need of forgiveness common

to all men, and of the universal blessing God offers to all men even before any particular Church transmits it to them under its particular forms. So I mean by sub-structure the nature of man just as God has created him, a being both animal and spiritual, free and responsible, such as he became after the Fall, guilty, tormented by guilt, and yet also forgiven.

I always remember a foreign patient who had precisely stated when she asked me for a consultation that she was not interested in religious matters and that she hoped this would not be an obstacle to a good contact between us, although she knew I was a believer. You can appreciate that I carefully confined myself to my technical function and took care not to speak to her of my faith.

She was suffering from psychological inhibitions. Then suddenly one day she said to me: 'I wonder if it isn't pride which paralyses me like this.'—'Everybody is proud,' I replied; 'everybody is equally proud; I am as proud as you are. But there are people who are stimulated by pride and others who are paralysed by it according to their psychological complexes.'

She showed the most keen astonishment: 'You are not proud,' she told me kindly. I had to disillusion her, for it is easily the most ineradicable sin I have! 'The proof,' I told her, 'is that I take a lot of trouble to cure you. Pride urges me on, and I should be very humiliated if I failed. I can struggle as much as I like against pride, but it is always there.'

There was a pause. Then she expressed her thoughts aloud: 'What you say is frightful! If everybody is proud whatever he does, then there is no solution.' 'Yes, there is a solution, one only, but I cannot tell you of it, as it is a religious one, and you have asked me not to talk to you about religion.' 'Tell me the solution all the same,' she replied. 'The solution is that I am a proud man who has been forgiven; if we are all proud, we are all also proud people who have been forgiven.'

You can see how imperceptibly we had passed, in spite of my reserve, from the psychological problem to the spiritual problem. For the question of guilt arises in every man, and it demands an answer. The answer is of a religious nature but it can be made in a very general manner which in no way prejudices the religious developments which will make it definite and explicit through the dogmas of a Church.

This basic datum, this assurance of the forgiveness of God and of His blessing would not be enough to edify and nurture the religious life either for us or for our patients. So the woman I mentioned was not long in asking to be instructed in the Christian faith and to receive baptism, which was no longer my function as a doctor. On the other hand, as you will clearly see,

by forbidding itself to make any spiritual reference, medicine
has been condemned to envisage no more than a partial aspect of
man. It can be said that today it no longer has a concept of man
at all.

But if a spiritual reference is reintroduced into medicine there is
also a risk of reintroducing the philosophical and theological
controversies from which it had to free itself three or four centuries ago. So we have to elaborate for our own generation a
concept of man which takes into account the entire man, including
his spiritual aspect, but which is valid and common for all men
whether they are believers or not, or whatever the Church to
which they belong.

It is to that task that Dr. Anton de Mol van Otterloo dedicated
himself together with all the collaborators he grouped around
him. He calls it 'basic anthropology' or 'pre-dogmatic anthropology', that is, a conception of man in his entirety, in the reality
of his life as he lives it, both physically, psychologically and
spiritually, even before any philosophical doctrine or any theological dogma gives a particular and defined formula for it.

Everything is mingled in life, and the Bible continually depicts
life in its unity and its complexity. It does not set the religious life
apart like a speciality reserved for theologians, it constantly links
the most concrete events of physical life—meals, tiredness, illness
—to the highest spiritual experiences. It suggests the unity of
man through images and symbols. I myself am particularly
sensitive to the poetry of the Bible, and I can speak boldly of it to
doctors since C. G. Jung reintroduced myths and poetry into
medicine. The account of the Garden of Eden, the enigmatic
figure of Melchizedek meting out the blessing of God, and all
the parables of Jesus express universal human truths.

Thus the 'metanoia' we have spoken about, this change of
mind which marks entry into the Kingdom of God, is for theologians a figure of religious conversion and of integration into
the Church. But in a more general way it is also a law of life
whose universal nature we as doctors and psychologists can
verify. There are only endless torments and a vicious circle of
misfortunes if a man represses his guilt and denounces the guilt of
others. The only peace with oneself and others lies in accepting
one's guilt and confessing it.

Thus a parable like that of the Prodigal Son expresses a religious
truth which the Church formulates in dogmas or in sacraments of
penance and absolution. But it also expresses in a quite general
way the condition of man as we can observe it as doctors. All
men are exiled, impoverished and all feel guilty; all yearn for the
wealth of the home they have abandoned, and for forgiveness.

Guilt is therefore a religious problem which interests theologians, a social problem which interests sociologists, and a psychological problem which interests psychologists. But it does not let itself be dissected. It is a human problem, a form of suffering peculiar to man, and of concern to the doctor because his vocation is the relief of all suffering.

REFERENCES

1. Dr. René Allendy, *Justice intérieure,* Paris, Denoël and Steele.
2. Prof. Dr. Karl Barth, 'Die Menschlichkeit Gottes', in *Menschlichkeit: Verhandlungen des schweizerischen reformierten Pfarrvereins,* Biel, Schüler, 1957.
3. Dr. H. Baruk, *Psychiatrie morale expérimentale,* Paris, P.U.F., 1945.
4. Dr. Théo Bovet, *L'art de trouver du temps,* Strasbourg, Oberlin, 1955.
5. Albert Camus, *The Rebel,* London, Hamish Hamilton, 1951.
6. Albert Camus, *The Plague,* London, Hamish Hamilton, 1948.
7. Maryse Choisy, 'Genèse de la culpabilité', *Psyché,* Paris, April-May 1948, p. 386.
8. J. Daniélou, 'Psychiatrie et "morales sans péché" ', in *Monde moderne et sens du péché,* Paris, Pierre Horay, 1957.
9. Suzanne de Diétrich, *Hommes libres,* Neuchâtel, Delachaux and Niestlé, 1957.
10. Prof. J. Dor, Inaugural Lecture: *Les Annales de chirurgie,* Paris, June 1957, no. 11-12.
11. Dr. Silvio G. Fanti, *J'ai peur, docteur* . . . , Neuchâtel, Delachaux and Niestlé, 1953.
12. Jean Guitton, 'La philosophie de la culpabilité', *Psyché,* Paris, April-May 1948, p. 542.
13. Jean Guitton, 'La conversion du pécheur, gloire de Dieu', *Monde moderne et sens du péché,* Paris, Pierre Horay, 1957.
14. Georges Gusdorf, *La découverte de soi,* Paris, P.U.F., 1948.
15. Heinz Häfner, *Schulderleben und Gewissen,* Stuttgart, 1953.
16. Dr. A. Hesnard, *Morale sans péché,* Paris, P.U.F., 1954.
17. Dr. A. Hesnard, *L'Univers morbide de la faute,* Paris, P.U.F., 1949.
18. Prof. Dr. Arthur Jores, 'Magie und Zauber in der modernen Medizin', *Deutsche Medizinische Wochenschrift,* Stuttgart, 17th June 1955, pp. 915-20.
19. Prof. C. G. Jung, *Aspects du drame contemporain,* Geneva, Georg, 1948.
20. Prof. C. G. Jung, *Psychology and Alchemy,* vol. 12 Collected Works, 1953, p. 14.
21. J. Lacroix, *Les sentiments et la vie morale,* Paris, P.U.F., 1953.
22. J. Lacroix, 'Morale sans péché', *Recherches et Débats,* Paris, May, 1955.

23. Dr. René Laforgue, 'La peste et la vertu', *Psyché*, Paris, April–May 1948, p. 406.

24. Dr. A. Maeder, *Vers la guérison de l'âme,* Neuchâtel, Delachaux and Niestlé 1946.

25. Bernard Martin. *Le ministère de la guérison dans l'Eglise,* Geneva, Labor and Fides, 1952.

26. H. Michaud, 'Anger', *Vocabulary of the Bible,* London, Lutterworth, 1958.

27. Dr. Charles-Henri Nodet, 'Psychiatrie et "morales sans péché" ', *Monde moderne et sens du péché,* Paris, Pierre Horay, 1957.

28. Dr. Charles-Henri Nodet, 'Position de saint Jérôme en face des problèmes sexuels', *Mystique et continence,* Etudes Carmélitaines, Bruges, Desclée de Brouwer, 1952.

29. Dr. Charles Odier, *Les deux sources, consciente et inconsciente de la vie morale,* Neuchâtel, La Baconnière, 1943.

30. Prof. H. Plügge, Über die Hoffnung. Situation I, *Spectrum,* Utrecht-Antwerp, 1954.

31. Review *Présences,* no. 59: *Malades et médecins,* The Priory of St. John, Champrosay (S.-&-O.), 2nd. qr. 1957.

32. Dr. Pierre Ponsoye, *L'Esprit, force biologique fondamentale,* Montpellier, Impr. Causse, Graille & Castelnau, 1942.

33. Paul Ricoeur, 'Morale sans péché', review *Esprit,* Paris, Aug.–Sept. 1954.

34. Dr. Jean de Rougemont, *Devenir médecin,* Lyon, Impr. Bosc, 1958.

35. Dr. J. Sarano, *La culpabilité*, Paris, Armand Colin, 1957.

36. Dr. André Sarradon, *Le sentiment de culpabilité, son rôle en pathologie interne,* from the author, 11, av. du Rove, Saint-Louis-Marseille, 1957.

37. Jean-Paul Sartre, *Existentialism and Humanism,* London, 1948.

38. Jean-Paul Sartre, *Esquisse d'une théorie des émotions,* Paris, Hermann, 1948.

39. Abbé Jean- P. Schaller, S.T.D., 'Les limites de la médecine et le Dr. Paul Tournier', *Laval médical,* Quebec, April 1954, vol. 19, no. 4.

40. Rev. Dr. J. Scharfenberg, 'Schuld und Schuldgefühle bei Martin Buber', *Wege zum Menschen,* Feb. 1958, Göttingen, Vandenhoeck & Ruprecht.

41. Jacques de Senarclens, *Héritiers de la Réformation,* Geneva, Labor & Fides, 1956.

42. Pierre-Henri Simon, 'Personnalisme chrétien et culpabilités collectives', *Monde moderne et sens du péché,* Paris, Pierre Horay, 1957.

43. Dr. Arnold Stocker, *Le traitement moral des nerveux,* Geneva, Rhône, 1945.

44. Max Thurian, *La confession,* Neuchâtel, Delachaux & Niestlé, 1953.

45. Dr. P. J. Waardenburg, 'Ehewahl und Nachkommen', *Geloof en Wetenschap,* no. 1, 1952, Loosduinen, Kleywegt.

46. Otto Weber, *Karl Barth's Church Dogmatics,* London, Lutterworth, 1953.

47. Hans Zulliger, *Umgang mit dem kindlichen Gewissen,* Stuttgart, Klett, 1953.

INDEX OF BIBLE REFERENCES

INDEX OF NAMES